2014
The Best Ten-Minute Plays

2014
The Best Ten-Minute Plays

Edited and with a Foreword
by Lawrence Harbison

Smith and Kraus Publishers

ISBN: 1-57525-886-2
ISBN: 978-1-57525-886-7
ISSN: 2164-2435

Typesetting and layout by Elizabeth E. Monteleone
Cover Design: Borderlands Press

Smith and Kraus Publishers

A Smith and Kraus book
177 Lyme Road, Hanover, NH 03755
Editorial 603.643.6431 To Order 1.877.668.8680
www.smithandkraus.com

Printed in the United States of America

TABLE OF CONTENTS

M= MALE ROLE —F= FEMALE ROLE

FOREWORD   11

    Lawrence Harbison

PLAYS FOR TWO ACTORS

CANDY LIKES YOUR STATUS   15

    Matt Henderson (2f)

COMMUNICATION GAP   23

    Bill Cissna (1m 1f)

dtf   31

    Bekah Brunstetter (1m 1f)

END OF THE RAINY SEASON   39

    Mark Rigney (1m 1f)

FILLER   47

    Andrew Biss (1m 1f)

GIRLS PRAY OR THE KETCHUP STIGMATA   55

    Alexis Kozak (2f)

GRACELAND   61

    Katie Thayer (2f)

HALFWAY   69

    Emily Schwend (2f)

How To Succeed In Romance
   Without Really Connecting 79
     Trace Crawford (1m 1f)

Lost And Found 91
     Jerry McGee (1m 1f)

Mandate 99
     Kelly Younger (2m)

Oblivion 109
     Paul Lewis (1m 1f)

Painting Seventeen 119
     Sharon E. Cooper (2f)

Perfect 127
     Maura Campbell (1m 1f)

Return Of The Curse 133
     Jack Neary (2m)

Ripple Effect 143
     Jon Spano (2m)

A Second Rapture 153
     James E. Marlow (1m 1f)

Something Like Loneliness 161
     Ryan Dowler (1m 1f)

Stubble 167
     Erin Mallon (1m 1f)

A Tall Order 175
     Sheri Wilner (1m 1f)

UNDER THE POMEGRANATE TREES   183
 Don Nigro (2f)

UNPRIMED   191
 John McKinney (1m 1f)

A WALK IN THE PUBLIC AREA   201
 Greg Kotis (1m 1f)

YOU BELONG TO ME   209
 Daniel Reitz (1m 1f)

PLAYS FOR 3 OR MORE ACTORS

ALL AMERICAN   219
 Mayank Keshaviah (5m)

AT THE FINISH   231
 Nick Gandiello (1m 2f)

BITE ME   243
 Nina Mansfield (2m 1f)

CAKE   251
 Sherry Kramer (2m 2f)

DETECTIVE STORIES   259
 Philip J. Kaplan (2m 1f)

EAST OF THE SUN   267
 Regina Taylor (2m 3f)

FULLY ACCESSIBLE   273
 Bruce Graham (1m 2f)

I Love You I Love You I Love You   283

    Josh Levine (2m 2f)

Intervention   291

    C.J. Ehrlich (3m 2f)

Lost In Thought   301

    Christopher Lockheardt (2m 1f)

Mothra vs. The Casting Director: An Allegory   309

    David Bar Katz (2m 1f)

Moving Day   317

    Kathryn O'Sullivan (3m 2f)

My Body   327

    Rachel Bublitz (1m 2f)

One Life   333

    Mark Cornell (3m 1f)

The Origin Story Of Lewis Hackett   343

    Ron Burch (3m 2f)

Parting Gifts   351

    Joe Calarco (2m 1f)

Pink, Grey, Maroon   361

    Jenny Lyn Bader (1m 2f)

The Proxy   369

    Philip J. Kaplan (2m 1f)

Rise   377

    Crystal Skillman (1m 3f)

Sacrifices   387

    Erin Moughon (4f)

SOMETHING FINE 395

    Eric Dufault (3f)

STONEHENGE 405

    Patricia Milton (1m 2f)

SUPERNOVA IN RESEDA 411

    Jerrod Bogard (1m 2f)

UNVEILED 421

    J. Thalia Cunningham (3f)

WHOSE BAG IS IT ANYWAY? 433

    Michele Markarian (1m 2f)

WITH HER OLD BOYFRIEND THERE WERE PATTERNS 443

    Eric Pfeffinger (1m 4f)

RIGHTS AND PERMISSION 450

PRODUCERS 455

In this volume, you will find fifty terrific new ten-minute plays, culled from the several hundred I read last year, all successfully produced during the 2013-2014 theatrical season. They are written in a variety of styles. Some are realistic plays; some are not. Some are comic (laughs); some are dramatic (no laughs). The ten-minute play form lends itself well to experimentation in style. A playwright can have fun with a device which couldn't be sustained as well in a longer play. Many of these plays employ such devices. I have also included a comprehensive list of theatres which do ten-minute plays.

In years past, playwrights who were just starting out wrote one-act plays of thirty to forty minutes in duration. One thinks of writers such as A. R. Gurney, Lanford Wilson, John Guare and several others. Now, new playwrights tend to work in the ten-minute play genre, largely because there are so many production opportunities. Twenty-five or so years ago, there were none. I was Senior Editor for Samuel French at that time, and it occurred to me that there might be a market for these very short plays. Actors Theatre of Louisville had been commissioning them for several years, for use by their Apprentice Company, and they assisted me in compiling an anthology of these plays, which did so well that Samuel French has published several more anthologies of ten-minute plays from ATL. For the first time, ten-minute plays were now published and widely available, and they started getting produced. There are now many ten-minute play festivals every year, not only in the U.S. but all over the world.

What makes a good ten-minute play? Well, first and foremost I have to like it. Isn't that what we mean when we call a play, a film, a novel "good?" We mean that it effectively portrays the world as I see it, written in a style which interests me. Aside from this, a good ten-minute play has to have the same elements that any good play must have: a strong conflict, interesting, well-drawn characters and compelling subject matter. It also has to have a clear beginning, middle and end. In other words, it's a full length play which runs about ten minutes. Many of the plays which are submitted to me each year are scenes, not complete plays; well-written scenes in many case, but scenes nonetheless. They leave me wanting more. I chose plays which are complete in and of themselves, which I believe will excite those of you who produce ten-minute plays; because if a play isn't produced, it's the proverbial sound of a tree falling in the forest far away. In the Rights & Permissions section at the back of this book you will find information on whom to contact when you decide which plays you want to produce, in order to acquire performance rights.

There are a few plays in this book by playwrights who are fairly well-known, such as Don Nigro, Greg Kotis, Regina Taylor and Bruce Graham, but most are by exciting new playwrights you've probably never heard of who I have no doubt will become far better known when their full-length plays start getting produced by major theatres, playwrights such as J. Thalia Cunningham, Maura Campbell, Emily Schwend, Sharon E. Cooper, James E. Marlow, John McKinney, Mayank Keshaviah, Erin Moughon and Eric Pfeffinger—and you read their work first here!

Lawrence Harbison
Brooklyn, New York

CANDY LIKES YOUR STATUS

Matt Henderson

ORIGINAL PRODUCTION:

Candy Likes Your Status was originally produced by Theatre Westminster as part of the Ten Minute New (And Nearly New) Play Festival October 3-6, 2013.

Directed by Joshua Scott

CAST:
CANDY: Courtney Edmondson
SANDY: Antonia Flamini

Festival produced by Terry Dana Jachimiak II, Director of Theatre at Westminster College

CHARACTERS:
> CANDY: twenty-two, a very optimistic recent college graduate
> SANDY: twenty-two, a very optimistic recent college graduate

SETTING: The virtual world of Facebook represented onstage. Present day. Various set pieces resembling the layout of Facebook may be used to indicate the setting.

NOTES: Projections showing the typed statements of Candy and Sandy may be considered, but aren't necessary. The lines containing extraneous letters should be pronounced as phonetically as possible; for example, "lifeeeee" should be pronounced like "lifey" but with the second syllable considerably elongated. Lines like "A;LSKDJFPOIZXJR" should be pronounced as nonsensical noises. Emoticons like ☺ or ☹ should be pronounced "smiley face" or "frowny face" accompanied by a physical demonstration of the emoticon.

> *(The stage on which all of our lives unfold: Facebook. A big sign saying "Facebook" in that unmistakable lettering hangs above the stage, looking down on all. CANDY enters wearing a college graduation robe and makes a funny kissy face pose. She speaks while holding this pose.)*

CANDY: OMG, commencement is today!!!! Four years have gone by so fast!!!! Look out world, here I comeeeeeeee!!!!! Lol

> *(SANDY enters wearing a college graduation robe and makes an even funnier kissy face pose. She speaks while holding this pose.)*

SANDY: OMG, commencement is today!!!!! Looking forward to the futureeeeee!!!! Watch out real world, I'm blowing you a kisseeeeeeee!!!!!

> *(CANDY and SANDY relax out of the kissy face pose and take off their graduation robes.)*

CANDY: Time to start job-hunting, guys!!! OMG A;LS-KDJF-POIZXJR I CAN'T WAIT!!!

SANDY: ZOMG, EVERYONE, I JUST SENT OUT MY FIRST RESUME!!!! GAHHHHHHHH!!!!!!

CANDY: Oh noes, you guys, I got a rejection letter!!! : (Oh well, I sent out plenty moreeeeeee!!!!!!

(SANDY turns to face CANDY to indicate that she is commenting on her status.)

SANDY: Sorry, you got a rejection letter, Candy, but don't worry you are awesome I'm sure you'll find an amazing jobbbbbbbbeeeeeeee!!!!!!

(CANDY turns to face SANDY to indicate that she is responding to the comment on her status.)

CANDY: Thanks, Sandy I hope you get an amazing jobbbbbbeeeeee tooooooooooo!!!!!!!!!!

SANDY: Yayyyyyy!!!!!! Lol

CANDY: Candy liked your comment "Yayyyyyy!!!!!! Lol"

(CANDY and SANDY both turn to face front again.)

SANDY: ZOMG YOU GUYS THEY WANT ME TO COME IN FOR AN INTERVIEW!!!!!

(CANDY turns to SANDY.)

CANDY: Candy likes your status.

(SANDY turns to CANDY.)

SANDY: Thanks for liking my status Candy don't worry I'm sure you'll get a job interview soooooooon!!!

CANDY: Yeah Candy I'm not worried about it lol. Although I am sooooo jealous lol. I kind of hate you lol. Jk lol. Hahahahahaha.

SANDY: Hahahahaha well I kind of hate you tooooo Candy you're such a loser lol jk shut up you know you're prettier and smarter than me.

CANDY: Yeeahhhhh well you're pretty much right there. Lol

SANDY: K

(There is an awkward silence. CANDY and SANDY face out. CANDY pulls out a mannequin of a very muscular shirtless man and poses with him with an even sillier kissy face.)

CANDY: Candy is in a relationship with Brian Buff-Muscles.

SANDY: *(turning to CANDY)* Sandy likes your relationship status.

CANDY: Thanks for liking my relationship status, Sandy, don't worry I'm sure you're gonna find a really amazing guy someday tooooooooooooooooooooooo!!!!!!!!!!!!!!!!!!!!!!!!!!!!

SANDY: Thanks, Candy, I wasn't really worried about it lol but go ahead rub your happiness in my face jk lol seriously I'm actually really happy for you guys lol

CANDY: You should be cause he's amaaaaaaaazingg

SANDY: Sandy likes your comment "You should be cause he's amaaaaaaaazingg"

(They both face out again.)

CANDY: Night out with Brian my loveeeeee. OMG never thought I would be this happy life is so GOOOOOOD

SANDY: Wish me luck you guys job interview is today fingers are crosseeeeeeeed!!!!

CANDY: *(turning to SANDY)* OMG good luck Sandyyyyyy!!! Brian and I will keep our fingers crosseeeeed!!!!!

SANDY: *(turning to CANDY)* Thankssssss!!!! Hope everything's going well with Brian and you're not sick of him already hahahahahahahahahahaha

CANDY: Lol nope he's amaaaaaaazingg

(Awkward silence.)

(Candy likes her own comment)

"Lol nope he's amaaaaaaazingg"

(They both face out.)

SANDY: I think the interview went well hope they want to hire me so I can move out of my parents' house and start my lifeeeeeee

CANDY: *(turning to SANDY)* Candy likes your status.

SANDY: Thanks, Candy!!!!

(Awkward silence. They both face out.)

CANDY: Candy went from being "In a relationship with Brian Buff-Muscles" to "Single."

SANDY: *(turning to CANDY)* OMG Candy I'm soooooooo sorry what went wrong?!?!?!?!?!?!?!?!?!?!

CANDY: *(turning to SANDY)* It's ok Sandy there are plenty of guys out there and now that we're both single we can go out and cruise the dating sceneeeeee

SANDY: We totally have to we need to hang out sometime I haven't seen you in so LONG AXKLKJL;N;LLJLJALK;SJDF

CANDY: AS;DLKJAL;SKJDFLJSLJAS;;LAJDSLKJSL;JF;AL DFS

SANDY: Sandy likes your comment "AS;DLKJAL;SKJDFLJSL JAS;;LAJDSLKJSL;JF;ALDFS"

(They both face out.)

CANDY: So sorry it ended but not sorry it happened. YOLO, guys. Time to move ONNNNNNEEEE!!!!!

SANDY: Just got a rejection letter, guys. : (Guess I have to start the job hunt againnnnnnn.

CANDY: *(turning to SANDY)* Don't worry Sandy you'll find a job and a boyfriend really really soon I'm sure of it

SANDY: *(turning to CANDY)* I hope so Candy I'm starting to get really depressed about it : (

CANDY: Candy likes your comment "I hope so Candy I'm starting to get really depressed about it : ("

(Awkward silence. They both face out.)

SANDY: Got another rejection letter. : (But on the bright side, this cute guy winked at me todayyyyyy.

CANDY: *(turning to SANDY)* Candy likes your status.

SANDY: *(turning to CANDY)* Thanks Candy we need to hang out soooooon!

(Awkward silence. They both face out.)

CANDY: OMG guys I got a job offer!!!!!! And it pays really well too!!!!! ASJLKJL;FKJSL;DF my life is startinggggg!!!!!!!!!

SANDY: *(turning to CANDY)* Candy that is so great so proud of you girl!!!! BTW when are we gonna hang out we need to have some drinks and celebrateeeeee

CANDY: *(turning to SANDY)* Thanks Sandy idk when I'm available I'm super-busy right now with the job and moving into my new apartment so happy to be out of the house and finally a real adult lol but I will let you know!!!!!!

SANDY: K

(They both face out.)

CANDY: So happy to be out of the house and on my own, can you imagine if I was 23 and still living in my parents' house omg I'd be such a loser but I'm getting out just in timeeeee

SANDY: I wore my special dress for the cute guy who winked and he didn't even notice me. : (

CANDY: *(turning to SANDY)* Candy likes your status.

SANDY: *(turning to CANDY)* Why are you liking that Candy it sucks lol how's the new job going

CANDY: Idk just cause you put it in a funny way haha The new job is amaaaaazingg

> *(They both face out.)*

SANDY: Got another rejection letter today and I sat next to the cute guy who winked on the bus and he didn't even say hi I'm starting to think he wasn't winking at me he was winking at somebody who was sitting behind me or just has some kind of funny tic with his eye : (

CANDY: *(turning to SANDY)* Candy likes your status.

> *(Awkward silence. They both face out. CANDY takes out her mannequin boyfriend again and makes an even more obnoxious kissy face.)*

> *(Candy went from being "Single" to "In a relationship with Brian Buff-Muscles")*

SANDY: *(turning to CANDY)* ZOMG when did this happen I thought you guys weren't together anymore wtf

CANDY: *(turning to SANDY)* We were only taking a breakkkkk but we couldn't stay away from each other and now we're soooooo happy

SANDY: Lol that's so funny rub your happiness in my face again lol jk but seriously lol it's so obnoxious lol stop being so happy hahahahahaha you make me so depressed roflmao

CANDY: Candy likes your comment "Lol that's so funny rub your happiness in my face again lol jk but seriously lol it's so obnoxious lol stop being so happy hahahahahaha you make me so depressed roflmao"

> *(They both face out.)*

SANDY: Got another rejection letter and don't even have money to go out anymore. : (

CANDY: *(turning to SANDY)* Candy likes your status. Awww things'll get better Sandy if you wanna hang out we don't even need to go anywhere we can just have movie night at my apartment or something

SANDY: *(turning to CANDY)* Really Candy? That would mean so much to me I've been so depressed I'd love to have some company and have fun like old timmmmmmmeeeeessssssss

CANDY: For realz

SANDY: What day is good for yooooooouuuuu

CANDY: Idk yet Brian and I haven't had a date night in so loooooooonnnnng so it depends on when he wants to go out but we need to do it soooooooooon

> *(Awkward silence. They both face out.)*

Going out with my loveeeee again omg we're so happy we're so happy we're sooooo happppppppppyyyyyyyyyyyy!!!!!!!

SANDY: Another rejection letter and my parents are annoying me about getting out of the house f my lifeeeee

CANDY: Had a hard day at work today but Brian brought me candyyyyy being in love is sooooo gooooooood

SANDY: Omg another rejection letter and I'm still single wtf is this my lifeeeee

CANDY: I LOVE MY JOB! I LOVE MY BOYFRIEND! I LOVE MY LIFE!!!!!!

SANDY: Another lonely day but I got two rejection letters so at least someone's thinking of me

CANDY: So boreddddd tonight Brian isn't hereeeee

SANDY: *(turning to CANDY)* Wanna have date night tonight Candy?

CANDY: *(turning to SANDY)* Idk I need to go to bed early tonight cause I got work super-early I'm tireddddddd lol

> *(They both face out.)*

SANDY: Another rejection today

CANDY: *(turning to SANDY)* Candy likes your status.

> *(They both face out. CANDY puts on a ring and poses with her mannequin.)*

> *(Candy went from being "In a relationship with Brian Buff-Muscles" to "Engaged to Brian Buff-Muscles")*

SANDY: *(turning to SANDY)* Congrats you guys good luck you're gonna need it

CANDY: Lol what's that supposed to mean?

SANDY: Lol idk

(Awkward silence. They both face out.)

Another day of rejection letters and being alone lol this is great

CANDY: *(turning to SANDY)* Candy likes your status.

SANDY: Six months of nothing but rejection letters and being single and not going out with anyone. Yayyyyyyyy.

CANDY: *(turning to SANDY)* Candy likes your status. *(facing out)* Candy went from being "Engaged to Brian Buff-Muscles" to "Married to Brian Buff-Muscles" OMG thanks for the well-wishes!!! A year ago, I was jobless and single and look at me now!!!!! Dreams can come trueeeeeee!!!! YOLO!!!!!!!!

SANDY: I think I'm going to kill myself today. Sorry, guys, I can't do this anymore. Hope you don't miss my Facebook posts when I'm gone. YOLO. Lol

(SANDY exits.)

CANDY: *(turning to where SANDY was)* Candy likes your status. Lol Sandy you're so funny you should totally go ahead and kill yourself jk hahahahahahaha but seriously we haven't hung out since last year you should totally come and check out our new apartment when are you free?!!!

(Awkward silence.)

Sandy are you there? Lol

(Awkward silence.)

K

(The Facebook sign gets pulled away to reveal SANDY hanging from a noose and making a really really obnoxious kissy face. CANDY does not notice it. Blackout.)

COMMUNICATION GAP

Bill Cissna

ORIGINAL PRODUCTION

Evening of Short Plays #24, Studio Theatre 106,
Greensboro Cultural Center, Greensboro, N.C.
February, 2011.
Directed by Randall C. Morris

CAST:
JAMES THOMAS: Skyler Whitfield
KATHERINE TURNER: Artemis Jamison

EoSP #24 was produced by the Greensboro Playwrights
Forum and the City Arts Drama Center, Stephen Hyers,
Managing Director

SECOND PRODUCTION

Vince Mazza ONE/Act Festival,
Brooklyn ONE Productions, St. John's Parish Hall,
Brooklyn, NY
October 11-13, 2013
Directed by Adriane Cole
Producer: Anthony Marino, Co-Founder/Artistic Director

CAST:
JAMES THOMAS: Hermes Del Villar
KATHERINE TURNER: Miranda Jean Larson

CHARACTERS:

JAMES THOMAS: twenty to twenty-five, decent-looking college student

KATHERINE TURNER: eighteen to twenty-three, totally gorgeous college student

In the present. KATHERINE sits at a café table in a bookstore coffee shop, with a glass with ice/beverage in front of her. JAMES approaches her hesitantly. He takes the other chair, which action she ignores. He leans over the table towards her.

JAMES: Hello? *(She picks up her cell or other hand-held, video-ready device from the table, fiddles with the controls to start recording a video, then lifts the phone to face JAMES.)* Aren't you Katherine?

KATHERINE: *(Stares at him through the video screen, not looking at him but at the screen.)*

JAMES: You're in my sōsh* class, right?

(With a long "o," as in, short for Sociology.)

KATHERINE: *(Turns the device to face herself.)* She recognizes the young man somewhat. He claims to be in her "sosh" class. It *could* be true. What's his name, she wonders? *(She turns the device back to face him. This back-and-forth with the device continues throughout.)*

JAMES: James. James Thomas.

KATHERINE: James Thomas, the young man says. He's already in trouble. Father wouldn't like that name at all, if she were to take him home to meet the folks for some obscure reason. Father has never trusted people who have two first names for their first and last names.

JAMES: I could change it.

KATHERINE: Well, he does show a certain level of flexibility that is either charming or scary. Hard to tell.

JAMES: I don't think I'm scary at all.

KATHERINE: Scary is in the eyes of the beholder, she retorts.

JAMES: This is kind of weird.

KATHERINE: What does James Thomas, Mister Two-First Names, know about weird, she wonders? Is he an escaped mental patient?

JAMES: I'm not an escaped mental patient! I'm in your sosh class.

KATHERINE: Attending a college sociology class is certainly no proof of sanity. Besides, he has only *claimed* to be in the class. To this point, however, he has offered no firm evidence.

JAMES: Sorry, I didn't carry my textbook along to the bookstore. They frown on people carrying other books in here.

KATHERINE: He seems to have a ready excuse.

JAMES: *(Fishes out his wallet.)* Here's my student I.D. Good enough?

KATHERINE: *(Takes it from him, studies it, shows it to the camera, eventually tosses it back on the table.)* His "proof" consists of an I.D. card that could be new, old, possibly faked. Though it does at least have his photo on it, which is helpful, yet inconclusive. Is he or is he not a fellow student, she contemplates, or is that just a diversion so that he can come on to her?

JAMES: What d'you mean, come on to you? I just sat down and tried to say "hello."

KATHERINE: He seems self-defensive when confronted with his questionable actions.

JAMES: Questionable? I'm in your sosh class and I just sat down to try to be friendly, because I recognized you when I came in. That's "questionable"?

KATHERINE: One wonders what lurks in this young man's past that makes him so sensitive to perceived criticism. Is it something hopelessly genetic, or were his parents some kind of monsters? Or perhaps he was an orphan with no parental guidance at all. Yes, that constant debate of nature versus nurture rears its ugly head once more in this coffee shop confrontation.

JAMES: My parents were … I mean, are … just fine, thank you very much.

KATHERINE: He admits it's a genetic problem.

JAMES: I do not! It's not a genetic problem. Wait a minute! It's not a problem at all. I mean, there's no problem. With me.

KATHERINE: She's not completely convinced yet that he's sane. Sitting down with strangers in bookstores suggests a certain wild streak in his character.

Lawrence Harbison   25

JAMES: You're not a stranger! I thought we made that clear in the beginning.

KATHERINE: Clear to him, perhaps. Though there's a certain familiarity to his visage, she notes. It's certainly conceivable that she's seen his face somewhere before.

JAMES: Because we're in sosh class together.

KATHERINE: Ah, right, the famous sosh class. With Professor Gilder.

JAMES: You know as well as I do it's Professor Smith.

KATHERINE: He's not quite as stupid as he looks.

JAMES: Oh, I look stupid?

KATHERINE: But Smith is a common name, she ponders. There are at least four Professor Smiths on campus.

JAMES: But only *one* Professor Smith in the Sociology department.

KATHERINE: Hah! Well played, she thinks, but doesn't want to give him the satisfaction of his temporary victory.

JAMES: But you just did!

KATHERINE: There are times when she's not totally sure what he's on about.

JAMES: *(Pauses for a moment to regroup.)* Can I buy you a coffee or something?

KATHERINE: "Or something"? That sounds awfully suspicious to her. Probably wants to feed her a roofie "or something." She's heard all about these date-rape drugs that men try to use on women out in public. His offer is probably overloaded with evil intent.

JAMES: What if it was just an innocent offer to buy you a drink and he really had no desire to date-rape you at all?

KATHERINE: Once again, he's trying to confuse her. She is, of course, deeply attractive and incredibly desirable, so it's entirely reasonable that he might be trying to slip her a Mickey, which is an expression she heard in some really old movie she picked up from Netflix.

JAMES: If nothing else, you do have a healthy ego. If only your sanity could match it.

KATHERINE: Is he trying to infer that she's off her nut?

JAMES: I've never been able to figure out the difference between "infer" and "imply," so I just can't answer that question.

KATHERINE: Avoidance. Another typical frat boy trick when he's trying to pick someone up.

JAMES: I don't belong to a fraternity.

KATHERINE: Black-balled?

JAMES: No, perfectly healthy, but that's neither here nor there. You called me a frat boy, and that's just not true. Or you inferred or implied it, anyway.

KATHERINE: Truth is a slippery slope when you're walking through the swamp.

JAMES: Not that anything else has, but that makes no sense at all.

KATHERINE: Her trick wording has turned the tables, and now he's the one who's confused.

JAMES: Not so. I've been confused from the very beginning.

KATHERINE: At first blush, she'd assumed he was fairly bright, being a college student and all. But this admission of ongoing confusion suggests that he may be a little on the dim side.

JAMES: Dim? I'm number three in my class. How about you?

KATHERINE: Suddenly he seems to be making a competition of it. As much as she would like to entertain the concept, she really doesn't see the point.

JAMES: Like life itself, there really doesn't seem to *be* any point. I thought we might have a normal conversation, but that, so far, seems to have very little chance of happening.

KATHERINE: Apparently the dim young man also thinks of himself as a psychic.

JAMES: I do not. It was just a wild guess, actually. Though all of the evidence to this point seems to support the unlikelihood of a sane chat.

KATHERINE: She begins to think he could be a worthy adversary.

JAMES: Adversary? I'm not all that interested in fighting over whether or not to buy you a beverage.

KATHERINE: This might be a good place to cue up *"Love is a Battlefield"* for background music.

JAMES: Love? Lord above.

KATHERINE: Now he's trying to be cute. Actually, it is kind of cute, one musical cultural reference following another. And he's not that bad-looking, either.

JAMES: Do you ever keep any of your thoughts to yourself, or is everything in the public domain?

KATHERINE: Why would she have anything to hide? And why would he think she did?

JAMES: I'm pretty sure I'm beginning to not think anything about you at all.

KATHERINE: To Katherine, this does not seem to bode well for a long-term relationship.

JAMES: We'll be lucky if it lasts *(looks at his watch)* for another five minutes.

KATHERINE: He seems to be the type who gives up easily.

JAMES: I've hiked the entire Appalachian Trail, completed two half-marathons, built a Habitat house with just two other people and after only ten years of trying, figured out a Rubik's Cube. I'm no quitter!

KATHERINE: Oh my god! Ego alert! Ego alert!

JAMES: Not at all. I was just trying to prove my point, or deny yours. Whatever other classes you might be taking, debate is clearly not one of them. Though I could postulate that you're studying abnormal psychology. Or better yet, you're a case study for that class. Yeah, that's it.

KATHERINE: *(Soberly, to her camera.)* Or maybe she just doesn't know how to talk to somebody other than through FaceBook.

JAMES: Ha! He's got her on the run now.

KATHERINE: *(Shaking off her momentary seriousness.)* What? Is he trying to take control of the situation?

JAMES: He is *in* control of the situation.

KATHERINE: It would be touching if it weren't so laughable.

JAMES: Do you see me laughing?

KATHERINE: It wouldn't be him laughing, it would be *me* laughing. Wait a minute. Now I'm confused.

JAMES: Ha! Victory is mine!

KATHERINE: It is not! No, wait, maybe he's right. No, *no*. That just can't be. I'm always in control.

JAMES: Maybe that's your problem.

KATHERINE: Problem? Is he suggesting I have some kind of problem?

JAMES: I'm suggesting you have some kind of problem, for sure.

KATHERINE: Insulted deeply, she invites him to leave her table, drinkless and as alone as he was when he arrived in this social environment.

JAMES: Well, you have the power to ask me to leave the table, but not the cafe. I'll just leave you to your … whatever it is you were doing when I came in.

KATHERINE: She thinks this is the best idea he's had all day, perhaps all year.

JAMES: It's been delightful not talking to you.

KATHERINE: He tries to leave on a high point.

JAMES: And does so *(as he walks off)* successfully!

KATHERINE: That went well! *(Talking directly into the video device again.)* I think that just about wraps up tonight's documentary subject: "Why is it that men have so much difficulty communicating with a woman?" Tomorrow night, perhaps we'll pick up on that long-delayed topic: "Why is it that Katherine seems to have so much difficulty finding someone to date?" *(She stares at the empty seat across from her, the space around her, the device; then slowly turns the device off and puts it down.)* Or maybe not.

   BLACKOUT

dtf

Bekah Brunstetter

ORIGINAL PRODUCTION
    Presented by LiveWire Chicago's VisionFest,
    17 July-2 August, 2013

    Directed by Julie Ritchey

    CAST:
    SARAH: Molly Bunder
    KEVIN: Nathan Drackett

KEVIN waits at a bar, stinking of nerves. Two whiskey neats sit in front of him. He takes off his blazer. Folds it in his lap. Reconsiders. Puts it back on. Rolls up the sleeves. Reconsiders. Rolls the sleeves back down. Sits. Touches his hair. Messes up his hair. Reconsiders. Smoothes his hair. Reconsiders. Does something to his hair that is somewhere inbetween smooth and mess. Clears his throat. Feels something he had for lunch in his teeth. Starts to pick. With perfect timing, SARAH softly approaches, stinking of am I pretty and will he murder me? And regret. She spots KEVIN picking his teeth. Considers running. Considers throwing herself into oncoming traffic or climbing onto his lap and telling him all of her secrets. Attraction. She approaches. He spots her. He's hooked. He stands up too fast, sending his bar stool plummeting.

SARAH:	KEVIN:
Hey, are you	Oh, sh—hey, I'm /Kevin
SARAH:	KEVIN:
Hey I'm Sarah	I'm Kevin
SARAH:	KEVIN:
Hi Kevin	Hellooooo Sarah!

SARAH: What?
KEVIN: What?
SARAH: Nothing.
KEVIN: Wait, what?

> *(Beat)*

You wanna sit down?
SARAH: Yeah, sure, let's sit. I'll sit. By which I mean, yes, I will sit. Okay, I'm sitting.

> *(She sits.)*

SARAH:	KEVIN:
I just saw a dog get hit by a car	I ordered you a—what?
SARAH:	KEVIN:
Sorry, what?	Like a dog?

SARAH:	KEVIN:
Yeah, but it was maybe a coyote?	Oh, my God, I'm so sorry. Is it—

SARAH:	KEVIN:
So I won't be eating lasagna for a while.	Fuck coyotes

SARAH:	KEVIN:
Yeah, fuck 'em. Demon dogs, ha ha—	Was that a lasagna joke?

SARAH: What?

KEVIN: Lasagna.

>   *(Beat)*

KEVIN: So I uh, I got you this Knob creek, not like *let's get you hammered* but you said you like it in your prof. File.

SARAH: I do! Indeed I do. So.

KEVIN: Hey, cheers.

SARAH: Cheers!

>   *(They clink.)*

KEVIN: So how was your day at the Library, the Mumford Branch, yeah?

SARAH: Yep! That's me. It was uh, it was nice and bookish. Only *two* homeless people tried to use the free computers to 'squeeze the seed,' as they say, probably also in France.

KEVIN: What the hell is that?

SARAH: Porn.

KEVIN: Seed—?

SARAH: Think about it—ha ha—

KEVIN: Like uh. Like incredibly small nuts.

SARAH: Ding!

>   *(They high five. They are both now shocked that they both did this. They fall in love. Hands quickly return to their laps. They are nervous as shit, both terrified of blowing this.)*

KEVIN: I think that's great, I really think that's great, that you're a librarian, dying breed.

SARAH: Well, I love books.

KEVIN: I like to smell them.

SARAH: Me too.

KEVIN: Me too. They have a uh, if you're hungry, they have really great brussel sprouts here, they uh, I've been here before. You said on your—that you're into them. They uh, they roast them? And there's something on there, it's like salt, but it's not salt. It's beyond salt.

SARAH: Cumin?

KEVIN: Maybe. Great spice. They uh, the texture's really great. Here. Really tender but then crispy. Not moist at all.

SARAH: That's a terrible word.

KEVIN:	SARAH:
Oh My God it's the worst word	It's almost as bas as 'casserole'

(Beat)

KEVIN: I really like what you said. About, um. About what you're looking for. I'm sorry to just say that right now, but I just wanted to put that out there, I thought it was incredibly honest and articulate, and I *also* prioritize cuddling over uh, the over stuff. Things.

(Beat)

And I *also* listen to Loretta Lynn when I'm sad.

SARAH: This is really embarrassing….

KEVIN: Yes. Yes it is.

SARAH: No, I mean. My app freaked out on me so I couldn't check your profile before I got here so I kind of have no idea who you are. Or which—I mean, I can't remember anything about you. And you know all of these things about me, you really looked, you really—

KEVIN: Well, I can *tell* you, with my mouth—

SARAH: Wait, are you the guy who makes his own cheese?

KEVIN: No, but now I want to go home and do that.

SARAH: You have a 'kid named Brandon and he is your heart?'

KEVIN: No children, to my knowledge.

SARAH: Are you the juice guy?

KEVIN: Can't say I am.

SARAH: You're the child actor! The grown one.

KEVIN: No, but I did do a local TV spot for my uncle's used mattress store in my youth, and yes it's on the internet, and no I cannot figure out how to take it down.

> *(SARAH laughs. Shows her uncensored self.)*

KEVIN: Ow.
SARAH: What?
KEVIN: You are really pretty.
SARAH: Thank you.
KEVIN: Thank you.
SARAH: Thank you. *(Beat)*
> What's your name thing? On the'—
KEVIN: Doesn't matter.
SARAH: No, what is it?
KEVIN: IamKevin.
SARAH: No it's not.
KEVIN: Yep. Nope. It's uh, it's dtf039.
SARAH: Ah.

> *(Beat)*

> What's dtf?
KEVIN: Nothing. It's a joke thing.
SARAH: What's it mean?
KEVIN: You really don't know?
SARAH: Nope?
KEVIN: Who are you?
SARAH: I'm Sarah.
KEVIN: Sarah, how did you come to be? Are you real?
SARAH: Pretty sure.
KEVIN: Kansas, yeah?
SARAH: Yup. My parents are still together, and everything.
KEVIN: Mine too.

> *(They smile at each other.)*

SARAH: Donuts then Friendship.
KEVIN: Yup!
SARAH: So . . . who are you?

> *(This stops KEVIN. What a question. How does one now answer this question, not in front of a computer? He wants to reach for one, he wants to hide under his com-*

*forter and think and type, but he can't. He motions for
another drink.)*

KEVIN: I am uh . . . I am Kevin.

SARAH: Hi Kevin.

KEVIN: Uh, hi. I am—27 years old. I'm from Connecticut. I
work in finance. I'm really good at pretending like I like to
watch sports. I'm an incredibly open person, I love to laugh.

SARAH: 'You're looking for someone who wants to laugh with
you through all of the sad and terrible things.'

KEVIN: Yeah.

SARAH: 'Penchant for microwave popcorn also a plus.'

KEVIN: *(kind of touched)* Nailed it.

SARAH: I remember. What else? Tell me a new thing.

KEVIN: Just one?

SARAH: Sure.

KEVIN: Well currently I'm uh, I'm sitting twelve to fourteen
inches from what I'm pretty sure is a hologram designed to
restore my faith in humanity and maybe also in love.

> *(Beat. SARAH smiles.)*

Wow. Mulligan.

SARAH: No, it's okay. I liked it.

KEVIN: it liked you.

(what am I saying?)

What?

SARAH: Can I ask—

KEVIN: No.

SARAH: Okay.

> *(Beat)*

Do you ever wish it didn't have to be like this?

KEVIN: We could sit at a table—

SARAH: No, I wish I could meet you. Like, in the world. Like on
a raft. Like at trivia.

KEVIN: Why?

SARAH: I guess I just. I guess I still feel like this means—Meeting you this way means—

KEVIN: Like it can't be real?

SARAH: Like I'm a robot? Like my feelings and preferences can
be quantified and measured and labeled. Turned into charts.

Like I'm all wire inside?

(Beat)

KEVIN: You can meet me in the world.
SARAH: Too late.
KEVIN: Nope.

(He gets up and goes. SARAH sits, confused. A few moments go by. KEVIN returns, walks right past her, not looking at her. SARAH smiles. A few moments later, KEVIN returns.)

Hey, have you seen a guy go by?
SARAH: A guy?
KEVIN: He's uh, he's about yay high, lumberjackish—
SARAH: Nope, haven't seen him.
KEVIN: Oh, well.

(Beat)

KEVIN: Mind if I join you while I wait?
SARAH: For your lumberjackish friend.
KEVIN: Yeah, he's probably just late. That guy. Always late.

(He sits next to her. Extends his hand.)

Nice to meet you. I'm Kevin.
SARAH: Sarah.
KEVIN: You hungry, Sarah?
SARAH: *Yes.*

(KEVIN motions to the bartender for a menu, takes a sip of his whiskey.)

Down to fuck!

(KEVIN spits. Laughs.)

KEVIN: I'm sorry?
SARAH: Dtf.
KEVIN: Nailed it.

(They cheers.)

But I don't mean really—I mean, I mean it ironically, with irony—
SARAH: *(all smile)* I know.

(Beat)

I know.

> *(Eyes locked, they face each other, plugged in, synapses throbbing, wires moving, unable to think of anything to say, at all.)*

END OF PLAY

END OF THE RAINY SEASON

Mark Rigney

PRODUCTION NOTES:

End Of The Rainy Season was first produced by the FU-SION Theatre Company (FUSIONnm.org) as the Jury Award-winning entry in their annual original short works festival, THE SEVEN, June 6-16, 2013 at The Cell Theatre in Albuquerque, NM.

Festival Producer: Dennis Gromelski
Festival Curator: Jen Grigg
Directed by Laurie Thomas
Lighting and Scenic Design by Richard K. Hogle
Sound Design by Brent Stevens
Property Design by Robyn Phillips
Production Stage Manager: Maria Lee Schmidt.

CAST:
JANINE: Kate Costello
AMEN: Marc Lynch

CHARACTERS:
>AMEN: Male, black. A village innkeeper in Togo.
>JANINE: Female, white. A U.S. grad student.

STAGE REQUIREMENTS: The ideal set would feature at least one door, plain chairs or stools, and a dilapidated counter. Several specific props are essential: A backpack, travel gear. A portable radio of some sort. An iPod, any variety. A table lamp. Two derelict boots.

PLACE: A gone-to-seed "hotel"—really a very meager *pensión* in Togo.

TIME: Between darkness and midnight, tonight.

>*Sounds of driving rain and gusting wind. A very bad night to be out and about. Welcome to the rainy season in Togo.*

>*Lights up on the middling "lobby" of a scruffy, run-down "hotel." Two doors would be ideal, one to the outside (rainy) world, and one leading elsewhere, in. There's also a counter, behind which sits AMEN OLYMPIO, black, aging, a Togo national, busily repairing a boot. Next to him: a lamp that doesn't work.*

>*The exterior door bangs open and in staggers JANINE, dripping, out of breath. Has she just been swimming? No. Just drenched by rain. She's a U.S. grad student, white, twenties.*

JANINE: Wow! It's pouring out there! Sorry, do you speak English? (*Off Amen's non-committal response*) Oh. (*Readying her limited Ewe*) Okay, let's see . . . *Medekuku, fica de*?
AMEN: "Where is the please?"
JANINE: No, no, I'm trying to say, "Do you have a room?" Wait. You just said—
AMEN: —Yes. I speak English. Also *Français*.
JANINE: Ah, *oui. Combien pour une salle*?
AMEN: But do I *have* a room? That is the first question.

JANINE: I did ask.

AMEN: I have one room.

JANINE: Okay, great. How much is it?

AMEN: It is not available.

JANINE: Oh. Someone else is already here?

AMEN: No.

JANINE: But someone reserved it?

AMEN: No.

JANINE: Look, sir, I'm sorry if I said something wrong, *babana-wo*, but it's pouring outside.

AMEN: Mmm, the rainy season, yes. Come back in the dry season. Togo, in the dry season, has at least a little potential.

JANINE: I like it fine during the wet season. When I can get a room.

> *(Janine begins to strip off gear, her backpack, etc.)*

AMEN: I told you. I don't have a room.

JANINE: No, you told me you have a room but that I can't use it.

AMEN: Is that all you have?

JANINE: I like to travel light.

AMEN: Light? (*Indicating the nearby lamp*) Like this?

JANINE: Light meaning without a lot of gear. Bags.

AMEN: Ah. Light. English is my fifth language, so.

JANINE: May I ask *why* I can't have the room?

AMEN: Do you know what I'm going to do next?

JANINE: Does it have to do with answering my question?

AMEN: You Americans. Always in a hurry.

JANINE: That is the stereotype, yes, but really this is about me, as a human, being wet.

AMEN: So you don't know the answer.

JANINE: I guess not, no.

> *(From behind the counter, Amen produces a portable (transistor?) radio and an iPod.)*

AMEN: Next, I will fix this. Then this. Then, hopefully, *(indicating the sad, broken lamp)* this.

JANINE: You can fix iPods?

AMEN: I can fix anything, and you would not believe how many things around here are broken.

JANINE: You can fix anything, but you won't give me a room.

AMEN: The truth? I can fix anything except this lamp. Also my country, which is probably maybe slightly more important.

JANINE: Well. Fixing a country, that's, you know, an ambitious project, for one night.

AMEN: My cousin's great uncle was the first president. Of all Togo.

JANINE: Great. Does that get me closer to a room?

AMEN: What do you think about ghosts?

JANINE: I don't think about ghosts.

AMEN: Mmm. Listen.

(Over or under the rain, a sound from behind the door. Rumbling?)

JANINE: Could be anything.

AMEN: I think maybe you're a ghost. Haunting this country. Doing I don't know what. Something probably not good for me, my people.

JANINE: If I were a ghost, I wouldn't want a room.

AMEN: You might.

JANINE: To what, haunt it? Look, this is the only place in the village. Please. *Medekuku.*

AMEN: What do you want from Togo?

JANINE: I told you, a room!

AMEN: No, that is what you want from me. What do you want from Togo?

JANINE: Nothing. I'm with Duke University, I'm doing research.

AMEN: Mmm, research.

JANINE: We're looking at big agribusiness, investment-based land transfers, who owns what. Are you even aware that most all the cropland northwest of here is now owned by the Chinese, Chongquing Seed Corporation?

AMEN: They pay well.

JANINE: A one-time fee.

AMEN: Yes. But enough that no one sane will turn them down. *(The radio, which he's been fiddling with, comes to life)* There. Another patient cured.

JANINE: You didn't use tools.

AMEN: I told you, I fix things.

JANINE: Can you make it stop raining?

AMEN: You have not answered my question.

JANINE: Not answered? I've answered, like, dozens of your questions!

AMEN: But not. What you want. From Togo.

JANINE: I told you, nothing.

AMEN: Researchers want nothing? You have risen above, you are beyond mortal needs?

JANINE: Okay, sure, yes. I would like to bring home enough compelling raw data for a thesis. To get my degree.

AMEN: Ah. So you will marry Togo to take her information, and you will divorce her for the sort of good life you can never have here.

JANINE: Or maybe I'll just catch my death of cold and die in your lobby.

AMEN: You're getting angry.

JANINE: Damn straight.

AMEN: I wonder, when that happens, what do you do with your anger?

JANINE: What do I do with it? I vent! I explode!

AMEN: Listen. You know how to work an iPod, yes?

JANINE: What the hell does that have to do with the price of tea in China?

AMEN: I don't know about the tea, but here. (*Handing over the iPod*) Try it.

JANINE: (*After doing so*) It's dead. Maybe recharge it?

AMEN: Wait, one moment. (*He performs unlikely mystical rites over the recalcitrant iPod*) There. Now try.

JANINE: (*Amazed that it now works*) Hang on. You're not saying you fixed that by wanting it to work.

AMEN: It's a small thing, an iPod. Easy. The things I really want to fix, so much more difficult.

JANINE: But you could make a fortune.

AMEN: Mmm, and I wouldn't even need a degree from Duke. But what I want, really? Is to fix Togo so that it is entirely uninteresting. Uninteresting to foreigners, people like you. I would like Togo to be a place you pass over, think nothing of, so that it can heal, become itself again. Now. I think you should go, because I think maybe you work yourself for this Chinese seed whatever-it-is, and the research you do will make it easier for them to buy more of our land.

JANINE: My research will actually most likely make it harder for big companies—Americans too, Agrisol or Jarch or whomever. But okay, sure, white people have been screwing you for centuries, yes. But in this moment? It's nasty outside and I am begging.

AMEN: The room is not available.

JANINE: Because it's haunted, or because you don't want to give it to me?

AMEN: Actually, both—and you should hope it's not haunted, because if it is, I cannot kick out the ghost. At least not today.

JANINE: All right. I'll bite. Why not?

AMEN: It's Tuesday. Very bad luck to kick out ghosts on Tuesday.

JANINE: Oh, for God's sake.

Janine marches over to the interior door and hauls it open. Instant CHAOS! Blinding light, cacophonous noise, howling, wind! Has she just opened the door to hell? It takes all her strength to shove the door closed.

JANINE: *(cont'd)* Holy shit.

Amen begins work stitching up another old boot.

AMEN: Ghosts, yes? Or something. Something very angry.

JANINE: Okay, fine. Can I just sleep here, in the lobby?

AMEN: My mother was a ghost, for a while. But very peaceful. She haunted the coffee plantation, the one just south of here, for, oh, two months. I think she missed her morning cup.

JANINE: Whatever's in there is nobody's mother.

AMEN: Mmm, no—but I thought at first maybe it was, that maybe it was a spirit, even my mother again, still angry about her coffee. But years went by, with more and more, you know, fury, and so I thought, no, what is behind that door is the history of the world. What could be angrier than that? But no. Wrong again. Only now, this month, did I discover the answer. What is in that room is me. My anger. All the rage I hold for my existence, and my country, and that has nowhere to go. And because I refuse to let it out, to let it fly into the

world where it could do real damage, my anger keeps growing larger and louder. Today it takes up an entire room. Next
year? I wonder how long that door can hold.

JANINE: That's the most one hundred percent ludicrous thing
I've ever heard.

AMEN: We play our parts very nicely, don't we? I, the African,
the mystical dark man who believes in spirits and phantoms.
In medicine that can fix an iPod just like that. And you, the
western white, always skeptical, so sure the world has nothing more to offer than what meets the eye.

JANINE: Where do you sleep?

AMEN: Here. On the floor. Blankets. There is room, if you want.
We can be as far apart as you wish.

JANINE: Thank you, *akpe meleo,* but at this point, I've got my
heart set on a bed. I assume, in there, you still have a bed?

AMEN: Of course, but—

JANINE: —Okay, then. How much?

AMEN: But you saw what's in there, you heard.

JANINE: Hey, you don't want my money, that's fine by me.

AMEN: No! You think I am a nice man, harmless? In there, I am
not!

JANINE: Last chance to make a buck.

AMEN: I will not be responsible.

JANINE: I know.

AMEN: What happens, happens.

JANINE: I got that, yeah. So look, last night I got a room for
one franc. But obviously this is special, a special room. How
about . . . ten dollars?

AMEN: That . . . that's a lot of money.

JANINE: I know. Sorry.

AMEN: You're really going in there?

JANINE: What, don't Togolese women do this sort of thing?
Take on a project, no matter how damaged and broken? They
don't say, "No worries, I can fix it. And if I can't, I'm strong
enough to take whatever comes. It'll be my cross to bear."
'Cos where I come from, women *like* bearing crosses. We're
damn near addicted.

AMEN: You're crazy.

JANINE: History of the world.

AMEN: I don't need you to fix my room. Or me.

JANINE: C'mon. Everybody needs a little fixing.

> *(As Janine approaches the door, a dangerous rumble sounds. But outside, has the rain stopped? Yes. Only drips remain.)*

AMEN: Wait. *Nkowode*?

JANINE: Janine. *Nkninye* Janine Anne Preston. Ms.

AMEN: Ms. I am Amen. Amen Olympio.

JANINE: Wish me luck, Amen. I might need it.

AMEN: *Hede nyuie.* And *mia dogo.*

JANINE: *Mia dogo*? I'm sorry, I don't know that.

AMEN: I say you do.

> *Janine opens the door. Not chaos this time, but a muted pulsing: visual, aural, somehow conciliatory. As Janine steps through the portal, the lights flicker, the noise level ramps briefly up, but then . . . the room draws a relieved sigh.*

> *As the lights on stage dim—as Amen is left temporarily alone—the lamp that he could never quite fix glows warmly to life. It, too, pulses. Like a heartbeat.*

> *END OF PLAY*

FILLER

Andrew Biss

ORIGINAL PRODUTION
　Produced by City Theatre of Independence in their 5th
　annual Original Playwrights Festival July 11-14 2013

　Directed by Lindsay Adams

　CAST:
　SHANE: Rob Ladd
　TATYANA: Jackie Coomes

CHARACTERS:

> SHANE: Tries to convey a macho image, but in truth is nervous and vulnerable. Perhaps a slight Cockney accent. Age open.
>
> TATYANA: Pragmatic, level-headed, but not without heart. Perhaps a slight Eastern European accent. Age open.

SETTING: An ominous and dimly lit stage.

TIME: The present.

> *At rise: The room is dimly lit. SHANE is seated in a chair, downstage C, holding his head in his hands. TATYANA paces back and forth, upstage. After a while, she stops and appears to peer out of a window, as if looking for something or someone. SHANE turns and observes her.*

SHANE: Any sign?

> *(pause.)*

TATYANA: Nothing.

SHANE: *(rubbing his face in his hands)*
Where the fuck is he?

> *(pause)*

TATYANA: I'm beginning to wonder if they haven't . . .

SHANE: Shut up! Don't! Don't even think it. We can't afford to.

TATYANA: He was careless. He was stupid. They could have easily . . .

SHANE: I said, shut it!

> *(Beat. He covers his face with his face hands again.)*

TATYANA: Yes, yes, bury your head in your hands—in the sand. But when you pull them away, the reality will still be there . . . waiting for you . . . for us both.

SHANE: I just need to think, that's all.

TATYANA: About what?

SHANE: About what we do . . . if he doesn't show up.

TATYANA: What's there to think about? If he doesn't show up... we're dead.

SHANE: *No!*

> *(He leaps from his chair and crosses to TATYANA, grabbing her roughly by the shoulders.)*

Listen to me, Tatyana, and listen good! He'll be here. I know he will. Something's happened. Something's screwed up his timing. But he'll be here. I know it.

> *(beat)*

And if he isn't . . . if he's . . . then we'll . . . change plans.

TATYANA: To what? There are no others. It all depends on him.

SHANE: No it doesn't! We still have options.

> *(beat)*

I just . . .

> *(He returns to the chair and rubs his head in hands once more.)*

TATYANA: Look, this is a one-way street. You knew the risks when you got into this. If you don't have the guts to follow through when things go wrong, then you should never have got involved to begin with. This operation can't afford people like you.

SHANE: Hey, it's not my fault he hasn't shown up. It's no good blaming me.

TATYANA: No one's blaming anyone. But if you can't keep your head in a crisis you shouldn't be in this business.

SHANE: It's keeping my head I'm concerned about. Now, instead of just standing there criticizing, why don't you try and help figure out how we're gonna get out of this mess if he doesn't show up.

TATYANA: He's not showing up.

SHANE: A real optimist you are, aren't you?

> *(beat)*

TATYANA: I think I've figured it out.

SHANE: Figured what out?

TATYANA: This. Us. All of this ... perpetual waiting.

SHANE: What's to figure out? We're waiting for him to show up, that's all.

TATYANA: But I told you ... he's not showing up.

SHANE: Not yet.

TATYANA: He's not showing up because he was never intended to show up.

>   *(beat)*

It's all a set up.

>   *(beat)*

SHANE: What are you talking about?

TATYANA: Us. This. We've been set up.

SHANE: By . . . by who?

TATYANA: I'll give you one guess.

>   *(beat)*

SHANE: I don't . . . I've no idea.

>   *(beat)*

TATYANA: The playwright.

SHANE: *(incredulous) What?*

TATYANA: You heard me.

SHANE: But . . . that's insane.

TATYANA: Is it? Think about it. Think about how neatly the last scene was resolved—how the scene following this one starts from an entirely different plot point.

SHANE: That doesn't mean anything.

TATYANA: No? Then why are we never mentioned again for the rest of the play?

SHANE: That's not true. We are. We are mentioned.

TATYANA: Near the end in a brief aside from a minor character to tie up a loose thread, that's all. The quick disposal of a thin subplot that was never intended to go anywhere in the first place.

SHANE: No . . . no, you've got it all wrong.

TATYANA: Shane, listen to me, this scene is completely unnecessary to the overall arc of the story. You know it and I know it. It neither propels the play forward nor adds anything of value to the central plot.

SHANE: And you . . . you really believe this?

TATYANA: I've had my suspicions for some time, but tonight … tonight the final pieces of the puzzle fell into place. You see, I'd often wondered why our characters were brought back from scene three in such a seemingly random and superfluous way. And tonight it hit me.

SHANE: What did?

TATYANA: This entire scene—/this completely meaningless waiting game—was added after he'd completed the original script.

SHANE: No!

TATYANA: I'm guessing somewhere around the third or fourth draft.

SHANE: But why? Why on earth would he do that?

TATYANA: Isn't it obvious? It wasn't long enough. He doubtless foresaw problems getting it produced if it didn't stretch to a full evening's entertainment, so he decided to...pad it out.

SHANE: Oh my God! That means...that means that we're . . .

TATYANA: Yes, Shane. It's time we faced the truth. And the truth is that you and I are little more than . . . filler.

SHANE: No!

(He begins pacing the stage, highly agitated.)

Jesus Christ, we've gotta do something! We can't just continue on like this!

TATYANA: Do what? We're merely pawns in this web of deceit. We have no say in it.

SHANE: But we have to do *something*. This is ridiculous. We'll be a laughing stock.

TATYANA: I fear it may already be too late.

SHANE: So . . . what happens now?

TATYANA: What always happens . . . we wait.

SHANE: I don't know that I can. Not now. Not now that I know

TATYANA: What choice do you have?

SHANE: But to stay here and just wait—knowing it's all pointless? Knowing we're just killing time because of a poorly structured play?

TATYANA: We've done it countless times before and we'll do it again.

SHANE: But that was before we knew. Oh God, this is … this is torture.

TATYANA: I doubt it's a walk in the park for the audience, either. Let's hope they remain intrigued enough by the mystery of who we're waiting for and don't start putting two and two together.

SHANE: This is unconscionable. How could he get away with it?

TATYANA: It doesn't matter how, the fact is he has. Anyway, it's nothing new—I see it all the time.

SHANE: I should have guessed. Why didn't I see it?

TATYANA: Don't blame yourself.

SHANE: I should have realized the whole concept was suspect. Two people just sitting around waiting for someone who never shows up—I mean, who could possibly find that interesting?

(TATYANA Shrugs.)

TATYANA: People are strange. Perhaps they read more into it— see it as some sort of ... I don't know ... metaphor.

SHANE: Well, I don't. I see it as a cheap cop-out from a lazy writer bankrupt of both ideas and principles.

(beat)

TATYANA: And yet still we wait.

SHANE: Not me. Not for much longer.

TATYANA: You have no choice, Shane. What's written is written. There's nothing to be done.

SHANE: But I . . . I can't be a party to this. It's a ... a waste of people's time.

TATYANA: Relax. They waste much more of it in far more trivial ways. At least with us they have a semi-respectable excuse.

SHANE: Which is what?

TATYANA: "I went to see a play."

(beat)

SHANE: So we just . . . wait . . . until the end?

TATYANA: Yes, Shane. I'm afraid so.

(beat)

SHANE: Oh, no!

TATYANA: What?

SHANE: Oh, shit!

TATYANA: What is it?

SHANE: I can't . . . I can't think straight, it's all...all this crap about the playwright and the scene, it's ... it's fucked with my head. I don't . . .

(beat)

I don't remember.

TATYANA: Don't remember what?

SHANE: How it ends.

TATYANA: Our scene?

SHANE: Yes.

TATYANA: It's nothing to worry about. It ends very simply.

(beat)

(It ends when the light goes out.)

SHANE: That's it?

TATYANA: Yes.

SHANE: All that waiting . . . all that hoping . . . and it all just ends . . . just like that?

TATYANA: Yes.

SHANE: So it was all ... pointless?

TATYANA: Well ... that depends on how you look at it.

SHANE: But we had all that hope—all that expectation. And then it just ends. Unfulfilled.

TATYANA: Not unfulfilled. Unanswered.

SHANE: Isn't that the same thing?

TATYANA: No. One is a dead end. The other is a question mark.

SHANE: You mean a mystery?

TATYANA: In a way.

SHANE: So it ... it was all worth it, then? Our scene did mean something after all?

TATYANA: In the grand scheme of the play, probably not. We have our turn in the spotlight, eventually the light goes out, and in truth, we're mentioned again but not really remembered.

SHANE: So ... so we really are just...filler?

TATYANA: I wouldn't say that.

(beat)

Now that I look at it, it's really not been that bad. We had our time together, you and me, and on the whole you were pretty good company to share it with.

(beat)

And anyway, it couldn't go on forever.

SHANE: No.

TATYANA: So, all in all, I'd say it was worth it.

SHANE: Yeah ... yeah, I think so, too.

TATYANA: Good. Now give me your hand.

SHANE: Why? This isn't a ... does it become a love scene?

TATYANA: No, Shane, mercifully not. But it is the end.

SHANE: It is?

TATYANA: Yes.

SHANE: Are you sure?

TATYANA: My memory's better than yours, remember?

SHANE: Oh, yeah. I'd forgotten.

>   *(He places his hand in TATYANA's.)*

TATYANA: Are you ready?

SHANE: For what?

TATYANA: For what comes next.

SHANE: And what's that?

TATYANA: Ah ... well, I'm afraid even I don't know the answer to that.

SHANE: Oh.

>   *(beat)*

That's okay.

TATYANA: Trust me?

SHANE: Yes.

>   *(beat)*

TATYANA: Very well, then...our moment's up. Time to go.

>   *(They both look skyward as the lights slowly fade down to black.)*

>   *END OF PLAY*

GIRLS PRAY, OR THE KETCHUP STIGMATA

Alexis Kozak

ORIGINAL PRODUCTION
Black Box Asbury Park
Anthony Ciccotelli
Artistic Director
Black Box Asbury Park

Gallery 13, Asbury Park, NJ: June 14th, 15th, 16th

Directed by Barbara Panas

CAST:
ALLIE: Mel Ridgway
LISA: Allie Brand

Finalist in the Miami City Theatre National Award for Short Playwriting Contest.

CHARACTERS:
> LISA: late-teens, early twenties. White high school girl. Street smarter.
> ALLIE: late-teens, early twenties. White high school girl. Book smarter.

TIME: The near present.

PLACE: A largely Spanish all girls Catholic high school.

> *All plays are about lies.*

> —David Mamet, Theatre

LIGHTS UP

LISA and ALLIE, two Catholic high school girls, wearing plaid skirts and white boxy blouses. LISA wears a v-neck school sweater and holds several ketchup packets. They are in the hallway or the locker room. Maybe they are in the school chapel!

LISA: Hold one ketchup packet in each hand. When I tap my pencil on my desk three times, you just squeeze them, like this, and then drop the packets.

ALLIE: But I have a white blouse.

LISA: Did you study?

ALLIE: No.

LISA: The Spanish final starts in fifteen minutes, so if you have a better idea, now is the time to say it.

ALLIE: My mom's gonna kill me.

LISA: Well you should have thought about that before you put a white blouse on this morning.

ALLIE: But it's our uniform.

LISA: You could have worn the school sweater, like I did.

ALLIE: It's the middle of June.

LISA: Oh sure. Now you're full of excuses. You weren't so full of excuses when we were out with Peter and Frank last night, were you?

ALLIE: I didn't even want to go.

LISA: I bet you didn't even want him to stick his tongue down your throat either. Just take the ketchup packets.

ALLIE: They're gonna think it's weird that you're wearing a sweater.

LISA: They're nuns. They're dumb. In fact, they're Sisters of Saint Joseph, which means they are especially dumb. They're as dumb as they come. I mean, if they were Sisters of the Sacred Heart or something, then yeah, maybe the sweater would be an issue.

ALLIE: My mom's gonna kill me if I get ketchup on my blouse. She's gonna make me wash it myself.

LISA: They're never going to make us take our final exams if we have the stigmata. Especially if *both* of us have it.

ALLIE: You think so?

LISA: How many times do you think they've had girls with stigmatas here at St. Rose's?

ALLIE: "Stigmata."

LISA: What?

ALLIE: The plural of stigmata is stigmata. It's like "deer" and "fish."

LISA: Deer and fish, great. I'm trying to save our asses here, and you're giving me grammar lessons. Then maybe you *are* ready for the final. How many girls do you think have had . . . "stigmata" here at St. Rose's?

ALLIE: Didn't Jenny Rodriguez have it?

LISA: Right. And that was like two years ago or something.

ALLIE: Do you really think they'll believe us?

LISA: *Two years?!* It's high time Hermana brought up a student holy enough to have the stigmata. Not just *any*body gets a stigmata.

ALLIE: But ketchup?

LISA: St. Augustine's Preparatory School for Boys is beating us six to four in stigmata over the last ten years. This will put us even. Who are we hurting? Jesus wouldn't want us to take our finals. He'd *tell* us to do this.

ALLIE: He would?

LISA: What kind of a student do you think He was? Look at him. He's the kind of kid who faked an injury to get out of something if I ever saw one.

ALLIE: Yeah?

LISA: In fact, where do you think ideas come from?

ALLIE: I don't know.

LISA: From God. They come from God. In which case, this one did. Sister Regina Michael practically told us in anatomy that all thoughts come from God.

ALLIE: She did?

LISA: She said that if God made chemicals—which he did—and thoughts are just chemicals bouncing around into patterns, then a thought is from God. I mean, that's pretty apparent, if you ask me.

ALLIE: That doesn't sound like something she'd say.

LISA: She "practically" said it.

ALLIE: Which means she didn't.

LISA: No.

ALLIE: It's a lie.

LISA: No, no, no. No it is not, which therefore it wouldn't be.

ALLIE: Why?

LISA: Because He told me.

ALLIE: Who?

LISA: God . . . Jesus . . . He said—

ALLIE: Wait, wait, wait! Jesus spoke to you , and you didn't tell me?!

LISA: I'm telling you now.

ALLIE: Why didn't you tell me before?

LISA: Because I didn't want you to get all worked up like this. I know how you get.

ALLIE: How do I get?!

LISA: He said, are you ready for this?, he said, "Your future depends on this. You're not ready for the test. Fake the stigmata."

ALLIE: He said that?

LISA: "But don't do it by yourself. Ask your best friend to do it with you."

ALLIE: … Really? He said, "Ask your best friend"?

LISA: He said, "Ask your best friend Allison."

ALLIE: He knew my name?

LISA: Yeah. Who would make up a story like that?

ALLIE: … Us?

LISA: Exactly, nobody. They always believe girls.

ALLIE: I don't know, Mary Alice.

LISA: Don't call me that.

ALLIE: But it's your name.

LISA: Call me "Lisa."

ALLIE: Fine, "Lisa." Not like there's a Saint Lisa.

LISA: Do you really want to go to Plan B?

ALLIE: What's Plan B?

LISA: Father Peter molesting us.

ALLIE: It's better than *this* plan. At least it's plausible. It happened. To Guadalupe. But she's ... you know.

LISA: What?

ALLIE: . . . Spanish. You know how they are.

LISA: Slutty?

ALLIE: Lisa!

LISA: What?!

ALLIE: I meant how the nuns always think they're super holy or whatever.

LISA: And the priests always think they're good in bed. "Ay! Ay! Papi!"

ALLIE: Lisa!

LISA: They've got zeal! Fervor!

ALLIE: No. I meant it's because they're poor.

LISA: We're poor too.

ALLIE: Yeah, but we're poor and white.

LISA: So?

ALLIE: Don't you pay attention in Church History? The Christ only appears to poor Spanish girls.

LISA: Oh shit.

ALLIE: In South America. And never in twos. Only in threes. You know?, because everything is in threes.

LISA: Allison Katherine Bernadette Mary O'Malley, you are a genius!

ALLIE: What did I say?

LISA: We'll ask Conchetta.

ALLIE: What?

LISA: To do it with us.

ALLIE: Lisa, no!

LISA: We'll be up versus St. Peter's by two!

ALLIE: Lisa.

LISA: Let's find Conchetta. She's usually in Sister Inez's room washing the black board with her tears.

ALLIE: Goodbye Hudson County Junior College, hello Hudson County Institute of Nothing.

LISA: Allison.

ALLIE: I'm just saying. We need to have a Plan C.

LIGHTS DOWN/END PLAY

GRACELAND

Katie Thayer

ORIGINAL PRODUCTION
Produced by Playwrights' Round Table of Orlando at the Orlando Shakespeare Center as part of Summer Shorts July 19-21, 26-28, 2013

Directed by Walter "Buddy" Fales
Stage Manager: Tara Rewis

CAST:
GRACE: Amy Cuccaro
PRISCILLA: Brittany Davies

CHARACTERS:
> GRACE: twenties-thirties, but she should seem older. A housewife from Ohio obsessed with Elvis.
> PRISCILLA: twenties-forties. A Southern waitress working in an Elvis themed diner.

SETTING: Present day, but it should feel older. An Elvis-themed diner in Memphis, Tennessee.

PLACE: Graceland

TIME: Present day.

We open on a small restaurant: one or two tables and sets of chairs, and a counter. Behind the counter is an exit to the kitchen. Somewhere out of the way. There is a mirror. After a moment, GRACE, who appears 20s-30s, wearing an overcoat, enters from the front door (offstage). A bell over the door JINGLES.

PRISCILLA, twenties-forties, in a waitress uniform, enters from the kitchen.

PRISCILLA: Well, hi there. How many'll it be?

GRACE: Two, please.

(Pricilla grabs menus and seats Grace.)

PRISCILLA: Here ya go, table for two, just like it was waitin for you to show up.

GRACE: Thanks.

PRISCILLA: Can I getcha something to drink?

GRACE: I'll just take a water—Oh, wait, do you have Pepsi Cola?

PRISCILLA: Let me guess: you're in town to see Graceland.

GRACE: How did you know?

PRISCILLA: The only folks in Memphis that want Pepsi Cola only want it because it was Elvis's favorite drink. Everyone else just orders a Coke.

GRACE: So, do you have—

PRISCILLA: Of course I have it. Can't have a restaurant this close to his house without catering to his devoted fans. Besides, I'm a huge fan myself.

(Brings her the Pepsi.)

GRACE: Yeah?

PRISCILLA: Oh, honey yes. Please, just look at the menu. It screams "Elvis."

(Grace reads the menu.)

GRACE: Oh . . . "Love Me Chicken Tenders". . . "Viva las Eggs" . . . "You Ain't Nothin but a Hot Dog" . . . What's the "Heartburn Hotel?"

PRISCILLA: That is our specialty! It's a feast that includes a peanut butter and banana sandwich, a cheeseburger, grape jelly, pork chops, sauerkraut, burned bacon, and mashed potatoes. For dessert, you get a complimentary bottle of Tums, and no guarantees you won't die on the toilet later, if you catch my drift.

GRACE: I think I do.

(after a moment)

I want it.

PRISCILLA: You sure?

GRACE: Yes, I want it all. Anything that Elvis liked or might have breathed on, I want.

PRISCILLA: Well, ya sold me. Do you want me to put it in now, or wait for your second person?

GRACE: Oh, I don't know what's taking my husband so long. He heard some kind of gr-gr-umpht sound when we were nearby. When I got out of the car he said he wanted to take a look at the problem. He's probably staring under the hood, pretending like he knows what he's looking at. Go ahead and put mine in. He should get bored pretty soon.

PRISCILLA: You got it. Say, where are you folks visiting from anyway?

(Priscilla writes some stuff down and brings it off to the kitchen. She does waitress-y stuff throughout the following.)

GRACE: Ohio. Columbus.

PRISCILLA: That's pretty good drive.

GRACE: I wouldn't call it good. But being cramped up forever was worth it. I'm finally here. Well, almost.

PRISCILLA: What's the occasion?

GRACE: It's our anniversary.

PRISCILLA: Well, congratulations!

GRACE: Thanks. We were supposed to come here for our honeymoon, but right before the wedding, I found out I was pregnant, so we moved the wedding up and starting saving for the baby instead.

PRISCILLA: You do what you've gotta do.

GRACE: Then we promised each other we'd come for our first anniversary . . . then our second . . . then it seemed like we never had the time or the money.

PRISCILLA: I know how that is. So why now?

GRACE: A few months ago I won a small jackpot in the lottery . . . not much as far as lotteries go, but it took some of the pressure off, satisfied a few bill collectors . . . and I took it as a sign. Here I have money basically being dumped in my lap. It's like God said, "Well, here you go. Now stop all that dreaming and go do it."

PRISCILLA: I think they call that destiny.

GRACE: Oh everything about Graceland is my destiny!

PRISCILLA: How so?

GRACE: Well, my name is Grace, so for starters, they named that place after me . . . or at least I like to think so.

PRISCILLA: You don't say. My mamma named me Priscilla. So, after Elvis got married, I'd always say he married the wrong Priscilla.

GRACE: That's amazing! I'm in Memphis, in an Elvis themed restaurant, and my waitress is named Pricilla. What else have you got for me? A cook named Lisa Marie?

PRISCILLA: No, but I do have a dog named Lisa Marie.

GRACE: A dog?

PRISCILLA: Well, I figured I'd never have a kid, so when I became a mommy to my hound dog, it just seemed fitting.

GRACE: I don't know if Ms. Presley would agree with you on that one.

PRISCILLA: Well, how about you?

GRACE: What about me?

PRISCILLA: What have you named after Elvis? Because I know it's something.

GRACE: Ha, well, when my son was born, I begged my husband to let me name him Elvis. But he thought a name like that would get him teased in school. I mean, can you imagine, sharing the name with the king of rock getting you teased? Anyway, we fought for a while, but ultimately compromised on naming him Aaron, which is—

PRISCILLA: Elvis's middle name.

(They share a moment.)

GRACE: I also had dogs named Dixie, Natalie, and Ginger at various points in my life. Although I didn't name Ginger after Ginger Alden, he dated her after I named that dog.

PRISCILLA: No way!

GRACE: Oh yeah, I thought I was psychic! The universe understood that Elvis could only date women who shared names with my animals! I was going to name the next one Grace just to see what happened, but I didn't get a chance.

PRISCILLA: Oh, I wish you had. What a neat experiment that would have been!

GRACE: Oh, I was already with my husband at the time . . . but I do think he would have understood.

PRISCILLA: Was he your free pass?

GRACE: My what?

PRISCILLA: You know, free pass . . . the one celebrity you would be allowed to sleep with?

GRACE: Oh . . . um . . . well, we never formally discussed it . . .

PRISCILLA: I'm sorry, I guess that's a bit crude.

GRACE: No, that's alright.

PRISCILLA: He woulda been my free pass too.

GRACE: Are you married?

PRISCILLA: Was. Twice.

GRACE: What happened . . . if you don't mind me asking?

PRISCILLA: I'm not shy. The first one ran off with my younger cousin, and the second one took too many not-so-free passes until I kicked him out.

GRACE: Oh, I'm sorry.

PRISCILLA: No sweat off my back. I've got this place, my records, Lisa Marie—

GRACE: Lisa M—

PRISCILLA: My dog.

GRACE: Oh. Right.

PRISCILLA: And, of course, no man could take the place of Elvis.

GRACE: Did you ever get to see him?

PRISCILLA: Unfortunately, no. You?

GRACE: Once.

PRISCILLA: What? You've been holding out on me!

(Priscilla grabs a seat with Grace.)

GRACE: I wasn't holding out, it just hadn't come up—

PRISCILLA: Honey, we have been talking about nothing else since you walked in that door. Now spill.

GRACE: So, when I was 16, he announced he would be playing in Cincinnati. I pleaded with my parents to let me go. My mother didn't want me to go because she didn't want me to be corrupted by Rock n Roll, and "Elvis the Pelvis," and well, my father didn't care enough to fight against her ruling. I was heartbroken. I locked myself in my room playing nothing but Elvis's sad songs for weeks. Then, about a week before the concert, Eugene Knickerbaucher . . . I swear that was his name . . . asked me out. He was a real nerd, I mean, who is named Eugene and is not a nerd? Well, I told him I would go out with him under one condition: he take me to that concert! He agreed. So, I made up this story for my parents that my friend Sally was having a sleepover, and got another friend to pretend to be her mom on the phone. Eugene borrowed his father's car, and we drove straight down to Cincinnati from school. We were right up front. Eugene tried to kiss me during CAN'T HELP FALLING IN LOVE WITH YOU, but I blocked him. And then, the most magical thing happened: He looked at me!

PRISCILLA: Eugene?

GRACE: No, Elvis! We locked eyes, and I swear he sang an entire verse just to me! I could have died in that moment.

PRISCILLA: Oh, I can't even imagine! Did you look stunning?

(Grace takes off her coat to reveal a very fifties-style dress.)

GRACE: Oh, of course! My hair and makeup were done to the nines! And I bought the most perfect dress.

PRISCILLA: What did it look like?

(Note: The following line can be changed slightly to echo the details of the costume, as long as it is a similar feel.)

GRACE: It was this beautiful polka dot pattern, belted and then it flared out.

PRISCILLA: Sort of like what you're wearing?

GRACE: No, it . . . Oh. Yes. This . . . this is the dress. I don't . . . huh.

PRISCILLA: What?

GRACE: I just haven't fit in this dress in years. I don't remember putting it on.

PRISCILLA: Well, that's curious.

(Grace gets up and walks around in it. She catches her reflection in the mirror.)

GRACE: Oh my God.

PRISCILLA: What?

GRACE: I look so . . . young.

PRISCILLA: You certainly do.

GRACE: I . . . I'm 73. What's happening?

PRISCILLA: It's okay.

GRACE: It's not okay . . . What's going on? Who are you?

PRISCILLA: I told you, I'm Pricilla—

GRACE: No, I mean how are you . . .WHAT are you—

PRISCILLA: Okay honey, take a deep breath. What's the last thing you remember before you walked in here?

GRACE: I—I don't know. My husband checking the car.

PRISCILLA: Is that really the last thing you remember?

GRACE: No? I guess . . .the noise. I remember the noise in the car. The gr-gr-umpht.

PRISCILLA: And then?

GRACE: My husband saying we should pull over.

PRISCILLA: And then?

GRACE: I don't . . . oh my God.

(after a moment)

The car . . . stalled. In the intersection. He . . . he banged on the car to get it to move but, it wouldn't budge. He got out to push it, and the light changed, and this truck came around the curve and— I'm . . . I'm dead, aren't I?

PRISCILLA: Yes.

(After a moment)

GRACE: And, my husband?

PRISCILLA: Fine. The truck missed him completely.

GRACE: I see. That's . . . good.

> *(After a moment)*

So, is this heaven? Are you . . . God?

PRISCILLA: Not quite. You've got just a little farther to Graceland.

GRACE: But I get to go?

PRISCILLA: Like you said, it's your destiny.

> *(Priscilla gestures to the front door. The bell over the front door JINGLES. A bright light shines from it. CAN'T HELP FALLING IN LOVE WITH YOU starts playing. It swells and fills the room. Grace looks around, and then decidedly walks into the light.)*

HALFWAY

Emily Schwend

ORIGINAL PRODUCTION
Produced by Lesser America in 2011.

Part of Lesser America's
Too Much Too Soon evening of original 10 minute plays
Theater for the New City
September 29 – October 9, 2011
Directed by Stephen Brackett & Portia Kreeger

Produced as part of the 2013 Humana Festival of New
American Plays at Actors Theatre of Louisville.

Actors Theatre of Louisville
April 6-7, 2013

Directed by Meredith McDonagh

CAST:
KAT: Rebecca Hart
MELISSA: Amy Lynn Stewart

CHARACTERS:
    KAT: late twenties
    MELISSA: mid twenties, her sister

PLACE: The kitchen in a halfway house in Northeast Texas

TIME: Saturday in the summer

> *A kitchen, the middle of the day, probably on the weekend. In Texas, in the summer.*
>
> *KAT and MELISSA, both in their mid-ish, late-ish 20s sit at the scrubbed table. The kitchen is clean but completely charm-less.*
>
> *A pan of pecan squares rests between them.*

KAT: Oh my God. I am so sorry .

MELISSA: It's not a big deal.

KAT: It is a big deal. It's a huge deal because like. Like you could have died. Here. In the kitchen. You could have died here and it would have been my fault.

MELISSA: It wouldn't have been your fault. It would have been the pecans' fault.

KAT: But I should know. Because I did know, like, at one point, like when we were kids, I did know that you were allergic to pecans, and I should, you know, I should still know. So.

MELISSA: Yeah, okay, but you handed me a pecan square, and you said to me, like you literally said to me "have a pecan square!" So. So if I just went ahead and took the pecan square and then bit into the pecan square, and then died, in this kitchen, well. That is not your fault. That is knowing suicide.

KAT: Still. I should have remembered. I should have remembered that. About you.

MELISSA: Well. I carry an epipen.

KAT: I just thought I'd, you know. Make something. And I don't know how to make a whole lot of things, but I do know how to make pecan squares. They had a class—well, I guess it wasn't really a class because we just like, watched this woman cook but we didn't get to cook or anything. And she made pecan squares. And meatloaf and chutney, but I figured it'd just be real weird to hand you a plate of meatloaf or, ah, or chutney, so. So I made the pecan squares.

MELISSA: Well. I appreciate it. Even if I can't eat 'em.

KAT: There's supposed to be more cooking classes, like I don't know when, but. So maybe there's something else I can make next time, 'cause I don't know how to make a whole lot by myself. And they don't have cookbooks here or nothing like that.

(Kat takes the pecan squares far away.)

There's other stuff. Non-pecan stuff. Not a lot of stuff. I have Oreos, if you want Oreos. In my bedroom. Like, locked in my bedroom because someone'll steal 'em if I leave 'em in the kitchen or anywhere else. I had to keep all the stuff for the pecan squares in my bedroom—even like, stuff like, like canola oil! Like canola oil that's in my dresser drawer next to my socks and stuff. So. So, anyway, there's Oreos. And I guess there's also canola oil. And, ah. Whatever else. Baking powder.

MELISSA: Maybe an Oreo.

KAT: Sure, all right. I'll be right back.

(Kat goes.)

MELISSA takes a moment. She looks around the kitchen; it's grim. She walks to a tiny window above the sink, peers out.

Outside the kitchen, there's an argument between two women. A loud argument.

(Kat returns, calling back after her:)

KAT: It's there on the sheet and you can talk to Sandy yourself and she'll tell you the same thing!

(She closes the door. She's rattled and a little pissed off.)

MELISSA: What was that?

KAT: Just—nothing. Just this bitch who's living here and she's like. Like she's a pain in my fucking ass.

MELISSA: I thought you were liking it here.

KAT: I mean. Yeah. Yeah, I am. But. Like, some of the women here are just. They're fucking crazy, that's what they are.

So I reserved the kitchen for an hour and like. And like that means they can't come in here for an hour and if they want to come in they have to knock and ask me and if they like. Need something then they have to get it before or after and like. Like fuck it. She's just being a pain in my ass.

MELISSA: We can go outside if you want. Or up to your room if it's ...

KAT: Can't go up in my room. It's not, well—and it's too hot. Outside. Anyway.

MELISSA: All right.

(A beat.)

(Kat takes off a rubber band sealing the box of Oreos. Pushes them towards Melissa.)

MELISSA: *(cont.)* Thanks, Kat.

KAT: Sure. I really wish they taught us some other kind of square.

(A beat.)

MELISSA: So how was it?

KAT: It was good. It was real good. It was real hard.

MELISSA: I bet.

KAT: But I think I figured some stuff out. Like a lot of stuff. Like, a lot a lot. And so. So it was real good. For that.

MELISSA: Okay .

KAT: And, ah. And I don't want to go back there, like. Like never again. But I am real glad I did. Like, I am so glad I did. I just. I feel like I'm in a whole new—like everything feels new. Everything feels like. Like if I can just keep it all the way it is, I can work it out all right. Like I'm in a whole new p lace, like in my head. Like I have a whole new head. And I'm gonna keep it that way, MELISSA, I swear it. I have like. A sponsor. And I go to meetings every week, and I have to do that, but I would do that any way even if I didn't have to do it. And they said I can even go more than once a week if I want to, because there's like. There's always s a meeting. That's what they said.

MELISSA: That's good.

KAT: Yeah.

MELISSA: That's real good to hear, Kat.

KAT: Yeah. Yeah. Hey, so.

> *(beat, she changes her mind)*

Did you see the plants on the terrace?

MELISSA: Yeah, they're real pretty.

KAT: They give you one when you get here. It's like. Your plant. Sometimes it's just a seed, but I got a plant because someone left early and left her plant here and. And so I got her plant. And I gotta keep it alive while I'm here, and then when I leave, I can take it with me if I want to. Or I can leave it here for someone else. I haven't decided what I want to do yet.

MELISSA: Well. You don't have to worry about that yet.

KAT: No. I know. I'll probably end up killing it any way. Never had a. You know. A knack. For plants. I even killed that cactus I got at that dude ranch in West Texas—remember that? Who kills a cactus?

MELISSA: Maybe it wasn't killed. Maybe it just died.

KAT: Maybe.

MELISSA: Or maybe it just looked like it was dead and so we got rid of it. That happens sometimes with flowers. They look like they're gone over to the other side, but then you give 'em a little water and they perk right back up. But I don't know if that's what a cactus does.

KAT: Well. I hope I don't kill the plant they gave me here, 'cause, you know, 'cause that would look just, real bad.

> *(beat)*

Peter couldn't come?

MELISSA: Not today.

KAT: Busy, I guess.

MELISSA: He's been working a lot. Weekends. And he's working from home now.

KAT: Oh, right.

MELISSA: And it's been a lot for him. All of this.

KAT: Right. I know. I know it. How's mom doing?

MELISSA: Good days and bad days. The physical therapy helps. I think.

KAT: That's good. That's real good.

MELISSA: She was asking about you this morning. When I went to see her.

KAT: Oh yeah?

MELISSA: She's worried. I mean, she doesn't know about—everything, but. She's worried about you. Like she always was.

KAT: Yeah.

MELISSA: You should go see her. Show her you're doing all right. She didn't believe me when I told her we found you again.

KAT: Yeah, well.

   (beat)

   I will. I mean, I want to, but I can't right now, 'cause it's out of the perimeter.

MELISSA: What do you mean?

KAT: I mean that for the first 30 days you're here, you can go two blocks in any direction, except north you can go three blocks because three blocks away is the SuperTarget and a while ago, like before I got here, some people complained about how there ain't really a whole lot in two blocks north and south and east and, you know, and there's this huge Super-Target three blocks north and so they put together this whole, you know, like a presentation about it and they voted on it and now the perimeter is three blocks going north, but still two blocks everywhere else. And no matter where you're going, you have to go with at least two other people and a chaperone, and the chaperones don't really like going out that much, so no one really goes out that much. But if we wanted to, and if they go with us, we can go to the SuperTarget.

   (beat)

   Some people got jobs working there. Like a sort of deal they did—the people who run this place and the people who run the SuperTarget—and so some people here can get jobs working there. Like after 30 days, you can do that, 'cause you can go anywhere. Not anywhere, but. But you can go to the SuperTarget by yourself, so. So I was thinking about doing that. After 30 days are up.

MELISSA: I think that'd be great.

KAT: Yeah, 'cause. 'Cause I know it's costing you money—you and Peter—a lot of money to help me pay for this place and

for the last place too, and I want you to know that I'm planning to pay you back. For all of it, however long it takes.

MELISSA: Well. We don't have to worry about that now.

KAT: Okay. Yeah. Okay. I just, I really have a real good feeling
about it. About being here and about working on my steps
and staying clean, and I have been, the whole time and like,
and that wasn't easy either, but I did it and I'm doing it, and
I swear to you, Melissa, I know I messed it up before, but it's
different this time. It's real different.

MELISSA: I know. I know you feel that way .

(beat)

KAT: And, ah. And I thought maybe you could bring Hailey next
time.

(beat)

Or like. Or I could see her after 30 days when I can go anywhere. Like outside the perimeter. You know?

MELISSA: We'll have to work something out. We'll have to see.

KAT: Because I was talking to my sponsor and she said that a
lot of women can get custody of their kids again. After, you
know, like I know it'll take time to like. To prove that I'm serious. And that I can do it. But she said that, like in my kind
of situation, where there's family support and where there
wasn't ever any kind of abuse or nothing like that, sometimes
it can work out.

(beat)

MELISSA: I don't think we should think that far ahead, Kat.

KAT: I want to think that far ahead.

MELISSA: Let's just wait, okay? See how this goes and then take
the next step.

KAT: Yeah. Yeah, all right.

MELISSA: She's doing real good though. She's talking a lot now,
I think it was just a few words back when, ah. When you left.
And she's just a little chatterbox now. Talks in these little
half-sentences. Like her own language. Like, ah. What's the
word. Shorthand. Like a shorthand language. It's real special.
She's real special, Kat.

KAT: I know. I know it.

MELISSA: There's a day care real close to the house, and they're great. The two ladies who run it are just great, and all of the day care teachers are grad students studying, you know, children's education and one of 'em is studying child psychology and so. So they're great too. She just loves it there, I have to tear her away when I'm picking her up.

KAT: God. I can't—I just miss her. So much.

MELISSA: Yeah. Yeah I know you do.

(beat)

I, ah. I don't think she remembers you, Kat.

(That cuts into Kat like a knife.)

(A long beat)

KAT: Right, ah. Do you, ah, do you want another Oreo? You can have one, I can't eat the whole box myself. Or I shouldn't, anyway.

MELISSA: All right.

(She takes an Oreo.)

KAT: I wish I could give you a glass of milk, you know? Like it almost feels stupid having this big bag of Oreos and then never having even a cup of milk to give you to eat 'em with, but. But milk barely lasts more'n a day in the fridge—someone uses it on her cereal or in her mac and cheese and so. Well. I guess I don't really like milk anyway, so even if no one was gonna drink my milk, maybe I still wouldn't have any in here to give you.

MELISSA: Well, you're lactose intolerant. Or you were, when we were kids.

KAT: Right. Well. I don't know if it's lactose intolerant, but I never did like it. Milk. Any kind of, ah. Milk product. You know, they make dinner here on Sundays, but no one eats it, or at least I don't eat it because it's always just some kind of casserole that's not so much a casserole as it is just a few potatoes or noodles or rice covered with melted processed cheese on the top. It's worse than family meal at the restaurant. Remember that? So godawful, and no one ate it, and then we had to serve burgers and fries all night long.

MELISSA: It got a little better once you left.

KAT: I just remember it was always cut up hot dogs and rice.

MELISSA: Sometimes noodles. Cut up hot dogs and noodles.

(A beat)

KAT: I know you don't believe me, but I'm going to do it, Melissa, I swear.

MELISSA: All right.

KAT: I swear to God, Melissa.

MELISSA: All right.

(And they sit in the kitchen together.)

END OF PLAY.

How to Succeed in Romance Without Really Connecting

Trace Crawford

ORIGINAL PRODUCTION

How to Succeed in Romance Without Really Connecting was originally produced by Future Tenant (Pittsburgh, PA) in November of 2010.

Directed by Todd Betker

CAST
MAN: Rob Gorman
WOMAN: Maggie Mayer
BOOK VOICE: Vince Ventura

SECOND PRODUCTION

It was subsequently produced by The Mirror Theatre (Los Angeles, CA) in June 2014.

Directed by Nova Mejia

CAST:
MAN: David Currier
WOMAN: Lauren Miscioscia
BOOK VOICE: Paul Calderon

Inquiries for productions should be sent to the author at: tracecrawford@gmail.com

CHARACTERS:

> MAN: Mid thirties. Divorced. For him, sex and romance in the modern world is a riddle wrapped in an enigma covered in chocolate and holding a knife—enticing, but confusing and a little bit scary. Fairly nervous and self-conscious, especially around younger women.

> WOMAN: Twenty-five, attractive. Full of energy and enthusiasm for life. Completely engrossed in the trappings of modern relationships (i.e. social networking, exhibitionism, and voyeurism) and loving it. A product of the "sex is the new handshake" generation. It is important that she is dressed in a manner appropriate for a typical first date—*slightly* revealing, perhaps, but don't go too far.

> BOOK VOICE: Male, any age, should have an air of wisdom (ala Walter Cronkite). The disembodied voice of a "How-to" guide for success in modern romance. At first, at least, the Book Voice is a parody of the Book in *How To Succeed in Business Without Really Trying*.

SETTING: A typical bachelor's efficiency apartment that could be found in any major city.

TIME: The present.

> *(SCENE: A typical bachelor's efficiency apartment found in any city: sofa, coffee table, an area defined as a kitchen.)*

> *(AT RISE: We hear multiple deadbolts unlock. The MAN enters with several shopping bags, fumbles to hit the light switch with his elbow and closes door—either real or mimed—and sets bags down on sofa. In a hurry, glances at watch for time. HE's running late.)*

MAN: Shit. *(HE fishes in a bag, pulls out a small book, and opens to the first chapter.)*
We're gonna have to do this quickly.

BOOK VOICE: Dear Reader: This little book is designed to tell you everything you need to know about the science of getting ahead with the woman of today.

> *(MAN turns front toward the audience, does a take, and turns the page in the book. Ala "How to Succeed in Business . . . ")*

Now let us assume that you are young, healthy, clear-eyed and eager, anxious to rise to the top of the modern romantic world. You can!

MAN: *(looking up)* I can!

> *(HE continues reading the book.)*

BOOK VOICE: If you have education, intelligence and financial security, so much the better. But remember that every day, millions of people manage to achieve success in seduction without any of these qualities. Just have courage and follow the simple steps in the chapters that follow. If you truly wish to be among the desired few, you can!

MAN: I can!

BOOK VOICE: Chapter One: How to arrange your environment.

MAN: Here we go.

BOOK VOICE: A good first step is to make your living space as inviting as possible.

> *(MAN surveys the squalor he calls home. Beat.)*

You can always dim the lights. *(HE does.)* No matter how revolting your home may be, it's nothing a little low lighting can't fix. However, never overlook the power of natural moonlight. Why not open the drapes and let Mother Nature work her magic?

BOOK VOICE: *(continued)*

> *(MAN x's DS and mimes opening large curtains at the fourth wall.)*

Next, be sure to light a few scented candles.

> *(HE scours through a bag, while still reading with the other hand.)*

Not only will this demonstrate your sensitive bohemian personality, but it will also mask your home's many underlying offensive odors.

MAN: *(Lighting candles. Genuinely impressed.)* Good stuff. Good stuff.

BOOK VOICE: As a little alcohol never hurt one's chance at romance, have a bottle of fine white wine chilled, awaiting the arrival of your guest.

MAN: *(Takes out a bottle of something cheap and nasty. Looks at bottle. Beat.)* I'll dim the lights a bit more.

(HE does. Puts wine in kitchen.)

BOOK VOICE: A vase of fresh roses can really liven up the romantic mood. If you cannot afford roses . . .

(MAN grabs a half-dead fern and places in on a table.)

then any sort of exotic wildflower can have the same effect.

(Beat.)

Next, it is very important that you have chosen the correct location to set up your telescope.

MAN: *(Stops dead in his tracks.)* What?

BOOK VOICE: I said, next it is very important that you have chosen the correct location to set up your telescope.

MAN: *(Not sure where this is headed . . .)* Okay . . .

(HE grabs a telescope on a tripod as he continues reading.)

BOOK VOICE: Obviously, it must be positioned facing a window with a view; however, since it is important to be considerate of your female companion's needs, you must be sure to also provide her with an optimal viewing location.

(HE stands holding the telescope, perplexed by what HE has just read.)

MAN: What?

BOOK VOICE: You have now set the stage for a wonderful, if not meaningful night of lovemaking.

(The doorbell rings.)

MAN: Shit.

(HE hurriedly tidies up–stuffing bags under cushions, puts book in his sport coat pocket. HE leaves the telescope standing in view upstage. HE is about to open the

door when he gets the book out to check something. The doorbell rings again.)

BOOK VOICE: Chapter Four: First Impressions. Your greeting sets the tone for the evening. Try to be suave.

MAN: *(Puts BOOK back in his coat. HE practices saying "hello" to himself a few times, then opening door, ala a bad 70's aftershave commercial...)* Hello.

WOMAN: *(Gleefully puts arm around MAN and takes a selfie with HER phone.)*
Smile! *(Types on phone.)* . . . and upload. *(Beat.)* Wow. Your place has a great Bohemian vibe. *(Inhales.)* Is that sandalwood?

MAN: It's—

WOMAN: You know, I never do this.

MAN: Do what?

WOMAN: Show up at a guy's apartment that I met online. But I saw in my feed that Janie thought you were OK, so then when you IM'd me, I figured, "Hey, what the hell", right?

> *(Please change Facebook references to what current social media trends dictate.)*

MAN: Right.

WOMAN: I mean, really, we owe her a lot. I never even would have friended you if it weren't for her. It's like you never know who's gonna turn out to be boring, or a jerk, or give you a roofie, chop you up, put you in a Hefty bag, and leave your body on the side of a deserted road. Am I right?

> *(SHE laughs enthusiastically.)*

MAN: *(With an uncomfortable chuckle.)* I know what you mean. Wanna sit? *(They do. Awkwardness.)* Can I get you a drink?

WOMAN: Please.

MAN: *(Getting up to pour wine.)* I like Janie. *(Awkwardness.)* Uh . . . how do you two know each other?

WOMAN: High school. We did the plays together. I always loved the attention, but she... Well, I think she would have been happier watching from the audience, or something.

> *(Awkwardness.)*

MAN: *(overlapping)* So, I—   WOMAN: *(overlapping)*
                                                    Well, what—

MAN: Oh, I'm sorry, you go ahead.

(Hands HER a glass of wine and sits.)

WOMAN: Well, I was just going to ask what made you decide to ask me out? I mean, you just commented on my posts every once in a while, and then—

(SHE receives an alert.)

hold on—

(Checks phone. Laughs. Texts.)

I know, right?! *(Back to HIM.)* I mean, I was just curious what made you want to... check me out?

MAN: I don't know. You're profile pic just looked so—

WOMAN: Oh, that—See, I took it like this . . . *(Demonstrates taking photo.)* I had my head at just the right angle . . .

MAN: Well, I don't want to sound cheesy, but in that picture you have this amazing look in your eyes. This light. And there was something about your smile—honest, but a little mischievous, maybe, and I thought—I think I could really like this person.

WOMAN: *(Alert. Laughs. Texts.)* He's not *that* old. *(To him.)* You wouldn't believe some of the messages I get from men because of that pic—You'd think I was like getting a money shot

(MAN chokes a bit on his wine.)

in it or something. Oh! Are you ok?

MAN: *(Recovering)* I'm . . . fine.

WOMAN: Good.

(Beat.)

I mean, just 'cause I want to stay in touch with my friends doesn't mean that I want you to send me a picture of your junk, you know?

MAN: I'm . . . sure.

WOMAN: Right . . . I mean, at least *chat* with me first.

MAN: I, uh . . . yeah, that's just what I . . .

(Panicked, HE flips through THE BOOK for advice as SHE begins . . .)

WOMAN: You know, I gotta tell you, I don't know if it's this great wine . . . *(Surveying the room.)* the romantic lighting, the intoxicating aroma, or your . . . *(Comes to the fern . . . doesn't know what to say here.)* beautiful house plant, but I just feel so connected to you right now.

MAN: *(Looking up from the book—"I can't believe this crap worked!")* You do?

WOMAN: *(Seductive, every syllable more sexual than the last.)* I do. Connected *and* attracted. *(Seductively)* Come here.

> *(HE does, but as HE gets there, SHE gets up, peppy, breaking the mood.)*

WOMAN: Just let me get my stuff!

MAN: *(Perplexed)* Your stuff?

WOMAN: Yeah, silly, I left it in the hall. I'll just grab my stuff and we can pick up right where we left off.

MAN: *(Confused, but excited. Stands and x's behind the sofa.)* Sure! Get . . . *(What could she possibly be getting?)* . . . whatever it is you need!

> *(WOMAN goes to hall and gets a few bags. SHE sets their contents in a row on the DS table. An odd assortment. Starts with a few sex toys, but then just gets weird—a hot water bottle, a baby's bib, a mini Statue of Liberty, a small kitchen appliance—whatever, use your imagination.)*

WOMAN: Let's see now . . . Ah yes . . . Well, we gotta have these. *(A box of condoms.)* . . . Oh, we'll need this *(a vibrator)* and this *(sex toy)* and this, and these and—ooh, I don't think you're ready for that—and . . .

> *(Keep going until you run out of items, or space. The weirder, the better.)*

and of course . . . this.

> *(An active webcam on a netbook or laptop so the audience can see live images.)*

MAN: *(Taking it all in. Beat.)* Whoa.

WOMAN: Now where were we?

> *(SHE lounges seductively. HE sits on edge of sofa, like a nervous rabbit.)*

MAN: Whoa.

WOMAN: I can't wait to get started.

MAN: Sure, sure.

WOMAN: Now . . . what should we use first?

> *(SHE sets up webcam. MAN is at a loss. HE looks at the objects, looks out to us, down, out, down, looks at HER, looks out—terrified. Opens BOOK for advice.)*

BOOK VOICE: Hell if I know! Kid, you're on your own.

> *(Sound of a car door closing. Car starts, peels out and drives off. MAN looks panicked. Frazzled, HE tosses BOOK away from him and screams.)*

MAN: AHHH!

WOMAN: *(As SHE finishes with webcam.)* Well? Where would you like to start?

MAN: Uh . . . *(Rises. Perhaps stalling a bit.)* Just let me just close the curtains first.

WOMAN: *(Honest, not seductive.)* Why would you want to do that?

MAN: I don't know. Someone might see.

WOMAN: *("Obviously . . .")* Well, yeah.

MAN: You mean you want people to . . . *(watch us have sex?)*

WOMAN: *("Obviously" —not perverted in any way, for her this is just "normal".)* Of course I do.

MAN: I don't know how I . . . *(feel about this.)*

WOMAN: What's the problem?

MAN: Nothing, I just . . . *(don't like the idea of doing that.)*

WOMAN: Ah, come on. This is the 21st century you're living in. You know that nothing feels real anymore unless somebody else is watching you do it.

> *(SHE gestures grandly towards audience.)*

MAN: *(Looks into house, does a take. Is horrified to see the audience watching.)*
Jesus!

> *(HE mimes quickly closing curtains at fourth wall. Really embarrassed.)*

WOMAN: What's wrong?

MAN: *(Still recovering.)* Nothing! I'm . . . I'm fine . . . I just . . . *(Still upset, HE "reopens" the mimed curtains and yells at the audience.)* You all should be ashamed of yourselves!

WOMAN: What's the matter?

MAN: Nothing. It's just, I . . . I mean, I don't even know them . . . How could they just sit there . . . staring!

WOMAN: Isn't that the point? Why bother to do anything if nobody's there to see it? Doesn't it feel more exciting when you're being watched? Doesn't it make you feel like you need to be doing something that matters every second of your life? Something important? Don't you feel more alive in front of an audience?

MAN: I never thought of . . . I mean . . . That isn't something I . . . *(ever considered until now.)*

WOMAN: *(Teasing.)* Ahhh, come on. Don't pretend. You know what I mean. *You're* the one that whipped it out before I even got here!

MAN: *(Shocked and confused.)* What!

WOMAN: *(Gestures to the telescope. Beat, then a realization.)* Or is that the game? I see. Come here. Momma will show you exactly what to do. *(Leads the MAN to the telescope. They are on opposite sides of it.)* Don't worry. I'll be gentle.

MAN: This is all very strange.

WOMAN: OOH! Nice! You're good at this . . . Here. Now, let's get all set up. *(SHE sensually hands HIM the telescope and leads him DS.)* There we go.

> *(SHE mimes opening the curtains, then points telescope at audience. SHE strokes the shaft of the telescope.)*

Now be gentle. Don't force it. Take it slow. Now open it up nice and wide *(the aperture)* Just angle yourself this way... and then gently... slide... it... in.

> *(SHE has helped him begin to look through the telescope at the audience.)*

That's it.

> *(Places HIS hand on the telescope. HE is twists the focus back and forth.)*

Oh yeah. Really get a good, hard, look. Not too fast. Don't rush it. Try to take them all in.

> *(Scanning the audience, slowly.)*

Good. Good.

> *(SHE crosses to the hallway.)*

Perfect. Just like that. Oh yeah.

(SHE exits and returns with her own telescope, which SHE sets up DS, pointed at the audience as well, but SHE is not physically close to MAN.)

Mmmmmmm, that's wonderful. Don't stop. A little to the left ...

(SHE uses her telescope, too. They are now in sync. They both focus on the same audience member. SHE gasps.)

Oh yea, that's the spot. The guy in the red shirt.

(THEY are both probably writhing a bit by this point.)

Come on, make him feel alive!

(Looking from place to place through their telescopes, in sync, as SHE speaks, nearing a sexual climax. Feel free to ad lib sounds and phrases.)

That's it. Over there. Perfect. Now move slowly. Nice and slow. Mmmm. Now Fast. Faster. Yes!

MAN:	WOMAN:
Oh yeah ...	*(Building to a climax.)*
Yeah ...	Yeah ...
This is ...	Yeah ...
I see...	Yeah ...
Wow!	Yeah ...
I can't believe ...	Yeah ...
Oh, yeah!	Yeah ...
I think I'm ...	Yeah ...
I think I'm ...	Yeah ...
I think I'm gonna—	Yeah ...
I think I'm gonna—	Yeah!
	Yeah!

(BOTH freeze in a position of extreme sexual intensity as the lights dim.)

BOOK VOICE: *(In a grand style.)* A renewed lease this story with it brings,

As sex today has no need for a bed.

Go forth, and talk of voyeuristic things.

You shall be pardoned and not punish-ed; — unless, of course, that's what you're into.

For never was there a story of more . . .

MAN: OH!   WOMAN: OH!

BOOK VOICE: Than how love's different, now we're all on show.

(Blackout.)

LOST AND FOUND

Jerry McGee

ORIGINAL PRODUCTION
The Gallery Players
16th Annual Black Box New Play Festival
199 14th Street
Brooklyn, NY 11215

May 30, 2013-June 2, 2013

Directed by Neal Kowalsky

CAST:
SHE: Katie Braden
HE: Brandon Ferraro

CHARACTERS:

> SHE: thirty to forty, driven business professional—eccentric, cheap, tight, obsessive, insists she is happy being over thirty-five.
>
> HE: twenty-something, always employed, always on the go, not yet thirty, trying to develop into an adult.

SETTING: Bare stage. Each is in a spotlight, unaware of the other. They communicate directly to the audience. No set is needed, nor any props.

> They are located in the Brooklyn Heights neighborhood of New York City, present day.

NOTE: These are NOT generic characters, but should be listed without names to keep the audience in suspense.

> *(SHE and HE are on opposite sides of the stage, talking to the audience, separately.)*

SHE: It was one of those mornings. I'd tossed and turned all night, nothing was working.

HE: It was one of those mornings. I'd tossed and turned all night, nothing was working.

SHE: Brushed my teeth, and flossed, yes I did,—to keep the dentist away—but didn't do the morning stretching.

HE: Brushed my teeth, yes, and flossed—I do it every morning —but couldn't do the push-ups and sit-ups. Not today.

SHE: The milk was sour so my coffee was ruined. Dry whole wheat toast with my One-A-Day. Is that a good breakfast?

HE: The milk was lumpy, so—no coffee. See what I mean, one of those days? Do Pop-Tarts really have half a daily vitamin pill? So I ate two. Don't look at me like that, I'm going to the gym tomorrow, I'll burn it off.

SHE: There's a Starbucks on Montague, I'll get one to take out, it always gets me going.

HE: There's a Starbucks on Montague, jump start my brain.

SHE: There goes my budget.

HE: But, there goes my budget.

SHE: My investment counselor told me, if I'd forgo the daily Starbucks and put that $5 in an interest bearing account I'd be comfortable in 24 years.

HE: Can you believe, my investment counselor told me, if I'd drop the daily Starbucks and put that $5 in an interest bearing account I'd be rich in 20 years.

SHE: How can that work?

HE: Through the miracle of compound interest.

SHE: All I know is, that's what she said.

HE: All I know is, that's what he said.

SHE: But one morning won't kill my future. And nothing's working.

HE: So maybe I won't do it. When the sugar kicks in I can fly to the R Train.

SHE: So I'm walking to the R, sipping my tall latte with skim milk, trying to keep it off my Ann Klein II coat because I really need to make a good impression today.

HE: If I promised my guy I would absolutely give up the morning Starbucks, would he advance me some of that fortune now? I need it, now. I'm not kidding.

SHE: I make it to the station, and make it down the stairs, and even through the turnstile. Didn't spill one drop. Am I good or what?

HE: Today is Sharon's birthday. I knew it was coming up. I did. Then I forgot.

SHE: Standing there, waiting for the slowest elevator in the world to come, I looked to see just how late I really was.

HE: Damn it! Didn't get her anything. She could be the one. It's not just the sex, which is great. We can talk. We can.

SHE: So I did the comedy routine of looking at my wrist and spilling the coffee. Disaster!

HE: With all the others, she talks. I listen. She talks. I listen. With Sharon, WE talk. We listen. I even like her.

SHE: I didn't spill on my coat. No. I'm not that stupid. My watch was gone.

HE: Please God, let me find something I can afford and get right away. I need it tonight! I'm not kidding!

SHE: I know I put it on. I did. I know it. I never leave the house without it. I always know what time it is! I'm a Virgo!

HE: I'll save every Starbucks penny. Every one. I swear! I walked down Montague, looked in the window at all the suckers pouring their investment money right down their throats, and passed it by.

SHE: I'm acting like a crazy lady. Frantic. Looking everywhere. I had it! I had it! Everyone else looks around, too. We scower the floor. Nothing!!!

HE: One day at a time. If I can make it to the subway I'm safe.

SHE: I must have left it at home. It was one of those mornings. It's on the dresser. It has to be. I'm really late. I can't go back. The elevator comes, I take it down to the train. (*growl of frustration!*)

HE: And then I see something. Gold, shiny, right there on the sidewalk. No one else sees it. I stop, pick it up. It's a watch. An old watch. But a ladies watch. Elgin, it says.

SHE: I get on the train, I'm still checking every pocket, cuffs, anywhere I could have put it, or it could have fallen into. Crazy lady on the subway. No one says a thing.

HE: Can I give her an old watch? I know I asked for something, but . . . this?!

SHE: At work all day I think. I visualize every step I took from the time I awoke until I entered the subway. A lot of blank spaces. My meetings were . . . I've been working up this presentation for three months and I don't remember what we did . . . I remember getting up, I remember dressing, I think I remember leaving the watch on the dresser because the milk was sour and I was not going to get a Starbucks today but then I had to anyway. Providence. Maybe Starbucks has it. Someone found it there and they have it at the counter. Everyone's a friend at Starbucks. Yes. Or it's on the dresser. Yes.

HE: At work I showed my find to Kevin. He's older and he knows about these things. He perked right up when I handed it to him.

SHE: It wasn't just any watch. I'm not really obsessive. Well, okay I am, but this was my Grandma Bee's watch. Her Lady Elgin. Wind-up like they all did then. Gold. With two diamonds. Small, but real diamonds. Elgin used to make them like that. I've had it cleaned and it runs great. Antiques are really the best, don't you think?

HE: Kevin says it's from the 50's and it's still running. Must be good. Elgin was the best American watch then. 17 jewels. 12 karat gold, two what look to be diamonds. This piece is worth some bucks.

SHE: I can't believe this.

HE: I can't believe it!

SHE: Maybe I'll go home at noon and get it. I always know what time it is!

HE: Put it in an antique case. Shine it up. "It was my grandmother's." She'd love it. It could work. *(to God)* Thank you!!!

SHE: Don't overreact. Is this over-reacting? I'm always over-reacting. It's at home on the dresser.

HE: Or is it too much? Is it a commitment? An antique watch sounds like a commitment. Is it like a ring?

SHE: Whenever anything is lost, look again. It's always right there where it's supposed to be. You just didn't see it.

HE: Okay, it's not my grandmother's watch, it's just a watch. Okay? It isn't a ring. It isn't that big a step. Just a birthday present.

SHE: I went home on lunch hour. It wasn't there. I knew I'd put it on! It wasn't at Starbucks. Nobody turned it in. I followed my exact footpath from home along Montague Street. Nothing. Looked and looked.

HE: Kevin said go to Jean's Silversmith on 45th Street and sell it. Buy her flowers.

SHE: Made frantic signs on bright pink paper from the promo department. 8½ x 11 sheets. "LOST ON MONTAGUE STREET. Old gold watch. Sentimental value. Reward." And I put my phone number, too. Risky, but I did it! Taped the signs on every light pole all along Montague. And, one in Starbucks' window. It was a two hour lunch. Two plus.

HE: I see Sharon at 7:30. Should have time to wrap it ok. On the way home need to buy fancy paper at the Hallmark store. This will work. Yes!

SHE: Hope springs eternal!

HE: Leave work early, find a box, wrap it, put it together, take a shower, shave again, be ready to Birthday it up right. Sharon's day. Sharon's Night. One we'll remember.

SHE: I call home every half hour. No messages on the machine. Not one. Not even condo share adverts. Is it turned on? Oh, God. Should have used my cell number. But that's personal!

HE: So I get home early on the R, and there on the railing at the Court St. subway station, "LOST ON MONTAGUE STREET. Old gold watch. Sentimental value. Reward."

SHE: I raced home. On the R. Should have taken a cab, but I need the cash in hand. I said REWARD.

HE: Reward.

SHE: How much is a reward?

HE: How much is the reward? On an old watch. (correction) On an Heirloom. For a sentimental item?

SHE: Big mouth. You can't just say "Reward" and not have a plan.

HE: What do you think?

SHE: Reward! I don't have reward money. Yes I do. No I don't. A new watch would cost me . . . it's not the same thing!

HE: What are we talking? A hundred? Twenty? Five?

SHE: Are the signs still up? Some do-gooders take them down to keep the neighborhood upscale. Ricky, my neighbor, takes fliers down. Rips them all down.

HE: More than Jean's Silversmith's? I should have checked, found a base price.

SHE: The sign at the R stop was gone. I'm going to kill Ricky. Maybe a message on the machine when I get there.

HE: "Sentimental Value." Now, a valuable item, like a laptop with all your files, would be a big reward. Sentimental? What do you think? Less? Or more.

SHE: No one ever returns anything. I've been around long enough to know that.

HE: It's too much. It's a commitment. Grandma's or no grandma's. A watch is a pre-engagement present.

SHE: The flier at Starbucks is still there. The other LOST signs are still up. Maybe Ricky didn't come out yet.

HE: Pre-engagement. Everyone knows that. Kevin knows that. I know that. Sharon knows that.

SHE: Maybe it fell behind the dresser, I didn't look there. Lost things are usually never lost. And, every sign is still up. Except the subway.

HE: *(On the phone)* Ringing, ringing, ringing. Kevin was right. Flowers would be the . . . Hello! *(to machine message)* I know you're not there. I know what number I called, just say "I'm not here leave a message," comeon comeon give me the beep . . .

SHE: Unlocking my door I can hear my machine. Someone's calling! I can't get the key in the . . . !

HE: I have your notice about losing a lady's watch. If you could describe it, I may have it. I found something today. So you can call me, oh I won't be home this evening, but

SHE: *(on phone)* Hello! I'm here, I'm here! I couldn't get in the door and I could hear you talking, leaving a message and oh! Oh!, oh!, give me a minute.

HE: It's okay, take your time.

SHE: And I dropped my keys and I twisted my ankle to get here before you hung up . . . !

HE: It's okay, I'm here. There's no rush.

SHE: Thank you. I've just been so upset all day I didn't know what I'd do and. You found my watch?! You have it?

HE: Well, I have a watch. I found it.

SHE: Where did you find it? Where was it?!

HE: Uh, where did you lose it?

SHE: What?!

HE: Well, I want to make sure it's yours. Anyone can say "Oh That's Mine!" But if you tell me

SHE: *(cuts him off)* On Montague Street somewhere, I'm sure. It had to be. It's a Lady Elgin watch, very small and it has a thin gold band with a sort of a braided look to it—the band, not the watch—, it's gold, the watch is gold, old gold, worn a bit on the rounded edges, it has two small di . . . shiny stones on the face. It was my grandmother's.

HE: You're kidding. It really was your grandmother's?

SHE : It was Grandma Bee's.

HE: Funny.

SHE: What?

HE: Nothing.

SHE: It's all I have to remember her by. And it keeps perfect time. And I wind it every night before I go to bed. And it calms me down. And I remember her lilac scent when she'd tuck me in bed sometimes and lean over to kiss my forehead and . . . I don't know what I'd do without it.

HE: Well, what you describe is exactly the watch I found. It was on the sidewalk on Montague Street, down from Starbucks . . . and you're right, it keeps exact time.

SHE: Oh, Thank You thank you thank you Thank You. I'm so glad you have it. Where are you? How can I get it? I said a reward, I don't know what, how much, how to repay you. Name your figure.

HE: Oh, well, listen . . .

SHE: Anything. Any figure at all! I mean it. I'm serious.

HE: Listen, it was your grandmother's, and

SHE: Whatever you want! Name it! I have cash. And I can write a check!

HE: *(stumbling)* Lady, I don't want any reward money, thanks. Why don't I meet you

SHE: You don't want any money?

HE: Why don't we meet, say, in front of Starbucks to hand it over. In, like, ten minutes? I'll hold it up so you'll know who I am.

SHE: Good, ten minutes! But, you have to take money.

HE: No I don't.

SHE: You must need something.

HE: You could help me pick out flowers. I'm not sure what's right.

SHE: Flowers?

HE: It's my girlfriend's birthday. I'm taking her to dinner and I thought I'd give her flowers. Would she like that?

SHE: She'd love it. Any woman would.

HE: Great. Meet you at the florist down from Starbucks. Across the street. You know the place?

SHE: Yes, Weir's! Beside the Church.

HE: That's it. Meet you in Ten. *(Hangs up)*

SHE: *(hangs up) (to audience)* He found it! It isn't lost! (beat) I'm paying for the flowers. *(beat)* And I'll slip him dinner money, too! I will!

HE: *(To audience)* Hey, do I need a reward? This morning I began an investment plan. In twenty years I'll be rich.

(Blackout)

MANDATE

Kelly Younger

ORIGINAL PRODUCTION

Mandate premiered at the Stella Adler Theatre in Hollywood, CA on July 10, 2013 as part of *Snapshots* produced by Nicki Georgi and Lara Wickes with the following cast (to whom the play is dedicated):

DREW: Drew Powell
MARC: Marc Valera

* Note in Drew's monologue with the "5 Bs" the final word Buffett is the singer Jimmy Buffett (pronounced with hard Ts) not buffet (as in a smorgasbord of food).

A crowded sports bar. Two bar stools. Two beer mugs. One bowl of peanuts. Sounds of basketball game on TV. In the blackout, DREW shouting "C'mon! Give it to me! You know you want to!" Then as the light come up we see him violently giving the Heimlich to MARC in an oddly homoerotic way. Marc launches a peanut from his mouth.

A moment of relief.

MARC: What the hell dude?

DREW: You're welcome.

MARC: I wasn't choking.

DREW: Sure you were.

MARC: I was eating a peanut.

DREW: That got lodged in your throat.

MARC: Not until you started crushing my lungs.

DREW: Wait, seriously? You weren't choking?

MARC: That's what I was trying to say but you were shouting and thrusting and Christ, where did you learn the Heimlich, prison?

DREW: *(hands to throat)* You gave the universal sign for choking.

MARC: I was just adjusting my collar. I told you I was coming straight from a haircut.

DREW: Oh. Itchy?

MARC: Yeah.

DREW: Well it looks great.

MARC: Thanks?

DREW: Guess that was pretty awkward.

MARC: Yeah. Awkward.

DREW: But you're fit, man. *(poking him)* Could feel a pretty tight little core while I was squeezing you.

MARC: Not any less awkward.

DREW: I put on some sympathy weight when Hillary first got pregnant—with Addison. She used to say we were having twins. One in her belly, one in mine. Then when we had Bridgie I was like, bring on the sweatpants!

(MARC lifts his beer, DREW quickly follows and overeagerly cheers him, almost smashing his mug.)

Here's to good friends. Tonight is kind of special.

(MARC doesn't really know how to respond.)

MARC: So, Beth told me you're a teacher.

DREW: Earth science and driver's ed. 124 kids. All girl's school.

MARC: All girls. That's a lot.

DREW: Don't have to tell me. But I can text 90 words in 2 minutes 26 seconds, so, you know, I'm kind of a popular teacher. And I know the words to every *One Direction* song. Go on. Try me.

MARC: With what?

DREW: *One Direction* challenge.

MARC: I don't know what that is.

DREW: Seriously? They're like *the Monkees* for the new generation.

(singing, throwing out boy-band gestures)

You don't know you're beautiful! Oh-oh! That's what—

MARC: *(cutting him off)* Jake's kind of more into *Star Wars*.

DREW: Ah, man. I'd give anything to have a son. Don't get me wrong, I love my girls. I'm just, you know, kind of out numbered. I brought out all my old action figures and the girls just wanted to have a pool party with Barbie and I was like, Bobo Fet does not swim.

MARC: He's way into it. I do this funny thing with Jake, whenever we go through the security gate at our condo, it opens automatically, but I put my hand up like a Jedi and act like I'm giving it a force push, and when it opens, you should see his face.

(Long moment)

DREW: *(with deep admiration)* You're amazing.

MARC: I'm sure you do loads of stuff like that.

DREW: Addison and Bridgie paint my toe nails. In fact, my toe nails are always painted. Wanna see?

MARC: I'm good.

DREW: Cool.

MARC: Cool.

(A moment)

DREW: Can I tell you a secret?

MARC: I think you just did.

DREW: I'm a brony.

MARC: A what?

DREW: A bro who likes My Little Pony.

MARC: That's a thing?

DREW: Huge. My girls got me hooked. We threw a party for the coronation episode where Princess Celestia finally gave Twilight Sparkle her wings. Man. That was a great night.

> *(beat)*

Friendship is magic.

> *(MARC takes a drink and DREW mirrors his every move.)*

This is nice. I'm really glad our wives set this up.

MARC: *(focusing on the game)* Yeah.

DREW: They totally knew we'd get along. And it's so hard, you know, with work and kids and everything, I mean, how do people even make friends any more? Especially guys, you know? Like there's no way guys just become friends like you did in college. Had a class together or in a frat or something. Now it's all about do the spouses get along, and what if they do but their kid is an asshole or the kids get along but the parents are assholes and do you want to be best friends?

MARC: *(beat)* What's that?

DREW: Do you want to be my best friend?

> *(MARC laughs, then stops.)*

MARC: You're serious.

DREW: I mean, like, unless you've already got one. Do you?

MARC: A best friend?

DREW: And wives don't count. I'm talking guy best friends. You already have one?

MARC: Dude. I haven't really thought about it like that since—

DREW: Since what?

MARC: Grade school.

DREW: So do ya?

MARC: I've got plenty of friends.

DREW: Not counting work.

MARC: Ok, yeah.

DREW: And not counting dads from your kid's school.

MARC: Ok. Yeah, still got 'em.

DREW: And not counting guys from college.

MARC: Ok.

DREW: Or Facebook.

MARC: Well who's left?

DREW: See?

MARC: You basically eliminated all my social circles.

DREW: Hillary's got like ten best girlfriends and they go out and they talk on the phone every day and confide in one another and chat about work and yoga and how their bodies are changing and does Beth still give you blow jobs?

MARC: Dude!

DREW: Because before we were married Hillary treated me like a popsicle on the Fourth of July but now I'm lucky to get one on my birthday. And this . . . this is what guys should talk about, right?

MARC: *(thinking)* No.

DREW: But our wives do all the time about everything and I mean everything like shopping and gossip and your yeast infection.

MARC: What the fuck! You know about that? And it was not a yeast infection.

(subtly adjusting his crotch)

It was a fungus.

DREW: Made of yeast. But don't be embarrassed bro, it happens. You just gotta wash better after the gym.

MARC: Dude. I don't need your hygiene advice.

DREW: Apparently you do, 'cause where do you think she heard about soaking the boys in vinegar? It's the only cure for when your balls are baking bread.

(Pats him a little too high on the thigh.)

You're welcome.

MARC: Can we please just watch the Lakers?

DREW: Oh. Are we moving too fast? Or you already have a best friend?

MARC: No. I mean, yeah . . . that's right, I do.

DREW: Who?

MARC: The best man at our wedding. JD. He lives in Baltimore now.

DREW: How often do you guys talk?

MARC: Enough. I guess.

DREW: Like, once a week, or what?

MARC: Like . . . I don't know. I guess—

(beat)

Huh. When was the last time I talked to him?

DREW: See? He was your best man and you don't even talk anymore.

MARC: We don't have to. He's just the kind of guy that just, you know, we don't need to talk a lot.

DREW: I'm not like that.

MARC: Really.

DREW: And I don't think most guys are either, we just think we're supposed to act that way.

MARC: Didn't you have a best man?

DREW: Hillary's brother. He doesn't like me all that much. Thinks I come on too strong.

MARC: *(beat)* Look, Drake.

DREW: Drew.

MARC: Sorry. Drew. Listen, Beth told me her friend from yoga . . . your wife . . . had a cool husband and we should meet up for a beer and I said, ok, sure, thinking we would just, you know, meet up for a beer, but, all this best friends forever kinda thing is just a little . . . I'm just not really . . . in the market for one, you know?

DREW: *(beat)* That's cool.

MARC: Let's just drink our beers, watch the game, be guys. In silence.

> *(DREW plays it off. They both watch the game. Then drew takes out a small pink notebook and pen, scratches something out.)*

What's that?

> *(eyeing his pad)*

Did you just cross my name off of some . . . list? What is this?

(picking up pad, reading)

"Possible candidates for my new best friend."

(He flips through pages. Clearly, a long list.)

How many . . . I'm at the bottom? Dave Scales is on here? That guy's a tool. How is he higher up on the list than me?

DREW: What's it matter now? I've run out of names.

MARC: Wait, seriously, you've done this with all these guys?

DREW: And none of them ever called for a second date.

MARC: Maybe because you're calling it a date.

DREW: What would you call it?

MARC: Just . . . hanging out. Grabbing a drink. Getting to know each other. Kind of like . . . kind of like . . . yeah, I guess . . .

(Stands, begins to pull wallet out.)

Look. You seem like a great guy.

DREW: Here we go again.

MARC: But it's not really a great time for me, right now, and I . . . what's happening?

(DREW's trying to keep it together, holding back tears. MARC eyes him, then DREW starts to lose it. MARC looks around. Clearly they have everyone's attention.)

You ok? Hey. Buddy.

DREW: *(through snot)* I'm not your buddy. You've made that perfectly clear.

MARC: Woah. Seriously, pal.

DREW: *(losing it)* I'm not your pal either. Or your amigo. Or your dawg. Or Edgar Allen Bro. I used to be fun. I lived my life by the 5 Bs. Beer. Bros. Babes. Ball. And Buffett.* Guys used to beg to hang out with me. But now I'm on list-serves with mommy and me groups. I have contact info for three different lactation consultants. Three! The last sporting event I went to was a Silpada jewelry party. I've become this overweight, pathetic, whiskered vagina! I don't know how to find my balls. You gotta help me!

(shouting)

I took care of your balls now it's your turn with my balls!

(He collapses into MARC, a blubbering mess. MARC is stunned, embarrassed, trapped. But then he pats DREW on the back.)

MARC: There there.

(But DREW is still weeping. This time, MARC actually pats him with sincerity, gently holding the big lug.)

Hey. It's ok. It's going to be ok.

(DREW eventually pulls himself together, embarrassed. He pats under his eyes with his ring fingers.)

DREW: Ok. I'm ok. I'm all right.

MARC: Look, man. I get it.

DREW: You're just saying that because I snotted on your sweater vest.

MARC: No, seriously. I do. I mean. If you asked me in high school if I would even be the kind of guy who wore sweater vests, I would have laughed right in your face. You think I wanted to grow up and be this sorry ass cubicle jockey who works sixty hours a week pushing numbers around? You want to hear something sad? The only thing I excel at . . . is Excel. I make good spreadsheets. That's it. And my freaking life has become this massive, over-organized spreadsheet with cells that just go on and on and on. It never ends. And it's sucking the life out of me, one spread-shit at a time.

(Bites his lip.)

Damnit. You're gonna make me cry now.

DREW: It's ok. Spreadsheets are hard.

MARC: They're really hard!

DREW: But it feels better to talk about, doesn't it.

(A moment. MARC nods.)

MARC: Look. I don't have a lot of time right now, with work and the kids and all, and, I don't know if I'm like best friend material here or anything but . . . you can keep my name on the list . . . if you want. And I'll . . . you know . . . I'll call you . . . for a second, you know, whatever this is. And maybe we can try it again. See where it goes. Cool?

DREW: Cool.

(They both stare forward in silence, watching the game. A big, delighted grin grows across DREW's face.)

We totally need nicknames

MARC: We totally do not.

BLACKOUT.

Productions:
    Subversive Shorts, Subversive Theatre Collective,
    Buffalo, NY
    June 14-July 7, 2013
    Directed by Michael Lodick

    Cast:
    GISELLE: Priscilla Young
    EDUARDO: Rolando Gomez

    Driftwood Players Theater Festival of Shorts,
    Edmonds, WA
    July 12-14, 2013 (Winner of Audience Favorite Award
    Directed by Paul Fleming

    Cast:
    GISELLE: Dawn Cornell
    EDUARDO: Steve Ruggles

CHARACTERS:
>GISELLE: an American doctor, early to mid fifties
>EDUARDO: a Uruguayan Jesuit priest, forties to fifties

SETTING and TIME: At a cafe in Montevideo, Uruguay, present day (2013)

>*Tango music underscoring quickly fades. Lights up on GISELLE and EDUARDO, seated at an outdoor cafe table.*

EDUARDO: They are called *alfajores*, these cookies. They are very popular here in Uruguay. The filling is *dulce de leche*. Perhaps you had them the last time you were here.

GISELLE: *Dulce de leche*, yes, of course. But *alfajores,* I don't recall. Your English, it's perfect.

EDUARDO: I attended seminary in California.

>*(beat)*

I was told that you were inquiring after my brother Tristan. Is this why you have come to Montevideo?

GISELLE: Yes.

EDUARDO: You have been here for how long?

GISELLE: About ten days. So, do I call you Father? I'm a Jewish girl from Pittsburgh and I've never—

EDUARDO: —You may call me Eduardo. So you have gone to a number of *milongas*, inquiring after him.

GISELLE: If you're looking for a tango dancer, you go to where they dance the—excuse me, but how did you know that?

EDUARDO: This is a small country. I first learned of your presence in this city over a week ago.

GISELLE: Listen, I don't want you to get the wrong idea. I'm not a stalker. I'm a doctor, a cardiologist with grown children. When we were here in 1983—my husband and I—Tristan gave us a private tango lesson. And I guess you can say that I was smitten with him. But thirty years is a long time. I understand that he's probably married—with kids, for all I know—but I'm just hoping to see him again, to say hello—

EDUARDO: —Tristan no longer lives in Uruguay.

GISELLE: Oh. I see. And, if I may ask, where—

EDUARDO:—I have not spoken with him for many years.

GISELLE: I'm sorry.

EDUARDO: I am sorry as well. But, as you see, I cannot help you.

GISELLE: I do see. And there's no one else who would be able to—

EDUARDO:—No.

GISELLE: Did he marry? If . . . I may ask.

EDUARDO: No.

GISELLE: Did he ever mention my name?

EDUARDO: No, not to me. Giselle is a very distinctive name. I would have remembered if he had mentioned your name.

(preparing to leave)

It was a pleasure to meet you. This cafe attracts many tango dancers, by the way.

GISELLE: *(shaken from her thoughts)* What?

EDUARDO: If you linger here a while, I'm sure you will see a dance or two. You can take some pictures, and bring back pleasant memories of your second trip to Uruguay.

GISELLE: Yes, of course.

(Eduardo begins to walk away.)

GISELLE: Wait. Don't go yet. Please, Eduardo . . . Father. Why didn't you contact me sooner? When you first learned that I was looking for your brother.

EDUARDO: *(with greater intensity, as he sits back down) Why* are you here looking for my brother? How did you meet him?

GISELLE: I told you: he gave a private dance lesson to me and my husband. We wanted to learn a few basic steps to take back home and show our friends. We thought it would be cute. Fun.

EDUARDO: And exactly how did you find him?

GISELLE: *(trying to recall)* How did we find him? We had a little time to spend in Montevideo, before the start of our week-long cruise. I believe we asked the concierge at the Hilton if he could recommend a private tango instructor. He's the one who put us in touch.

EDUARDO: You are certain this was the Hilton hotel.

GISELLE: We're talking about 1983. Thirty years ago. But, yes. As a matter of fact. The concierge at the Hilton arranged for us to meet a young woman—on a street corner in the Old City.

EDUARDO: And you arrived there how? By taxi?

GISELLE: Yes. By taxi, if I'm not mistaken, and then we walked with her to an apartment nearby. On the fourth floor, no elevator. That's where she introduced us to Tristan. There was an old phonograph, as I recall—

EDUARDO: —And so you had a tango lesson of, what? An hour? And you fell in love with him then.

GISELLE: The tango is a very romantic dance. The music . . . 'You lead from the heart,' I remember him telling my husband. And he danced with me to demonstrate, of course. Dancing the tango to old phonograph records on a first trip to South America. And then there were those beautiful eyes of his. How could a girl not fall in love just a little?

EDUARDO: And that was the last time you saw him.

GISELLE: Yes. Our ship departed for Rio the next morning.

EDUARDO: You're sure of that.

GISELLE: I'm sure.

EDUARDO: Did your husband ever know that you fell in love with your tango instructor?

GISELLE: I . . . feel like I'm at confession. But the answer is no. No. We're divorced now, but that has nothing to do with any of this.

EDUARDO: And did you ever demonstrate the tango steps you learned to your friends?

GISELLE: We never spoke of the tango lesson again. Why are you asking all these questions of me?

EDUARDO: It may be valuable evidence in the reconstruction of a crime.

GISELLE: A crime? What crime? Falling in love? Where is your brother?

EDUARDO: What do you remember of Montevideo in 1983?

GISELLE: I don't know . . . a South American city, much like the one I see today. Grand plazas and pockets of squalor. Too much traffic. Restaurants and cafes that stay open very late—

EDUARDO: —Giselle. Montevideo was a city at war. The signs of war were everywhere.

GISELLE: We probably heard some talk of turmoil, yes. But—and I mean this with no disrespect but in all honesty—it was not very apparent to us at the time. Perhaps we did not wish to know. We were tourists. I was an innocent. In the fullest sense of the word.

EDUARDO: Did you know that Tristan was in great danger when you met him? That he was in hiding?

GISELLE: In hiding? But . . . I had no idea he was political.

EDUARDO: We were all political. It was a very hard time, and we all had to make hard choices. How well did you know my brother?

GISELLE: I told you: I just saw him that one time.

EDUARDO: You saw him that one time, and yet you were able to conclude that he was not political—

GISELLE: —I simply thought of him as a musician, a tango dancer—

(a beat)

What happened, Eduardo?

EDUARDO: He was abducted by the secret police and executed several weeks later.

GISELLE: Oh, no.

(a beat, then very quietly)

When?

EDUARDO: In September of 1983, just around the time you were visiting the city with your husband.

GISELLE: How awful. I am so sorry.

EDUARDO: This was during the final days of the dictatorship. If Tristan had been more careful. . . It took me many years to forgive him for his carelessness. The police tracked down their enemies by whatever means possible: torture, blackmail, phone taps, paid informants and innocents alike people who became unwitting links in the government's web of surveillance.

GISELLE: Are you saying that they may have found your brother by following my husband and me?

EDUARDO: No. This much is certain. It was not on that occasion that they tracked down my brother.

GISELLE: Oh, thank God.

EDUARDO: We have sufficient knowledge of the facts to say that they did not take my brother away on that day. So, you see, you have no complicity in this case.

GISELLE: *(beat)* How do you know this?

EDUARDO: Because when they finally tracked down Tristan, it was through the information provided to the authorities by a concierge at the *Sheraton* hotel. And it was by following a woman who was by herself. A lone *gringa*, it was said. It was at first rumored that she was an informant for the military police, but it was later concluded that she was unaware of being used in this manner. Her name was Giselle, also. But that could not have been you, since on the one occasion you saw Tristan it was with your husband. So, you see, you have no complicity in this case.

GISELLE: Complicity? Why do you keep talking about complicity? I was falling in love!

EDUARDO: Regardless. The facts are clear. As you have already said, you are an innocent.

GISELLE: *(after a long beat)* What if I were to tell you that I went back the next day.

EDUARDO: Is that a hypothetical question or a statement of fact?

GISELLE: I went back. The next day, for another lesson. We actually had another day to spend—

EDUARDO:—And this was with your husband as well?

GISELLE: My husband wasn't feeling well. I told him that I was going out to do some sightseeing. I spoke with . . . the hotel concierge. I asked him if he could help me get in touch with a tango dancer named Tristan Ferrer. He made some phone calls—

EDUARDO: —This was the concierge at the Hilton.

GISELLE: No. I . . . I walked over to the Sheraton, and implied that I was a guest there. I didn't want my husband to somehow find out—

EDUARDO: —Do you remember the name of the concierge?

GISELLE: This was thirty years ago. How could I possibly—

EDUARDO:—His name was Sid!

GISELLE: How do you know that? Why do you ask me questions you already know the answer to?

EDUARDO: Perhaps because you seem curiously unwilling to ask them of yourself.

GISELLE: *(beat)* His name *was* Sid. I remember now. It was such an unusual name for a South American. He arranged for a taxi to drop me off on a corner in the *Barrio Reus*. The same girl was there—Ana was her name—and she took me to a different apartment, a smaller one.

EDUARDO: There was a record player in that room as well.

GISELLE: Yes.

EDUARDO: But there was no tango lesson on that day.

GISELLE: I don't remember.

EDUARDO: You would have only had an hour or so, before you had to be back at the Hilton, so that your husband would not suspect—

GISELLE:—Yes. You're right, of course.

EDUARDO: My brother offered you an iced coffee and *alfajores*, after which you and he made love.

> *(pulling out an old envelope and giving it to her)*

And you wrote down this address—a post office box in Pennsylvania—and Tristan promised to write to you, and yet you never heard from him.

GISELLE: It remained an unsolved mystery tugging at my heart. He said he would write—and yet he didn't. Why? Wasn't I pretty enough? Had he simply been toying with me? Or . . . did something happen? What was the silence trying to tell me? There are certain questions that you carry with you forever. Not to attempt to answer them would be intolerable.

EDUARDO: What did you see when you left the apartment that day? Do you remember a car?

GISELLE: A car?

EDUARDO: A car parked at the curb. With people inside.

GISELLE: Yes. No. I mean, there *was* a car, and I didn't look inside, but I sensed that there were a number of people packed inside. Maybe it was sitting very close to the pavement. How else would one get such an impression?

EDUARDO: Perhaps by looking through the windows.

GISELLE: No! For some reason I recall the scent of cigarette smoke and cloves. But I had this visceral feeling—an internal warning—that it was best not to look inside in the car.

EDUARDO: Except you did—

GISELLE: —That it was best to walk on. And that's what I did. I walked on to the corner and hailed a taxi. I did not look back.

(beat)

That was *them*, wasn't it? They were waiting for me to leave.

EDUARDO: What did you see inside the car, Giselle?

GISELLE: I didn't—

EDUARDO: —But you did!

GISELLE: I saw Ana! She was bound and gagged and looking right at *me*. And I saw men—several men. I couldn't make sense of what I was seeing. I was scared . . . terrified. What could I do? Call the police? They *were* the police, weren't they? All I knew was that I was in way over my head. I needed to get back to the hotel, to my *husband*.

(beat)

Oh, God. How old were they?

EDUARDO: Tristan was twenty-six. Ana twenty-four. Her, they let go after a few weeks.

GISELLE: *(with a gasp)* So young. I'm so sorry. So sorry.

EDUARDO: It surprises you that Tristan was twenty-six?

GISELLE: No. It makes sense. I was the same age. But now that seems so young to me. It's just not fair. What . . . should I do now?

EDUARDO: What should you do? There is nothing more to be done. Your mystery is solved. You shall return home. I shall return to my work. We shall continue to live our lives.

Someone has turned on recorded tango music.

EDUARDO: Look. I told you there would be dancers here.

GISELLE: But you must hate me. Please don't hate me.

EDUARDO: Ay, Giselle. How could I hate you? Do you think I have never been in love myself?

(beat)

This tango of ours. It conceals as much as it reveals. Tristan used to say that it could take you past the point of safe return, to the edge of oblivion. A dangerous proposition, don't you think—for a dance. But, look at those two. Do you see how the music seems to compel them forward?

(beat)

There is nothing you could have done, Giselle.

GISELLE: Did you . . . ever find him?

EDUARDO: Eventually, yes. We buried him in the cemetery in Colonia, near the Rio de la Plata.

GISELLE: Colonia. Is that very far from here?

EDUARDO: In Uruguay, nothing is very far from here. This is a very small country.

(a beat as they watch the dancers)

Tomorrow—

GISELLE: —Yes?

EDUARDO: Tomorrow—if you are free—I will take you there.

(They watch the dancers for a long moment.)

MUSIC SWELLS. BLACKOUT.

PAINTING SEVENTEEN

Sharon E. Cooper

ORIGINAL PRODUCTION

Painting Seventeen was originally inspired by the Matisse painting *Odalisque with Red Culottes* (painted 1921) and was originally produced as part of the "Matisse Plays" with The Milk Can Theatre Company at the Michael Weller Theatre, February, 2005, in New York City. The original director was Bobbi Masters. Lesley Miller played 30 and Cotton Wright played 17.

The play was further developed and revised in The CRY HAVOC Workshop in 2012 and was mounted as part of "Sharon's Shorts" in Planet Connections Festival, June 2013. Joanna Strange was the director. Kerry Flanagan played 30 and Evelyn Spahr played 17. Both actresses were nominated for "Best Actress" in the Short Play category and Evelyn Spahr won. "Painting Seventeen" won Outstanding Overall Production of a Short Play.

Playwright's notes: It is important to show that Saskia, 17, is "inside" the painting. One thing that worked effectively is placing a frame around Saskia on the floor so she is literally "trapped." Further, it is important in casting that the actors look similar. That said, if you have actors with different hair colors, you may add the line "I dyed my hair" in place of 30s line "the same color hair." While Saskia, 30, looks directly at 17, 17 can never see 30.

CHARACTERS:

> SASKIA: thirty, any race/ethnicity, jaded, attractive but doesn't know it; feels like she's lived a long, time
>
> SASKIA: seventeen, the same racial/ethnic background as Saski, thirty; feisty; lives only in the present and longs to have a real life

> *SASKIA: seventeen, is inside a frame and wears loose lingerie pants and a tank top.*

> *SASKIA: thirty, wears a bulky sweatshirt.*

> *Saskia, thirty, has been working on her self-portrait all day and occasionally paints on an easel directly in front of her.*

SASKIA, 17: *(dramatically)* I am the naked woman in the painting *by the stairs.*

SASKIA, 30: Will you quit your whining? You have clothes on—not to mention the yellow walls and bed made for a goddess—but no stairs, sorry. And those beautiful breasts. You lie back and they're still perfect. Do you think my breasts ever looked like that?

17: I don't know, did they?

30: Seventeen years old.

> *(17 looks around for someone else.)*

17: Who's seventeen?

30: You. Take a good look in the mirror. This is the best you'll ever look.

17: I don't have a mirror.

30: Well, then, trust me.

17: I feel—

30: Uh—no one asked you how you feel.

17: How can you create something and then be so mean?

30: Parents do it all the time. Hey, look at our parents.

17: Our mother told us to take a good look in the mirror, didn't she?

30: What do you know?

17: Nothing. So what exactly do you look like?

30: Like you, only older. When I smile, my face moves and lines form—

17: That sounds so great.

30: Wrinkles?

17: No. Smiling! We have people to smile with? Tell me every detail. Do *we* have children?

30: No, *we* have a divorce. Be grateful *we* don't have children. *They* would be miserable.

(17 twirls around her enclosed space.)

17: A divorce! How exciting.

30: I wish you would stop moving around.

17: We were married! We were married!

30: How do you know about these things?

17: Because I'm super smart. She tries to smell the fake flowers next to her bed. These suck.

30: Those roses remind me of Brooklyn Botanical gardens.

17: Did we meet our one true prince in the gardens?

30: No, I met my first love, Mike, at Myrtle Beach.

17: Mike—what a romantic name!

30: It's actually a pretty common name. Bill, Bob, Mike, John— common names.

17: Oh.

30: But we have a great name.

17: What is it?

30: Saskia.

17: Wow—Saskia! Saskia and Mike!

30: I was looking at the ocean; the water was cold on my ankles and my hat flew off my head. I turned around, and it was in his hand. We walked over to this group of rocks.

17: I knew it! The rock garden!

30: Weelll, they were big and slippery rocks with sharp edges—

17: That's so romantic!

30: He did play with my hair—

17: While the sun was setting!

30: We knew immediately that we liked each other. I said I was just out of a relationship and wanted to take things *slowly*. I almost fell off the rock when he agreed . . . .We had sex that night.

17: Is that slowly?

30: Yes. Uh, no. Well—

17: Love at first sight!

30: You could say that.

17: And I bet we shared intimate secrets until all hours—What's it like to kiss someone? To have them touch your face—to have your nose near their nose, your elbow—

30: Amazing.

17: He was your soul mate. I can hear it in your voice.

30: We tried having children. I kept losing them.

17: Where did they go?

30: Never mind. He moved in with one of my girlfriends from high school—Mary Ellen—she was like me—the same color hair—we were both transplants to the south.

17: *(romantically)* The South. Wait—where are we now?

30: Born in New York. Raised in South Carolina. College in Virginia. Married Mike in South Carolina. Divorced in New York. A fling in Paris. Well, I haven't told you about that yet. And now, New York. Try to keep up with the story.

17: *(overlapping)* Do I know her? Mary Ellen? If I'm seventeen and we were in high school and best friends with Mary Ellen—

30: She wasn't my best friend.

17: Oh. I was hoping we were best friends. Can I remember her if I try really, really hard?

(17 tries really, really hard.)

30: You're two dimensional; you have no memories.

17: *Come on, tell me everything.* Every detail. What it's like— love, friendship, pain, loss, lovers, moving, blowing bubbles, spitting—

30: Spitting? You want to know what it's like to spit?

17: I want to know what it's like to breathe.

30: When I finish this painting, people are going to admire you. You will be beautiful. Frozen.

17: I don't want frozen; I want life. Spill it. Every detail: 18, 19, 20, 21, 22—

30: After fifty, maybe even forty, men don't admire you at all. Overnight, you go from being a piece of meat, dealing with the "woohoos" and the "hey babies" to a fly who moves through the world with no one watching. And you think about getting rid of the dark circles under your eyes and the varicose vein on your right shin. You could be a naked woman on the stairs, and no one would even notice. You're invisible.

17: Wow—are you forty or fifty?

30: Thirty. But I see it coming.

17: You make the future sound like so much fun.

30: It gets much worse. All of it.

17: I want to experience it. Every second. I think you should paint me a staircase, and I will walk right outta here.

(17 tries to leave the painting. It's clearly not working.)

30: *(overlapping)* I can't. Stay where it's safe.

17: I don't want safe. I want freedom. These four walls are a prison. Paint me a staircase; let me out of here!

30: It sucks out here. I wouldn't mind living in a painting for a while.

17: It's numb here.

30: Numb sounds like a welcome change.

17: I would choose pain over numb any day.

30: That's because you've never experienced it.

17: I don't like what you've become.

30: I don't like you either.

17: Then why do you want to be me?

30: I *was* you. And you are an *assignment*.

17: What are you talking about?

30: I am taking a class at a community college—

17: I love college!

30: Shut up! I was assigned to do a modern version of a Matisse painting and for some God-awful reason, I'm painting *you*.

17: We turned out so mean, Saskia. You can't see how quiet it is here. The color that never changes. There's no future, no past. And your present is stale like old bread. But your breasts look great—because they're not real. You can say "best friends" and "marriage" and "divorce" but you don't get to experience it. But oh my God, if I got to smell real flowers, if I got to walk on the beach, if I got to sit in a rock garden, I would never come back.

30: *(overlapping)* In three months from now, the first boy you ever loved—

17: I knew it! I knew I had a first love!

30: *(overlapping)* He'll die in a car accident on Avril road. And your parents will get divorced when you're twenty-one, after they've been married twenty-five years—and you'll act like it doesn't bother you at all. And you'll work like a dog to have time to paint—you'll do temp jobs and waitress and work in a bookstore. Your sister will die from cancer—

17: I have a sister?

30: And you'll get married quietly, without much fanfare. And your marriage will feel like a trap while you're in it and a loss when it's gone. You'll find someone new, take one more chance at love, follow him to Paris, stroll and look at Matisse paintings and realize the paintings are more real than the relationship. Do you want to hear more?

17: Yes! Yes! What's my sister's name? Was she my best friend?

30: She was a History teacher for one year. When she got cancer, her students wrote her everyday. She joked that her students were nicer to her when she was in the hospital than in the classroom.

17: I would love to know her now.

30: Me, too. When I was seventeen, it felt like the right age—like this would be my age forever. And my parents would be forty-something and my grandparents sixty-something, and it would always be that way. Like a painting. Thirty felt so far away at seventeen. And my breasts never turned out how they were supposed to be.

(17 jumps up.)

17: Maybe you're hiding behind a difficult decade where you paint in boring pastels. Maybe you've forgotten the sweet moments that skirted the edges of despair—

30: You sound like a poet.

17: We are poets. And painters. And passionate. You may know the facts, but I know what's possible.

30: You don't sound so numb now.

17: What are you saying? Oh my God, am I alive? Is this life, like right now? *(squealing with glee)* Eeehh! Did you paint me a staircase? How can I ever thank you? Will I get to be thirty something and forty something, get married, divorced, know my sister, go to Paris, and be best friends with sooo many people. I can't wait to—

(30 walks behind the painting to gather new colors to finish the painting.)

17: Saskia? Saskia? Why aren't you answering me?

30: Sometimes, when it's late at night, my paint brush on the canvas sounds like rain, and I imagine lovers from all over the world touching elbows, touching noses, shifting their bodies so they fit just right, even if it's just for a moment. And I look at you. The one I come home to. Happy Birthday, by the way.

17: I'm seventeen, today, like today, like it's my actual birthday! Eeeks!

30: Forever.

17: Oh. Right. And you're thirty.

30: How did you—

17: I'm super smart. And—you said it before, you know—

(30 is putting the final touches on the painting.)

17: You aren't going to paint me a staircase, are you?

30: You make seventeen sound like sooo much fun. I miss that.

17: Being seventeen?

30: Fun. I could die here with you in these four walls, and I can't do that. I have to go. It's due. And it's time.

17: Oh. Well. Heck. Don't worry about me. I'm fine. I'm—two dimensional . . . Our mom—she was just feeling bad about herself. It wasn't her fault—or your fault. It was no one's fault. . . .You look great.

30: You can't see me.

17: So what.

17 moves her arm into her final resting place. It is above her head, as in the Matisse painting, Odalisque with Red Culottes.

(30 walks to the door, stops and turns around.)

30: Bye 17.

17: Bye 30.

(30 turns and leaves.)

(Fade to black.)

End play.

PERFECT

Maura Campbell

ORIGINAL PRODUCTION
   Perfect was first presented in Burlington, Vermont as part
   of the Off Center For The Dramatic Art's Third Annual
   Fringe Festival on November 8, 2013, with the following

   Directed by Laura Roald

   CAST:
   MAN: Bob Carmody
   WOMAN: Mary Scripps

CHARACTERS

> MAN: Sixties, a regular "Joe"
> WOMAN: Sixties, still beautiful

SETTING: A café, or park. A place where people arrange to meet someone they haven't seen in a long, long time.

> *A MAN sits and waits. After a moment, a WOMAN enters. She sits down next to him, but not too close. A pause.*

MAN: Afternoon.

> *(She smiles briefly. They resume sitting and waiting. He looks at his watch. Their eyes meet. He looks away politely. Looks past her as if watching for someone. He looks at his watch again.)*

MAN: Great weather.

WOMAN: Actually, it's a little cold.

MAN: Oh, would you like my jacket?

WOMAN: No, thank you.

MAN: I don't mean to be forward. I mean, about the jacket. It's just that I'm actually warm so I was going to take it off anyway.

> *(He takes it off.)*

And it's small, besides. So if you did want to put it on and forgot to give it back—not that I think you seem like you'd forget anything, more like I would forget to remind you. I wouldn't miss it, that's what I'm getting to. I'm planning to donate it to the Salvation Army, not that I think you would be interested in anything used—

WOMAN: Are you waiting for someone? Because you seem very nervous.

MAN: I'll say I'm nervous. You'd be nervous, too, not that you seem the nervous type, just that I believe anyone would be nervous under my circumstances.

WOMAN: What circumstances are those?

MAN: Oh, you wouldn't be interested. Not that you look like you don't have interests. Or aren't curious. I'll bet you're curious about a lot of things. Just probably not old men on park benches with small jackets. And—

(He reaches into his pocket.)

MAN: Perfect. Story of my life.

WOMAN: Excuse me?

MAN: Nothing. Um, if a woman comes by looking for me—

WOMAN: Looking for you?

MAN: You're right. I am waiting for someone. I don't think she's coming, though. But if she does . . . Dang it all, I'll leave a note.

WOMAN: She's late?

MAN: I've been waiting an hour. *(He smiles kindly.)* Sorry, not your problem. Not that you have an attitude of any kind. You look like the kind of person that is sympathetic. Well, I know you're sympathetic, because you've been putting up with me for the past, well, I guess it's only been a couple of minutes. You wouldn't have a piece of paper, would you?

WOMAN: I might, let me see . . . Here.

MAN: Thank you.

WOMAN: You say you're been waiting an hour?

MAN: Yes, um, you wouldn't have a pencil?

WOMAN: I thought you'd say that.

MAN: You did?

WOMAN: You look the type.

MAN: What do you mean?

WOMAN: Who forgets things.

MAN: Really? How can you tell?

WOMAN: A woman knows these sorts of things. It's instinctive. Could you have the time mixed up?

MAN: What? No, the letter said two o'clock. Now it's three. Does that say three?

WOMAN: Sometimes you get time mixed up, I'll bet.

MAN: No, I'm very punctual. Well, actually, I'm usually early. Usually I'm very early. Once I showed up to a funeral and the guy hadn't even died yet.

WOMAN: See? So maybe you've got the time mixed up.

MAN: I'll be damned. What else can you tell about me?

WOMAN: I'll bet you played soccer when you were young.

MAN: I did! I did play soccer! I was goalie.

WOMAN: Of course.

MAN: Of course?

WOMAN: You've got the look.

MAN: What look?

WOMAN: The Savior look. You look like someone who doesn't need to be the center of attention but is there in a pinch when needed.

MAN: Steady Eddy. If my name was Eddy, they'd call me Steady Eddy. Kind of boring, I guess.

WOMAN: Nonsense. Where would we be if we didn't have dependable types?

MAN: Yeah, but why does it have to be me? Why can't I be the daredevil, man about town—I'd settle for simply being a bit eccentric.

WOMAN: I'll bet you're Catholic.

MAN: Now this is getting uncanny! What else can you tell?

WOMAN: You like Italian food.

MAN: Like it? I love it! This is incredible. I had spaghetti for lunch, I—Do I have some on my chin?

WOMAN: You're just easy to read.

MAN: One more thing. Tell me one more thing.

WOMAN: I'll bet you married your high school sweetheart.

MAN: Wrong!

WOMAN: Really?

MAN: I married the girl I took to the prom. My sweetheart, well, there was a sweetheart but I didn't marry her.

WOMAN: Why didn't you?

MAN: She didn't know I was alive. So I did the next best thing. I married my second choice. I knew it then, I know it now. So when we got divorced I gave her everything. It was only fair.

WOMAN: What did she look like?

MAN: My wife?

WOMAN: No, your . . . sweetheart.

MAN: Oh, she had a great figure. Not too skinny, not too plump. Kind of short, but then, kind of tall. And smile, when she smiled it was like the whole world lit up. Brown hair with gold all over the place.

WOMAN: I know something else.

MAN: What's that?

WOMAN: I know she liked you, too.

MAN: How could you know that?

WOMAN: Because *I* like you. Anyone would.

MAN: Well, I'm lucky you sat down. What a nice thing to say.

WOMAN: How long has it been since . . .

MAN: Forty-five years this June. I haven't seen her since graduation. But I know I'll recognize her. That is, if she shows up which is looking more and more unlikely.

WOMAN: Forty-five years is a long time.

MAN: You don't know Cathy. She's got this great bone structure in her face.

WOMAN: Really?

MAN: She was a figure skater, you know.

WOMAN: How would I know that?

MAN: Oh, course you wouldn't. I just feel like I know you now, that's all. You remind me of my mother. Not that you look like her and, well, she's dead, too. But she was always soothing. Kind of comfortable to be around.

WOMAN: Like an old blanket.

MAN: Exactly!

WOMAN: This Cathy, was she shy?

MAN: Not too shy, not too outgoing.

WOMAN: She sounds wishy washy. First you say she wasn't skinny, then you say she wasn't plump.

MAN: It's hard to describe someone like—

WOMAN: Then you say she was kind of short, then kind of tall. Well, what was she?

MAN: She was perfect. There! That describes it. Kind of like you.

WOMAN: No one's perfect.

MAN: I suppose you're right. Of course you're right.

WOMAN: Now you sound wishy washy.

MAN: Do I?

WOMAN: I suppose that's why you were able to marry the girl you took to the prom.

MAN: I think you're right.

WOMAN: Would you quit agreeing with me?

MAN: All right.

WOMAN: Have you ever had an original thought?

MAN: *(Thinks)* I'm not sure.

WOMAN: Well, that does it. I knew this was a mistake.

MAN: Pardon me?

WOMAN: Did you ever wonder why that girl wasn't at the prom?

MAN: The—you mean—

WOMAN: You don't think I noticed you looking at me every day for four years?

MAN: But I——

WOMAN: Didn't it ever occur to you that I expected to be asked?

MAN: I don't believe this.

WOMAN: I turned down two other boys. I was waiting for you to ask me!

MAN: Cathy?

WOMAN: Forty-five years later I don't look so perfect, do I?

MAN: Cathy.

WOMAN: I'll see you.

MAN: It's just . . . you look so young. I couldn't imagine that you could be my age.

WOMAN: *(Pause)* Oh, Frank.

> *(She sits back down.)*

> *Black out.*

RETURN OF THE CURSE

Jack Neary

ORIGINAL PRODUCTION
> Originally produced at the 2013 Boston Theater Marathon,
> May 12, 2013, Boston Center for the Arts

> Directed by Jack Neary

> CAST:
> RUSTY: Andrew Dolan
> BEN: Kirk Trach

CHARACTERS:

> RUSTY is in his fifties, essentially a street person with street smarts and a glib tongue. He is an inveterate Boston Red Sox fan.
>
> BEN is Ben Harrington, in his thirties, the General Manager of the Boston Red Sox. Straight-laced and officious.

SETTING: The play takes place in Ben's Fenway Park office, some time in 2013.

> *The Fenway Park office of Red Sox General Manager Ben Harrington. All we need for our purposes is something that resembles a desk, and a chair.*
>
> *At rise, RUSTY, around 50, is seated in the chair. His clothing is ill-fitting and tasteless. He wears an ancient and decrepit Red Sox cap. One of his legs is bouncing nervously, jogging the ratty briefcase he holds on his lap up and down. He appears to be mumbling incoherently, although before long, we recognize the introduction to Neil Diamond's "Sweet Caroline." Ultimately, he reaches the verse, and begins to sing.*

RUSTY: *(humming in the dark)*

> *(LIGHTS UP. Both his legs are bouncing, the briefcase is flying.)*

SWEET CAROLINE . . . BA BA BA . . . Good times never seemed so good.
SO GOOD! SO GOOD! SO . . .!!!!"

> *(The briefcase is out of control.)*
>
> *(BEN HARRINGTON enters. He's in his mid-thirties, dry and unemotional.)*
>
> *(Rusty sees Ben. Stops singing abruptly.)*

BEN: Thank God. You came.
RUSTY: Are you him?
BEN: *(moves to desk)* Yes. Ben Harrington.

RUSTY: How'd you find me?

BEN: That's not important.

RUSTY: The dickhead. I bet it was the dickhead.

BEN: Theo?

RUSTY: See? Everybody knows who the dickhead is.

BEN: When he left, he gave me this card . . .

(shows card)

He said I should call this number . . .

RUSTY: He had his chance with me. He blew it.

BEN: He said . . . you were in possession of something that might solve any problems that might come up with the team.

RUSTY: Yeah. Did he tell you what that something was?

BEN: Yes.

RUSTY: Oh. Good. So you tell me. Say it. Say it out loud what it is I have that you want that will solve any problems that might come up with the team.

BEN: Well . . . I think we both understand . . .

RUSTY: No. You gotta say it. You gotta say what I got which is what you want. He laughed at me.

(a la Thurston Howell III)

Ha Ha Ha. Like that. Fuckin' Yuppie. Right in my face.

So, no. You gotta say it. I got what?

BEN: The . . . uh . . . the . . .

RUSTY: Say it, Benny. Say it!

BEN: The Curse. He said . . . you had . . . the Curse.

RUSTY: Aha! See, I knew he believed me, that snotty little blunderkind! Threw me outa here like I'm Grady Little the morning after Game 7 in '03. I fixed his wagon, though! And I did it sooooo smooth. So smooooth. I am a smoothy. Maybe you've noticed. I am smooth! I was so pissed, I decided to really hurt him. I let him win for a while. A World Series, even. Set him up, like. Made him feel like they don't need me. Then he gets comfortable and all smarty pants for a couple years and BAM! I hit him with Lugo!

BEN: We won another World Series with Lugo.

RUSTY: In SPITE of Lugo, you mean. Lugo was a zit waiting to be squeezed, and I squeezed him in '08 and '09! That was the real Lugo. So smooooooooth, I was, with that. The Lugothing.

BEN: He said . . . if you give it to me, I can control it.

RUSTY: Yeah. Like I control it now. If I give it to you.

BEN: How does it work?

RUSTY: The dickhead didn't tell you?

BEN: No. He was very . . . circumspect about the whole thing.

RUSTY: He was, huh?

BEN: Yes.

RUSTY: That sounds like him.

BEN: Yes.

RUSTY: Circumspect.

BEN: Yes.

RUSTY: What does it mean?

BEN: *(rattled)* How does it work! We don't have much time! Jeez, if Larry ever knew I was in here talking with you, he'd . . .

RUSTY: Okay, Benny, don't get a run in your sanitaries. Did the dickhead tell you about the guy at the trough?

BEN: He did mention something about a trough.

RUSTY: Big fat guy in a trenchcoat. Standin' next to me back then when they had the troughs in the men's rooms here at Fenway. Trench coat guy had a Yankee uniform underneath. I could see the pinstripes. I knew who it was. Hot dogs hangin' out of his pockets . . .

BEN: But how could it possibly have been . . .

RUSTY: Benny! Don't fight me on this! It was right out of the *Twilight Zone*, but I was there! And it was him! Case closed!

BEN: Babe Ruth . . . ?

RUSTY: Mustard. Relish, drippin' down his pants. The whole deal. Disgusting. Gives me this.

    (indicates briefcase)

Tells me it'll be worth it to me if I opened it in the park every once in a while. So I do. When I do, I start gettin' money in the mail. Cash. A lot of cash. Five grand a pop. But every time I open it, something bad happens to them. Dent. Buckner. Schiraldi. Grady.

BEN: And all you have to do is open it?

RUSTY: That's it.

BEN: *(reaches for it)* What's inside? Rusty leaps from his seat in a crazed effort to keep Ben away from the case.

RUSTY: NO! NO, YOU DON'T! NO WAY! YOU DON'T WAN-
NA SEE WHAT'S IN HERE! NO FRIGGIN' WAY, BABY!
NO WAY!

BEN: Okay. Okay. I'm sorry.

RUSTY: You remember that old Catholic story the nuns used to
tell you, about the Blessed Mother appearing to some Mexican kid or something, leaving a note from God. Pope reads
the note, shits a brick, keels over dead? Remember that?

BEN: I'm not Catholic.

RUSTY: Too bad. Good story. But it's like that. You can't look
in here.

BEN: I'd shit a brick.

RUSTY: At least.

BEN: But . . . if you give it to me . . .

RUSTY: Who says I'm gonna give it to you?

BEN: I don't think you'd be here if you didn't plan to give it to
me.

RUSTY: I hate this fuckin' thing.

BEN: So . . . .?

RUSTY: But I need it!

BEN: Why?

RUSTY: It's the economy, stupid! I tried to lay off! I had a few
bucks saved up from before '04! Dickhead'll tell you I was
here to give it to him then. I wanted to get rid of the guilt!
But he wouldn't take it! So I just stopped opening it. I felt
better and they won but I just got poorer andpoorer. Finally, I couldn't take it anymore and in the offseason a couple of
years ago, I opened it up three times!

BEN: Three times?

RUSTY: Crawford, Gonzalez and Bobby Jenks!

BEN: Cost us millions!

RUSTY: But I ate like a Kardashian! The chubby one!

BEN: Jesus.

RUSTY: Then I got greedy. I enjoyed the lifestyle. The comfort.
The dough. I wanted more. So one day, I'm standin' outside
Popeye's Chicken, chompin' on a drumstick . . .

BEN: No . . .

RUSTY: I look across the street, Beckett's walkin' by . . .

BEN: No . . .

RUSTY: "Josh," I holler! "You gotta try this stuff!" He goes in. I open the case. He orders about twelve buckets, sends 'em over to the clubhouse.

BEN: It was the Curse!

RUSTY: Of course it was the Curse! You think you can have the best record in baseball for four months and then turn into the '62 Mets overnight if it ain't the Curse?

BEN: My God!

RUSTY: *(beat)* And then there was Valentine.

BEN: Bobby? What about him? That wasn't the Curse. That was Larry. He made me do it.

RUSTY: Larry didn't make nobody do nothin'! Thanksgiving, November 24, 2011, I'm at my sister's as usual, and as usual I had too much to eat. You wouldn't know it to look at me, but I'm a big eater. Especially on Thanksgiving. So I get back to my apartment that night and I'm bushed. I throw my shoes in the closet and I don't notice it but the briefcase falls off the shelf, bangs on the floor and opens up. The tryptophan kicks in and I sleep for, like, 20 hours. Next day, November twenty-five, Red Sox meet with Valentine and the briefcase is open. 69 and 93. Case closed.

BEN: It was the Curse!

RUSTY: OF COURSE IT WAS THE CURSE!!! Who in his right mind would hire Bobby Valentine to take over a team full of chicken eaters and assholes? It was the Curse!!!!

BEN: I want it. I need it. I'll buy it.

RUSTY: You bet your ass you'll buy it. If I agree to sell it to you.

BEN: How much?

RUSTY: Well, you gotta understand, I'm no spring chicken. Pardon the pun. Is that a pun? Who gives a shit? I ain't goin' out and takin' a civil service exam, you know what I mean? I gotta leave here with an annuity. You saved a lot of money this past off-season, didn't you?

BEN: Well, we were prudent, and we . . .

RUSTY: You were cheap! You think Josh Hamilton was gonna show up and host coke parties in the bullpen between innings? You were cheap! You got money! I want it!

BEN: Okay. Fine. How much?

RUSTY: I want what you gave Ortiz.

BEN: Twenty-six million?

RUSTY: Over two years. I'm in no rush.

BEN: You're out of your mind.

RUSTY: What's your point?

BEN: I'm not giving you twenty-six million dollars for a brief-case.

RUSTY: No. You're giving me twenty-six million for what's IN the briefcase.

BEN: *(moves toward Rusty)* What IS in the briefcase?

RUSTY: *(running away)* NO! Twenty-six million, sight unseen. You transfer the money to my bank account, I give you the case. What you do with it after that . . . I don't give a crap. If I were you, I'd stick it in the basement and never open it again. You look inside, it's your funeral. And I mean that literally. Remember the Pope!

(gives Ben a slip of paper)

Here's the account. Call John. Get it done.

BEN: You think I'm going to call John Henry and ask him to transfer twenty-six million dollars to the bank account of some stranger?

RUSTY: What do you mean, stranger? I introduced him to his wife.

BEN: Linda?

RUSTY: Is that her name? All I know is I was busin' tables at the Alibi Bar in 2008. I see John Henry sittin' with Wer-ner. I'm pickin' up a coupla glasses at the table next to them. Werner gets up to go to the head. I spill a full glass of beer all over this brunette chick. I tell her to go sit next to John while I wipe up the beer. She does. I figure she's safe 'cause this guy's like fifty years older than her.Lit-tle did I know. The rest is history. I introduced him to his wife. Call him.

BEN: No.

RUSTY: Call him or I take this and never bring it back!

BEN: No.

RUSTY: Call him or I take this and never bring it back and open it every time you have a lead in the ninth.

BEN: No.

RUSTY: CALL HIM OR I'LL BRING THIS OVER TO DUS-
TIN PEDROIA'S HOUSE AND SIT OUTSIDE UNTIL
HE TRIPS OVER THE SPRINKLER IN HIS YARD AND
BREAKS BOTH ANKLES!!!

BEN: OKAY! Okay . . . .

*(Ben takes out his cell and punches in a number as
he walks out of the office. Rusty sits and starts in with
"Sweet Caroline" again.)*

RUSTY: Hand, touchin' hand. Reachin' out. Touchin' me.
Touchin' you . . . .SWEET CAROLINE . . . BA BA BA . . .
Good times never seemed so good. SO GOOD! SO GOOD!
SO . . . !!!!"

*(The briefcase is out of control on his lap. Ben re-
enters.)*

BEN: All right. It's done.

RUSTY: *(takes out his cell)* Just let me make sure . . .

BEN: It won't be posted yet.

RUSTY: Sure it will. What, you never seen 24?

(waits)

Uh . . . .yep! There it is! Good old BOA iPhone ap.

(hands briefcase to Ben)

There you go, Benny. Take my advice . . . right in the basement. Put it out of your mind. Do NOT . . . look inside.

BEN: You're sure this is the only Curse?

RUSTY: The only one I got. I got nothin' to do with them pink
hats!

(sings)

Good times never seemed so good. SO GOOD! SO GOOD!
SO GOOD!

(And Rusty is gone.)

*(Ben takes a deep breath, and walks with the case
over to his desk. Puts the briefcase down on the desk.
Stares at it. Looks around. He is alone. He will do it.
He will open the briefcase. Slowly, carefully, he does.
He looks inside. His face begins to shape into a wild*

contortion. Pain and fear and astonishment and panic sets in. There is a frightening, ominous musical chord as the lights.)

BLACKOUT.

THE END.

RIPPLE EFFECT

Jon Spano

ORIGINAL PRODUCTION

Ripple Effect was first produced at Theatre Three (Port Jefferson, New York) throughout March, 2013, and featured Steve McCoy (Peter) and James Schultz (Chaz) with direction by Jeffrey Sanzel. *Ripple Effect* was subsequently staged by the American Globe Theatre's Fifteen-Minute Play Festival in New York City.

CHARACTERS:

> PETER: Male. Late fifties. Weathered, world-weary, short-tempered. Still physically fit. He's lived in New York a long time and has buried a lot of friends.
> CHAZ: Male. Mid twenties. Any ethnicity. Buoyant energy, sometimes naïve. Service oriented and patient.

SETTING: Peter's modest apartment. Men's clothing. Cardboard boxes. Minimal furniture.

TIME AND PLACE: Now. New York City.

SYNOPSIS: As Peter (a fify-eight year old former gay rights activist) prepares to donate his spouse's clothing to Housing Works. Chaz, (the charity's young volunteer) arrives to assist. As the world-weariness of the older man clashes with the self-entitlement of the younger, a deeper understanding of life, loss, and love emerges.

> *Lights pop on. PETER, in his late fifties, holds his front door open for CHAZ, an energetic man in his twenties, stands tentatively in the doorway.*

PETER: Ah, good, right on time. Come in, come in.

> *(CHAZ, wary, enters the apartment. PETER and CHAZ shake hands.)*

CHAZ: I'm Chaz.
PETER: Chaz. Like Cher's son?
CHAZ: Exactly.
PETER: *(Checking out Chaz.)* Not exactly.
CHAZ: And you're Mr. Bartlett.
PETER: I am.
CHAZ: Like the pear.

> *(PETER conveys disapproval. CHAZ surveys the space, dozens of shirts and pants piled high or neatly folded. Several packing boxes scattered about.)*

You're donating all this?
PETER: I know. A person accumulates so much crap over time.

(Folding, packing)

I was going to deliver it all myself, but I threw out my back, so—Help!

CHAZ: Where do I start?

PETER: No-no, let me finish. You just sit.

CHAZ: My manager only gave me half-an-hour.

PETER: Sit down, Chaz.

(CHAZ sits as PETER continues folding and packing.)

So, how long have you been with Housing Works?

CHAZ: *(bashful)* This is my first day.

PETER: And what do you they pay you?

CHAZ: No-no, it's not my regular—I volunteer.

PETER: Ah, volunteer work. Good for the soul.

CHAZ: And even better for those we help.

PETER: Of course.

CHAZ: You ever volunteer for anything?

PETER: No. Lots of activism, though. Back in the day, before you were born.

CHAZ: I'm twenty-five.

PETER: Like I said.

CHAZ: I studied all that in college, though.

PETER: All what?

CHAZ: Activism. Act-Up.

PETER: What makes you think I was with Act-Up?

CHAZ: Educated guess?

PETER: Well, you're right.

CHAZ: "Silence = Death." That was awesome.

PETER: Shutting down the New York Stock Exchange . . . interrupting Mass at St. Patrick's Cathedral . . . storming emergency rooms at hospitals and demanding more beds and gurneys and *respect*. That was Act-Up.—You don't know what bullying *is* till a cop lands a blow to your skull with his Billy Club and a sneer.

CHAZ: I wrote a paper on it, too. Beginning with the Stonewall Riot and the first Gay Pride Parade? And all the way up to marriage equality.

PETER: Well, good for you.

CHAZ: I got an "A."

PETER: So did Hester Prynne.—So tell me: What do guys your age do now on Gay Pride Day? Other than skip the parade and head straight to the pier dance with their boyfriends?

CHAZ: I don't have a boyfriend.

PETER: Mmmnnn.

CHAZ: And frankly, from what I've read, you probably attended your share of dances at the um, um,—Oh, darn!—what were they called at the end of the last century? *(Deliberately playing dumb.)*

Oh, yeah: "Discotheques!"

PETER: Hah, hah, hah. You can write all the papers you want. But they're no substitute for walking the walk.

CHAZ: Let's not go there now, huh?

PETER: Go where?

CHAZ: You think just because I didn't grow up in the 80's that I don't know anything. And maybe you think I take my freedoms and rights for granted and think my life's been a stroll down Easy Street because of *Will & Grace* and *Glee* and *Modern Family*.

PETER: Yes, I think that.

CHAZ: And you probably think I have no appreciation for any of the accomplishments of my gay ancestors.

PETER: Predecessors!

CHAZ: It's true: There are lots of guys my age who think like that.

PETER: But you're different?

CHAZ: I marched against Prop 8 down at Union Square. Because one day I want to get married, just like you are.

PETER: How do you know I'm married?

CHAZ: *(pointing)* Because in that picture on the mantel you're kissing another man in front of City Hall. And you're both dressed in tuxedos. And you're wearing a wedding ring.

(PETER glances at his ring then continues to pack.)

PETER: Protest of any kind has a sort of ripple effect, don't you think? Someone throws a rock into the lake and makes a splash and the smaller waves undulate outward and somehow . . . change happens. So thank you—I mean it—for marching against Prop 8.

CHAZ: You're welcome. And thank you for marching against . . . everything else.

(Looking around.)

You have an amazing number of IZODs.

PETER: None of this is mine.

CHAZ: But you said—

PETER: I said "a *person*" accumulates, not "*I*" accumulate.

CHAZ: Then whose stuff is this?

PETER: Rick's.

CHAZ: Your husband's?

PETER: People should really organize their belongings before they decide to die because leaving a mess behind for someone else to clean up is just not good estate planning. God, that man never threw out so much as an old sock!

CHAZ: Oh.—So all of this is—? So, how long were you and Rick, um—?

PETER: Twenty-three years total, the last two of them legally and happily married.— Hand me that box will you?

(CHAZ hands PETER an empty box. PETER holds up a shirt, smells it, smiles.)

CHAZ: Does it still smell like him?

PETER: No, it smells like laundry detergent.

(Holding up the actual shirt.)

But this, *this* smells like Rick. It was the last thing he wore.

(PETER smells the shirt. He has a distinctly different reaction. Pause. PETER resumes packing.)

CHAZ: So Rick, he . . . he died of AIDS-related causes? Or from the meds? Because I hear the side-effects are really—

PETER: What makes you think that?

CHAZ: Well, you said about Act-Up, for one. And then obviously your generation was greatly impacted by—

PETER: Only mine?

CHAZ: Well, the numbers—

PETER: Numbers?

CHAZ: The stats on deaths in the gay community from AIDS and AIDS-related causes between 1981 and 1997 are like, crazy.

PETER: We didn't all get it.

CHAZ: Well, no, not *all* but, I mean, *most*.

PETER: And you didn't have to have AIDS to protest against the Church or Wall Street.

CHAZ: No, of course, I didn't mean to imply—

PETER: And what really makes my skin crawl is, unlike my *ancient* generation at least you guys know it's out there. Yet somehow you're still getting infected.

CHAZ: Yeah, but you guys are the one who started it.

(PETER is stung.)

PETER: See, this is when everyone who's twenty-something appears equally stupid. Because no matter what you've studied at NYU or what rallies you've marched in or how much your parents spoil you, you are *not* entitled to ignorance.

CHAZ: I'm not apologizing for being twenty-five.

PETER: You should.

CHAZ: Alright, screw this. I'm leaving now. I'll call Housing Works and ask them to send someone else.

(CHAZ heads towards the door. PETER stops him.)

PETER: YOUR YOUTH ISN'T BEING DEVOURED BY SOME UNIMAGINABLE TERROR. YOUR COMMUNITY ISN'T DYING EN MASSE IN A COMPLETELY INDIFFERENT AND DOWNRIGHT HOSTILE SOCIETY!

CHAZ: Would it make you happier if it was?

PETER: You'll never know that kind of daily torment! Or loss!

CHAZ: Sorry I didn't survive the Gay Holocaust!

PETER: We couldn't pop a morning-after pill following a night of reckless sex. We didn't have social networks to spread the word. To educate society. We did it all on foot. And we literally bled to death doing it.

CHAZ: Do you have AIDS?

PETER: No.

CHAZ: Are you dying?

PETER: No!

CHAZ: Then stop grandstanding. It makes you sound really old.

PETER: Right. And now the old man has to take a piss.

(PETER exits to the offstage bathroom to pee.)

CHAZ: *(Towards Peter)* I'm sorry about your husband, Mr. Bartlett. If it makes any difference, my mother died last year.

PETER: Chaz, you have my sympathy.

CHAZ: It's probably not the same as losing a spouse.

PETER: Having lost a wonderful mother myself, I can assure you there is no comparison.

CHAZ: How long's it been since Rick—?

PETER: Three months. Every morning I wake up and hope it'll be easier to get out of bed and make it to the agency on time. It isn't. I don't. —He used to say the dumbest things. Drove me crazy.

CHAZ: What kind of things?

PETER: Ricky had a knack for stating the obvious: We'd go for a walk on a clear day and he'd say, "The sky sure is blue." And in the spring he'd say, "Look how green the leaves are." And we'd go to the garden and he go, "Boy the flowers are really pretty." And I'd want to say, "Of course the sky is blue. What color should it be on a sunny day? Of course the leaves are green. It's fucking June! Naturally the flowers are pretty. They're *flowers*, you moron!"

(PETER fumes. Silence.)

I never had the chance to say goodbye. Sometimes death is less a process than it is a, a moment.

CHAZ: My mom died in a car crash. So sudden I couldn't make sense of it. It took me a very long time to cry.

PETER: So this time you know what I mean. *(Pause)*
You have a beautiful smile, Chaz. Like Ricky's.

(CHAZ, suddenly uncomfortable, looks around. The clothes are packed up by now.)

CHAZ: Look! You finished packing.

PETER: Part of me wants to keep it all but you reach a point, you can't bear the sight of it anymore. A red tie with little elves worn once to a Christmas party . . . a t-shirt from a tchotchke shop in Cape May . . . a pin button from the '96 Democratic Convention . . . Daily reminders of what is now and forever out of reach.

CHAZ: I know I'm young and I've never been in love, not like, not like you have.

PETER: You will. Be prepared.

CHAZ: But I see how much you miss him.

(It's too much for Peter to bear and time for Chaz to leave.)

PETER: All right, then, Chaz, Chaz, Chazzy, my boy: Take it all away!

(CHAZ abruptly stops packing.)

Well . . . ?—Don't look at me like that!

CHAZ: Like what?

PETER: Like Rick did, when he'd do something naughty like feed Rambo scraps of bacon under the table, which really used to make me—

CHAZ: Mr. Bartlett, what's your first name?

PETER: Peter.

CHAZ: Will you do me a favor, Peter?

PETER: What, what kind of —?

CHAZ: Will you . . . close your eyes for me?

PETER: Close my— ? I don't understand.

CHAZ: Just. Please? PETER: Why?

CHAZ: I need to do something.

PETER: What?

CHAZ: It's nothing freaky. But it might help.

PETER: Help what?

CHAZ: Help you.

PETER: I don't need any—

CHAZ: Yes, you do. I did. With my mom. And don't look at me like you don't know what I'm talking about.

PETER: I don't really think this is the time or place for—

CHAZ: Then when, Peter? How much longer are you going to torture yourself?

PETER: I'm not—! I don't—!

CHAZ: Bullshit. That's bullshit and you know it.

PETER: Well, so, um—What, what are you going to do?

CHAZ: You'll have to close your eyes.

PETER: I don't like surprises.

CHAZ: It's not a surprise. It's a gift. And you can only receive it if you close your eyes.

(PETER deliberates.)

Oh, come on, Peter! Just close your goddamn eyes for a minute, will you?

(PETER tentatively closes his eyes. Silence.)

PETER: This is . . . interesting.

CHAZ: Good. No peeking, now. Are you peeking?

PETER: No, Chaz.

CHAZ: I'm no longer Chaz.

PETER: Not—?

CHAZ: I want you to think of him. Think of Rick.

PETER: Of —*What?!*

CHAZ: Just do it!

PETER: Are you out of your—?!

CHAZ: Give me the benefit of the doubt here, alright, Peter? —Or I'll make you lift all those boxes yourself and you'll wind up lying flat on your back for the next month.

> *(Silence.)*

You with me?

> *(PETER nods.)*

Good. Alright. Now . . . I want you to think of you and Rick walking together.

PETER: Walking?

CHAZ: Maybe it's a year ago, or when you first met or somewhere in between. A beach or a park. —Do you have it?

> *(PETER nods.)*

Alright. Now keep thinking of him. Really think of him.

> *(PETER nods.)*

See Rick up close. His wavy black hair. Feel his breath on your face, sweet like mango. And you can smell him, like the smell of his shirt. And feel the heat off his skin.
And you're looking into his eyes. He's smiling at you, with that same boyish smile he had the day you first met.

> *(CHAZ softly kisses PETER on the mouth.)*

Keep your eyes closed!

> *(As he speaks, CHAZ sets the boxes into the hall.)*

Okay, now, imagine Rick's talking to you. That my words are his. When I speak, it's Rick, alright?—It's me, Rick. Ricky. And I just want to say . . . Good*bye.*

(Inching backwards towards the door.)

Goodbye, Peter.

(Stepping into the hall.)

Goodbye, Peter.

(Gently closing the door)

Goodbye. I love you . . . Peter.

(CHAZ has gone. PETER opens his eyes, takes in the emptiness. PETER takes Rick's shirt, nuzzles it against his face.)

PETER: The sky . . . sure is . . . blue . . . .The grass is . . . .so green . . . The flowers are so . . . pretty . . . .

(PETER weeps, at last. Blackout.)

END OF PLAY

A Second Rapture

James E. Marlow

Original Production
>
> "What He Didn't See" a.k.a. "A Second Rapture"
> by the Hovey Players, Waltham, MA.
> July 12-13, and 19-20, 2013
>
> Directed by Michael Haddad
>
> Cast:
> RITA: Ginny Carpenter
> FRED: Lou Fuoco

CHARACTERS:
> FRED: Forty-two, Disheveled upon his return home after a week on a mountain top.
>
> RITA: Thirty-nine, Has dinner and a surprise or two ready for him.

SYNOPSIS: When Fred returns from his unsuccessful religious pilgrimage, and expected rapture, he finds that his wife Rita has planned for his absence in his absence.

SETTING: Contemporary kitchen with dining table. The recent past and near future.

> *FRED, forty-two, tired, unshaven, clothes wrinkled, carrying a couple of empty water bottles, walks into the kitchen, carrying a coat over his arm. RITA, 39, is at the stove and looks up only briefly as he walks in. She is as neat and prim as he is the opposite.*

RITA: You're back. I thought you would be.

FRED: I know you did. Thanks for wiring the bus money.

RITA: What took you so long?

FRED: I was afraid you'd say "I told you so."

RITA: Did the congregation get cold on the mountain-side?

FRED: Yeah. Thanks for making me take the sweater.

RITA: I learned something the first time.

FRED: Are you suggesting—?

RITA: *I* try not to repeat myself. Sit. I've got food on the stove.

FRED: I will. I'm tired. (*He sits.*)

RITA: I guess the last last dinner together was not the last.

FRED: You're a good cook, Rita. You've turned blonde on me.

RITA: I've been busy. Like it?

FRED: Sure. Makes you look younger. I almost don't recognize you.

RITA: Tell me, anything interesting happen on the mountain-side?

FRED: You mean—besides—

RITA: Of course. I know what didn't happen—which is not interesting.

FRED: Well, I saw that William O'Brien brought money with him.

RITA: Whatever for? What was he going to buy? Or was he going to try to bribe someone in authority?

FRED: That's what we asked him. As a joke. At first.

RITA: And?

FRED: He said, "for emergencies."

RITA: That's lame.

FRED: "Like what?" we all asked. He did look a little ashamed.

RITA: I can just see him. Did he finally own up?

FRED: He did. "To get home, in case."

RITA: No! Oh ye of little faith.

FRED: That's exactly what the minister said.

RITA: Wouldn't he loan you any?

FRED: What? Money? No. We'd burned it.

RITA: You burned his money? How much?

FRED: Couple thousand, I think.

RITA: And he let you?

FRED: It was either that or go home. Early.

RITA: He's divorced, so—

FRED: Right. So nobody at home anyway.

RITA: To send *him* money.

FRED: He wasn't the only one who broke the rules.

RITA: Oh, good. Who else?

FRED: Helena.

RITA: If I'd known *she* was going to be there, I might have come.

FRED: You're wrong about her.

RITA: I'm not wrong. I've seen her make eyes at you.

FRED: She's near-sighted. It looks like she makes eyes at every man.

RITA: But *you* notice. I've seen your limp smile.

FRED: Limp? Just what do you mean by that?

RITA: One side of your mouth. It says, "I am pleased by your interest but I am officially with *her*," by which you meant your wife. Me.

> *(RITA lays a plate of food down in front of him and sits down across from.)*

FRED: I don't smile. Besides, no use giving her a smile she can't see.

RITA: Aren't you frugal? How much did she bring?—that near-sighted vamp.

FRED: How much?

RITA: Money.

FRED: No money. But she brought her compact. You know, lipstick, powder, mirror, and so on. And she wasn't the only one.

RITA: Why am I not surprised? Who else trespassed?

FRED: Arlen brought his cell-phone.

RITA: Wonderful! Was he going to call during or afterwards?

FRED: He wouldn't say.

RITA: Probably during, so he could gloat. What happened to your phone?

FRED: The minister hurled it off the mountain side.

RITA: With so many lapses in the faithful no wonder it didn't come off.

FRED: That's what the minister said. It was our fault. Dinner is good. How have you been?

RITA: I've been thinking. I decided that if you came back this time, I didn't want you back.

FRED: Really? Rita, dear, I can see that you are really annoyed with me.

RITA: Why should I be annoyed with you?

FRED: *I* don't know. All I did was follow my beliefs. What's wrong with that?

RITA: Oh, nothing, I'm sure, except for the little detail of leaving me behind.

FRED: I told you to come with me.

RITA: I had a job.

FRED: So did I!

RITA: I still have one. What did you expect me to do when you were whisked away? And, tell me the truth, you never expected to be back.

FRED: Of course not! Or I wouldn't have gone in the first place.

RITA: Second place, second time.

FRED: I was *so* sure this time.

RITA: There! You are admitting that you chose to leave me behind.

FRED: What could I do? You wouldn't come.

RITA: And what could I do? You wouldn't stay.

FRED: I don't like where this is going.

RITA: And I don't like your going. I thought, when we were married, it was "til death do us part."

FRED: Well, nobody died. And I'm back.

RITA: Oh, but you planned to be parted—only, not by death. *That* would have been one for the courts when I sued for divorce.

FRED: It isn't like I was cheating on you!

RITA: No? There was no woman, true, but you were being unfaithful, planning to *live*—separately. A kind of divine divorce.

FRED: Only for the time being! We would be joined later.

RITA: So, in planning to cheat death, you were willing to leave me. This time I figured it out.

FRED: Rita, dear, you should respect the depth of my faith.

RITA: A faith would save you from the pains of death and translate you straight to heaven.

FRED: Only if one is worthy.

RITA: And you were. But really, is a man who abandons his wife—a man who wants to be carried off to heaven and to leave his wife behind to suffer all by herself whatever happens at the end of the world—is such a man even worthy of going to heaven?

FRED: How can you say that?

RITA: It wasn't heroic, that's for certain. And, by avoiding death, you certainly weren't going to martyr yourself for your faith, were you? You would live!

FRED: I am sorry you don't see.

RITA: Oh, I see it all too well. You chose to leave me behind. But I didn't despair I got some things accomplished. I got the house sold.

FRED: What? You what? You're kidding?

RITA: You told me to take care of myself, didn't you?

FRED: But that fast?

RITA: It's a nice house, and I said "motivated seller."

FRED: I wish you hadn't.

RITA: Hadn't what? Said motivated?

FRED: Sold the house. What was the hurry?

RITA: I knew it was much too big for one person.

FRED: How could you be sure I wouldn't be back?

RITA: *(Pause.)* Oh, I was pretty sure you would be.

FRED: What? And you sold the house anyway?

RITA: And the cars. I bought a new convertible.

FRED: You sold both cars?

RITA: Down to one now. Mine. Yard sale was last Saturday.

FRED: Yard sale?

RITA: Remember? I said, "what should I do with your stuff?" And you said you wouldn't be needing your stuff.

FRED: Not my new golf-clubs!

RITA: Buying new ones was short-sighted, wasn't it? But also the boat; your shotguns.

FRED: Not the Browning!

RITA: I doubt that there is any hunting in heaven. Your suits didn't fetch much.

FRED: Why would you sell my suits? How am I supposed to work?

RITA: You quit your job. Remember?

FRED: I could ask for it back!

RITA: You don't have a car to get there. Besides, I doubt that they would want you back.

FRED: What makes you say that?

RITA: My sense of reality. You probably don't have much leverage since you made your announcement. Or was it pronouncement?

FRED: What am I supposed to do now?

RITA: Well, maybe Arlen or Helena (if she recognizes you with her glasses on) or William can put you up.

FRED: Are you trying to say that in a choice between you and God, I should have chosen you?

RITA: Not at all. God united us in marriage. Therefore, it looks to me like God and I are on the same side. I'd ask you to consider who or what is on the other side, but I doubt that your beliefs allow you to go there.

FRED: I'm sorry you turned out to be so small-minded, Rita. I expected more of you.

RITA: How could you? I wasn't as worthy as you. I see all that now.

FRED: You clearly don't get it, Rita.

RITA: Oh, I think I do.

FRED: It's called rapture, Rita! Rapture is to find yourself in the presence of God.

RITA: Unfortunately, the rapture has been postponed. What I can promise you is that our *rupture* will not be. Here's my lawyer's card. Call him. Oh, you can have the dishes. Au revoir; oh, but we won't be seeing each other again; adieu then, but how and when we get to God is the issue, isn't it? Adios? I give up. Bye, Fred.

(RITA rises, puts on a coat, and walks out.)

End of the Play.

SOMETHING LIKE LONELINESS

Ryan Dowler

ORIGINAL PRODUCTION

Something Like Loneliness premiered at Cultural Development Corporation's 2010 SourFestival in Washington D.C. It was performed as part of the 34th Marathon of One Act PLays at Ensemble Studio Theatre in 2013.

Directed by Colette Robert

CAST:
DAN: Chris Wight
MIA: Jane Pfitsch

CHARACTERS:
>DAN: twenty to forty-five.
>MIA: twenty to forty-five.

SETTING: Mia's Apartment. Morning

>*(DAN knocks on the door to MIA's apartment.)*

>*(MIA answers.)*

MIA: Do I know you?

DAN: I don't think we've met. My name's Dan. I live in the apartment right above you.

MIA: Oh. Nice to meet you. The space between your floor and my ceiling is like nothing. I don't have to turn on NPR in the morning. I just listen to yours. What can I do for you?

DAN: That sound that you make when you have an orgasm. I can hear that. I can hear it upstairs.

MIA: Oh.

DAN: And I'd like to have it.

MIA: You want to have an orgasm with me?

DAN: No. No, I don't want to have an orgasm. I want to have *your* orgasm. I want to keep it.

>*(He produces a piece of tupperware.)*

In here.

MIA: What the fuck? You brought that with you?

>*(Beat. MIA walks off. She re-enters with a sealed piece of Tupperware.)*

MIA: I've already got one right here. But you have to tell me why you want it.

DAN: Because my life is terrible and I need something to get me through. Because when I hear you I get the unyielding sense that a moment can be sucked from your throat and strung up like lights along the ceiling of your room the second that first forced breath leaves your lips. That's what I want.

MIA: And, so—what? You're gonna jerk off to it?

DAN: (*honestly*) No. The truth is—actually, it's embarrassing.

MIA: Well then forget about it.

DAN: (*honestly*) I just—I'm having trouble carrying on. I wake up in the morning and I just stare at the ceiling in despair, sometimes for hours. I guess I thought maybe— you'll think this is dumb—I thought I could listen to it in the morning and it might give me some adrenaline— motivate me to get up and start the day.

MIA: And what do I get in return?

DAN: See? I knew you'd say that. That's why I brought these.

(He kneels down and begins pulling Tupperware out of his bag.)

MIA: What do you have?

DAN: I've got me cracking open a PBR.

MIA: I've heard that one. A lot.

(He pulls out another one.)

DAN: You don't want this one.

(He sets it aside. Pulls another.)

I have me sneezing on a quiet day.

MIA: I want the one from when you're cooking dinner. I can hear you say out loud all the ingredients as you gather them. And then when you stir you kind of sing, "Mix it around. Mix it around."

DAN: You want that? I can go get it.

MIA: No. Something more meaningful.

(pointing to the one he set aside)

What's that one?

DAN: You can't have that one. Come on. I have a lot of good ones. I have the sound my cat makes when she's snoring. This one's the sound of a book falling off the shelf. I have crying.

MIA: I don't want crying.

DAN: Crying can be a good one, if it's over something honest. That's why people listen to sad songs.

MIA: Something honest like what?

DAN: Like loneliness. Like loss.

MIA: Have you been crying over a loss?

DAN: I lived with a woman for three years. We did everything together. We were really in love and then one day she was gone.

She left me with an empty apartment and a whole closet full of these. So once a week for the last year, I've been going down to Southland Springs, a place we used to hang out. I sit down in the grass every Sunday morning and I let a couple go. Open them up and just let the wind carry them out over the water.

MIA: Why Sunday mornings? Are you religious?

DAN: I'm religious about Sunday mornings.

MIA: And you want my orgasm to wake you up in the morning. Because you miss the sex.

DAN: I don't miss the orgasms. They were the first sounds to go. I do miss the unzipping, the unbuttoning, the sounds of the fabric as it slides away, off a leg, off a bed, through the floor and out into the void that exists between the first small kiss of a suggestion after dinner and the last labored breath before the thing is over. But you know what I miss more?

MIA: What?

DAN: The sound of a girl sliding on jeans early in the morning.

> *(beat)*

You know the sound of a mother giving birth?

MIA: Not intimately. But I'm pretty sure I have an idea.

DAN: If the sound of a mother giving birth were the same as the sound of a girl sliding on a pair of jeans in the morning, then babies wouldn't cry when they were born. No, they'd climb out of the womb happily, put on a pot of coffee, and hop into the shower.

MIA: What else did you have to let go of?

DAN: Her voice talking through the bathroom door was a hard one to let go of. I held on to that one for a year. The sound of a champagne flute shattering in the sink as it slips through her fingers.

MIA: When my boyfriend left me, all he left was the sound of his terrible impersonations and the sound of me asking, "Who is that supposed to be?" And the sound of him saying," Listen some more." And the sound of me saying, "I still don't know." And the sound of him saying,

> *(beat)*

"It's you."

DAN: Did he leave the sound a long kiss makes? She did. If you haven't listened in a while, then listen. Listen to the sound a long kiss makes. It's nothing like the abrasive dry smack of a short kiss.

MIA: Which were the last to go?

DAN: The last one. Her turning the pages of a new book with her long fingers in the afternoon.

(indicating the set aside Tupperware)

And then this one.

MIA: Can I hear it?

DAN: You don't wanna hear this one. It's like a glimpse of your parents in love long before you were born. A bittersweet moment of such private unaffected tenderness, it can put you in bed for weeks.

MIA: I want to hear it.

DAN: It sounds too much like happiness.

MIA: Happiness sounds good. Will you at least tell me what it sounds like?

DAN: It sounds like silence. The silence of Sunday mornings when we got up and went straight to church.

MIA: So you are religious?

DAN: Not that kind of church. The silence of the service in our living room. Hot coffee and Tim Russert on Meet the Press. With Gwen Ifill and David Brooks singing back-up. It's an entire symphony of coffee sips, sighs, drags off a joint, toast buttering, blanket tugging, newspaper folding, and sock-covered feet rubbing together.

MIA: Why do you still have it?

DAN: No reason.

MIA: Then why don't you—?

DAN:—I'm getting rid of it . . . I mean I was . . . . I was on my way now—I was—I'm gonna let it go eventually. Trust me.

(She gives him her Tupperware.)

MIA: I've got something else.

(She exits, returning with another piece of Tupperware.)

DAN: What's this?

MIA: It's nothing. Just take it.

DAN: You won't tell me?

MIA: It's me sliding on a pair of jeans in the morning.

DAN: I can't take this.

MIA: Take it.

DAN: Are you sure?

MIA: When you first wake up, do the orgasm, then do the jeans. You'll be all set for the day.

> *(beat)*

Just one thing.

> *(indicating the Sunday Mornings Tupperware)*

I want that one. That's the one I want.

DAN: You want this?

MIA: I want your Sunday mornings.

DAN: It's a very intimate thing to give away to a neighbor.

MIA: And an orgasm isn't?

DAN: But for me to let it go forever.

MIA: I'm not gonna live it, Dan. You're the only one who can do that. And you did it.

> *(beat)*

I'm your neighbor. I'll only be listening.

> *End of Play*

STUBBLE

Erin Mallon

ORIGINAL PRODUCTION
    Date: August 26, 2013
    Company: Cherry Picking 2013–The Year of the Fear
    Venue: The Wild Project, NYC
    Producer: mtp (cherrypickingnyc@gmail.com,
    917.882.9246)

    Directed by Clare Mottola

    CAST:
    KATE: Nicole Golden
    DAN: Chris Tomaino

CHARACTERS:
KATE: Thirties to Forties
DAN: Thirties to Forties

SETTING: The auditorium at Klinger Middle School

TIME: 8pm

Lights up on a 7th grade school dance. "The Sweetest Thing" by U2 plays. Two adults stand by the punch bowl, a deliberate bit of distance between them. They pretend to be engrossed in chaperoning the children, smiling broadly, but they are clearly distracted by each other's presence. They bop awkwardly to the music. After a few moments, Kate breaks their silence.

KATE: So!

(Dan immediately whips his head toward her and laughs boisterously.)

(Quick beat. Kate stares.)

DAN: Oh. I'm sorry, I thought you said something funny.

KATE: Did I? I don't think I did! I don't usually say funny things, do I?

DAN: No no, you don't, I'm sorry. / How's the Thoreau lesson going, are the kids liking it?—

KATE: No, I'm sorry! I like that you assumed I was being funny. Oh, Thoreau's fantastic! Yeah, the kids love Walden, thanks for asking. How bout you, you still working on Dante's Inferno with your class?

DAN: Yes.

(Beat.)

That was strange what I did a moment ago, sorry about that . . . I'm realizing now that someone told me a joke this morning, and it was still stuck in my head. That was why I laughed.

KATE: You had a joke stuck in your head? What was it? What was the joke? Can you tell me the joke? I'd love to hear the joke!

DAN: Suuuuure . . . . Yeah. Ok . . . .

(A beat as he racks his mind for a joke. She waits patiently, smiling.)

Ok, great. Yes. So it starts with—

(Kate laughs heartily. Quick beat. Dan stares.)

KATE: Oh. You didn't tell it yet, did you. The joke.

DAN: No, not yet.

KATE: I just thought you—I guess I . . . I'm sorry. Please, go ahead, tell the joke!

DAN: Actually. I'd rather not now.

KATE: Oh please tell it!

DAN: No thank you.

KATE: But I'm sure it was going to be very funny!

DAN: You know, I feel like an ass and you're not helping!

(Quick beat.)

Shit, I said ass! Fuck, I said Shit! Motherf—

(Quick beat.)

My apologies.

(Quick beat.)

Would you like some punch? The kids sure do seem to be enjoying it.

KATE: Please.

(He pours and hands her a cup.)

KATE: Thanks Dan.

DAN: Sure thing Kate.

(They smile and lock eyes for a moment, then quickly break their gaze. A beat while they bop to the music. Dan breaks the silence.)

DAN: *(referring to the punch)* Pink, huh?

KATE: *(referring to the music)* You think? It sounds more like Bono to me. *(note: she consistently pronounces this BEAU-no. Rhymes with faux-no).*

DAN: What?

KATE: Bono! I love U2.

(Quick beat.)

DAN: You do?

KATE: Yes. So much.

DAN: Wait. Did I say I loved you?

KATE: I'm sorry?

DAN: You just said you "loved me too."

KATE: Oh, no, no, no! I love U2! The band! Bono!

DAN: *(pronouncing it "BEAU-no" as well)* Oh! Bono!!!!

> *(Quick beat.)*

> *(They laugh uproariously. It gets uncomfortable quickly and subsides.)*

> *(They bop to the music in silence. Dan breaks the silence again.)*

DAN: You were about to say something before. Wh-wh-what were you about to say before?

KATE: Before . . . ?

DAN: Before the whole—

KATE: Oh yes! I have good news! You ready?

DAN: Sure.

KATE: Guess who is set to direct "The Sound of Music" here this Spring?

DAN: You????

KATE: Me!!!

DAN: Ahhhhhh!!!!

KATE: Ahhhhhhh!!!!!

> *(They leap into a hug, full bodies pressed together, jumping up and down in a steady rhythm.)*

DAN: Congratulations Kate!!!!

KATE: Thank you Dan!!!

DAN: A dream realized!!!

KATE: I'm so happy!!!

> *(They stop abruptly, realizing what they're doing. They separate.)*

DAN: Proud of you.

KATE: Thanks.

> *(Beat. They both stare off in opposite directions looking like they wanna die, especially Dan. Dan breaks their silence one more time.)*

DAN: Will there be lederhosen?

KATE: Hm? What?

DAN: In the production. Will there be lederhosen? You can't do The Sound of Music without copious amounts of lederhosen!

KATE: Oh, well, I suppose that's up to Doris. She's in charge of costumes so—

DAN: Then we better tell Doris to get on it A-S-A-P! Where is she? Is she here? Because I'll tell her myself!! I'll tell her, she'd better import you the best lederhosen that Germany has to offer/ because that's what you deserve!

KATE: I think the play is set in Austria—

DAN: Fine! Australian lederhosen then. You deserve authenticity! And what's going on with casting?/ Who's playing Captain Von Trapp? He'd better be top notch!

KATE: Well, we're going to hold auditions next week—Dan, are you ok?

DAN: This is your directorial debut Kate! It has to be perfect! AS PERFECT AS YOU ARE! How's the set design coming along? Do we have hills yet? Those hills better be majestic, or somebody's gonna answer to me, I'll tell you that much. And I think the real question we should all be asking ourselves is WHO THE HELL IS GOING TO PLAY ROLFE??!!?

(Beat. Dan is panting.)

KATE: Dan? What's going on? And remind me who Rolfe is.

DAN: 17-year old messenger boy. Sings with Liesel.

KATE: Right, thank you.

(Dan walks over to her and stands very close.)

What are you doing?

DAN: Let's cut the bullshit. It's been years. I fuckin' love you. It's a fact. So let's do this shit and let's do it now.

(A long beat. Then another. Then another still. Finally . . .)

KATE: Get under the table.

DAN: What?

KATE: Get under the goddamn punch table before I take you in front of all these 7th graders.

Lawrence Harbison   171

DAN: Really?

KATE: Go!

> *(They scurry under the table and sit very close. Dan immediately giggles and rocks back and forth like a little kid.)*

DAN: Oh man, we're gonna do it arent' we!

KATE: I think we are!

DAN: We're gonna do it under a table at a school dance!

KATE: Uh huh!

DAN: I feel like I'm twelve again.

> *(Quick beat.)*

Came out wrong. Didn't do this at twelve. So you like me too? Is that what I'm gathering from all this?

KATE: Yes!

DAN: You "like-like" me?

KATE: I like-like you!

DAN: SO EXCITED!

KATE: Me too!

DAN: Oh wow, I've never been this close to your face before. You're GORGEOUS!

KATE: So are you! Hey, your beard hair is a slightly different color than your head hair!

> *(Tiniest beat.)*

DAN: Huh? What?

KATE: It's reddish!!!

DAN: Yeah, well apparently the shaving cream I used when I was a teenager carried carcinogens in it, and now my chin and cheeks are forever tainted!

KATE: That's so bad ass, I love it!

DAN: Oh, OK, good! You have an eyebrow piercing?

KATE: *(brightly)* Nope, it's a mole!

DAN: Oh.

> *(Beat. Dan looks horrified.)*

KATE: Is that—a problem?

DAN: No, moles are . . . good.

KATE: Oh good, I think so too! Oh wow!

DAN: What?

KATE: Your neckbeard is fascinating!

DAN: *(body stiffening)* My what?

KATE: All this stubble you have here. You shave your neck, don't you!

DAN: No way!

KATE: Don't be embarrassed! Neckbeards are sexy. You know who else had a neckbeard?

DAN: No.

KATE: Thoreau.

DAN: He did?

KATE: Yup! Check out his photo on Wikipedia sometime. That shit went all the way down to his collarbones.

(Kate starts nuzzling her face in his neck.)

Mmmmm . . . . I wanna call you neckbeard. Can neckbeard be the thing I call you that no one else calls you so that when I call you it we always feel close to one another?

Dan Well, I don't really love—

(She tweaks his nipple.)

DAN: Oooohlalala you're tweaking my nipple!

KATE: I am.

DAN: Well stop!

(He slaps her hand away like a little child. A long beat. She stares at him.)

I don't like that. Being examined like that.

KATE: Who is examining you? I'm not examining you.

DAN: You are! What gives you the right to - to- to-

KATE: To what?

DAN: I do a-a-a-a LOT of work to-to-to-to . . . . hide things. And then you just come in and say "Oh I see your neckbeard! Let me call you neckbeard!"

KATE: I think it's sexy! I told you that!

DAN: I don't care what you think! I don't need you to approve of me! I don't need to explain myself to you! AND YOU'RE NOT SUPPOSED TO HAVE A MOLE!

KATE: Dan, why are you acting like this? We were having fun.

DAN: I'm getting out from under here.

(He moves to climb out.)

KATE: *(trying to hold him in place)* Please stay! I won't call you neckbeard. And we don't have to do anything, let's just sit here a little while longer, ok?

DAN: Get. Off!

> *(She lets go and he hits his head on the table, hard. It hurts.)*

Fuck. Ow.

KATE: *(reaching to his head)* I'm sorry!

DAN: Don't!

KATE: Dan, can't we just—

> *(He climbs out from under the table.)*

> *(Kate waits a few moments then climbs out too.)*

> *(They stand in silence, watching the kids.)*

KATE: Dan, can't we—

> *(Silence.)*

Dan?

DAN: Would you like some punch? The kids sure do seem to be enjoying it.

KATE: No, I—

(Beat.)

Please.

He pours and hands her a cup.

KATE: *(eyes welling)* Thanks Dan.

DAN: Sure thing Kate.

> *(They stare straight ahead, watching the kids.)*

> *End of Play.*

A Tall Order

Sheri Wilner

ORIGINAL PRODUCTION
    Thirst Theatre
    Minneapolis, MN.
    May - June 2006.

    Directed by Sheri Wilner

    CAST:
    SHE: Alayne Hopkins
    HE: Casey Greig

    2013 production
    City Theatre's Summer Shorts
    Miami, FL
    June 7 – 30, 2013

    Directed by Mcley Lafrance

    CAST:
    SHE: Renata Eastlick
    HE: Rayner Garranchan

CHARACTERS:
     SHE: Age twenty-five to thirty-five
     HE: Age twenty to five-thirty-five

SETTING: A restaurant*

> *PLAYWRIGHT'S NOTE: The restaurant in the play is named Christo's, but producers of the play should feel free to change the restaurant name to a local favorite.*

(SHE and HE sit at a table, menus open.)

HE: Quite a menu, huh? Any idea what you want to or—?

> *(SHE snaps her fingers and time stops. What follows takes place in the space of a second.)*

SHE: *(focusing intently on her menu)* OK. Here goes. Choose wisely. Choose well. What do I want? A salad? Good god woman, no! You can't get a salad. That's the kiss of death. Every man on the planet has an "I used to go out with a woman who only ordered salad" story. Those tales of terror are told in locker rooms, golf carts and barrooms everywhere.

HE: *(as if talking to his buddies)* They had this enormous menu. Prime rib, manicotti, pork chops, *everything*. And she says, 'I'll just have a salad.'"

SHE: And all his buddies will nod their head in solemn acknowledgement. Yes, we know what that means:

HE: *(to his friends)* A brittle, uptight neurotic so accustomed to starving and depriving herself, she thinks nothing of depriving you too.

SHE: To them "salad" is a synonym for

HE: *(to his friends)* Frigid, fussy . . . unsound. Having sex with her was like playing ultimate frisbee with a tiny, overbred dog.

SHE: No, I have to show him I'm made of stronger stuff. That I can eat meat. I'll get the pork chops or a rack of ribs. No, a Black Angus steak.

> *(to him:)*

You'd like that, wouldn't you?

HE: Women who use all thirty-two teeth are sexy.

SHE/HE: Yeah!

HE: Because they bite. They tear flesh off the bone.

SHE/HE: Grrr.

SHE: But then again he might think I'm:

HE: Too aggressive.

SHE: I'm:

HE: Too masculine.

SHE: And envision it's his flesh between my teeth. His bones falling in splinters onto my plate.

You can't show them any muscle, any force. Don't make the "Tony" mistake again.

Kissing, caressing, wrestling on the couch. Pinned down I was supposed to say, "OK, OK stop, stop." But I felt power. My taut muscles felt the limpness in his. And then: Blam! I flipped him off the couch and onto the floor.

(SHE and HE look into each other's eyes.)

And that look in his eyes told me I blew it. It was over before his back hit the broadloom.

You can't be stronger than they are. Physically, emotionally. Financially. They can't endure it. Black Angus beef says:

(Directly to him:)

I can overpower you. Prime rib says:

(Directly to him:)

My strength just might be greater than yours. Could you handle that?

HE: *(to his friends)* There was just . . . I don't know . . . a toughness to her, you know? I think it was actually hormonal.

SHE: Skip the beef. Pass on the salad. Avoid the extremes. Nothing too herbivore. Nothing too carnivore. Chicken. There you go. Chicken might be good. Chicken doesn't say frigid. Chicken doesn't say strong. Chicken's a safe choice. But maybe too safe. Chicken is boring. Chicken is monotony. I don't care what they put on it. Chicken is chicken.

(He'll think:)

HE: Wow. How . . . bland. Nothing but bedroom sex with her. Nothing but tourist trap vacations, toolboxes and neckties for birthday gifts, spicy recipes prepared mild. Assumptions that risks shouldn't be taken, money should be saved, safety comes first.

SHE: He'll look at the chicken on my plate and see his whole future on a bed of rice. He'll see:

HE: My father's life. One long, sad compromise.

SHE: I have to excite him. I have to order something that will make him say:

HE: Woo hoo! I'm in for one *wild ride* with this one! Life with her is like a nonstop fireworks finale. She just keeps sending herself up into the sky and bursting into colors that take my breath away.

SHE: That's the ticket! Go for some thing exotic, something wild.

(SHE searches the menu.)

The Pignoli Encrusted Chilean Sea Bass! That says:

HE: Spontaneous.

SHE: That says:

HE: Untamed.

SHE: That costs:

HE: Thirty-one dollars?!

SHE: The most expensive item on the menu. He'll think:

HE: Sixty-hour work weeks. Just to keep up, just to keep her happy. Just to keep from feeling like I can't give her what she wants.

SHE: You cannot choose the most expensive thing. Or the cheapest. Aim for three dollars right of center, which would be… Pasta. Pasta? Bad idea. Bad, bad idea. To brazenly go for the carbs. If he considers me overweight:

HE: Pasta. So that explains the slight chubbiness and her less then perfect figure.

SHE: Maybe I'll see what other women are eating. Is that like cheating on a test? Screw it.

Time has stopped. No one will know.

(SHE stands.)

No. Wait. What if I choose some self-sabotaging defeatist? Some relationship kamikaze who gives such crucial minutiae no thought? That would really suck if someone else's veal cacciatore screwed up my relationship. Maybe I'll say I'm not hungry. Maybe I'll say I'm fasting. Maybe I'll go into the kitchen and cook something myself. Were there specials? Specials are good. Specials say:

HE: She takes risks.

SHE: Or even:

HE: She's fearless!

SHE: So where are the specials? Where are the specials? Oh god! There are no specials! No chalkboards. No menu inserts. No awkward recitation by the waiter. Why aren't there any specials? Screw you, Christo, for your unspecialized menu! Wait! I know! If he

SHE: *(cont.)* orders first, then I can say, "I'll have what he's having." That's the way to go. That's smart second date ordering. I could say it in a playful flirty voice that makes him immediately know he's spending the night. *(Directly to him, seductively:)* I'll have what he's having.

HE: And you know I'll give it to you, baby.

SHE: Yeah. I'll just say, "Gee, I can't decide. Why don't you order first?"

(beat)

OK, first of all, don't ever, ever say "Gee." Secondly, stay away from that "can't decide thing." They hate that. They like a woman who knows her own mind. Who's not going to make them:

HE: Search Netflix for an hour.

SHE: Or ask their opinion about:

HE: Fifteen different black dresses.

SHE: That to him are:

HE: Indistinguishable.

SHE: He wants me to know what I want. I can feel it. I can feel his expectation.

(HE sits at the edge of his seat, grips the table and stares at her intensely.)

He's waiting for my answer. I can see the smile poised and ready to appear on his face when I say something:

HE: Surprising, unexpected, sexy.

SHE: And I can also see it ready to drop when he realizes I'm:

HE: Just another dime-a-dozen marriage-minded mediocrity.

SHE: Everything depends on this, everything hangs on my order.

> *(SHE looks at the menu and then at her date. SHE looks at the menu and then at her date. SHE looks at the menu, but then:)*

Screw it! No, screw you! Screw you for putting me through this! *I am not what I eat!* It all starts now. This order is going to set the tone for the whole relationship. I am going to order exactly what I want without giving him a single thought. That's what he's about to do right? That's what men always do. Choose an entrée without fearing the consequences.

That's me from now on, and I'll make sure he sees that:

HE: She just ordered something *with no regard* to the effect it will have on me.

SHE: That will excite him. That will make him want me. For once in my life a man will want me more than I want him and that shift will happen precisely the moment I place my order. So what's it gonna be, huh? What do I want? What do I really, really want?

> *(SHE makes her decision and then snaps her fingers. Time resumes.)*

HE:—der?

SHE: I would like . . . Someone who will love all my flaws as much as he'll love all my strengths. Someone I'm not afraid to reveal the parts of me that feel ugly, weak and broken. Someone I can completely expose myself to. And who will completely expose himself to me. I would like a man who takes my life in his hands

HE: and feels responsible for it.

SHE:	HE:
And who will place his life in mine	And who will place her life in mine.

HE: Someone who suffers if I suffer.

SHE: Who feels elated when I'm elated.

HE: Two arms that will always hold.

SHE: Two ears that will always hear.

HE: Two eyes that will always shine into mine.

SHE: A partner.

HE: In everything.

SHE: HE:
A partner in everything.   A partner in everything.
SHE: And a diet cherry Coke.

END OF PLAY

Under the Pomegranate Trees

Don Nigro

Original Production

Under the Pomegranate Trees was first presented in New York City by Nylon Fusion Theatre Company at the Gene Frankel Theatre on July 2, 2013. This production featured Matilda Brown and Lily DePaula, and was directed by Robert Verlaque.

CHARACTERS:
PATTY: a blond girl, nineteen
SHARON: a brunette, nineteen

SETTING: The back yard of an apartment near the campus of Arizona State University in Tempe, Arizona, in the autumn of 1968. Night. Two lawn chairs.

Patty and Sharon, two nineteen year old coeds, sitting on lawn chairs in the back yard of an apartment near the campus of Arizona State University in Tempe, in the autumn of the year 1968. They're wearing swim suits and drinking beer. It's night, but we can see them by moonlight. Patty is blonde, Sharon brunette.

PATTY: It's finally cooling off a little bit. I had too much sun. This is not the climate for me. I burn easily. I'm highly combustible.

SHARON: You've got to be more careful.

PATTY: I'm not careful. That's my trademark. I could spontaneously combust at any moment.

SHARON: You're extremely fair skinned.

PATTY: You're lucky. You tan, and I go all lobstery. I envy brunettes. I really do.

SHARON: No you don't.

PATTY: Okay, I don't. Well, sometimes I do. I get tired of being looked at.

SHARON: No you don't.

PATTY: You know what? You and I have known each other way too long.

SHARON: This is true.

PATTY: I was thinking about the pomegranate trees. Do you remember?

SHARON: I remember.

PATTY: How cool it was there? That long row of them, with the dirt pathway underneath, by the playing fields?

SHARON: It was nice there.

PATTY: I loved it there.

SHARON: It was really nice.

PATTY: What was that girl's name?

SHARON: Which girl? There were a lot of girls.

PATTY: The one who used to pull her dress up. She used to pull her dress up, for the boys.

SHARON: I don't remember that.

PATTY: Yes you do. She liked to tease them. She was a tease. She'd show them more and more. Right in front of everybody.

SHARON: Cindy.

PATTY: Was it Cindy? The one with the horse?

SHARON: Shelley had the horse.

PATTY: Then it was Cindy.

SHARON: I wonder what happened to her.

PATTY: She's probably on drugs.

SHARON: Everybody's on drugs.

PATTY: I don't mean casually. I mean seriously on drugs. Cindy was one messed up puppy.

SHARON: She was really smart.

PATTY: She was very smart, but she was totally messed up. Probably at home. Some sort of molestation in that family.

SHARON: You think so?

PATTY: Why else would she do that?

SHARON: Maybe she just liked to lift up her skirt for boys. Maybe it was a power thing.

PATTY: I don't think so.

SHARON: You were swimming naked with some of those same boys last summer.

PATTY: So? What's your point?

SHARON: My point is, what's the difference?

PATTY: There's a lot of difference.

SHARON: What is it?

PATTY: Well, we were just swimming.

SHARON: You were completely naked, Patty.

PATTY: Yes, but we were swimming.

SHARON: But you liked it, didn't you?

PATTY: I like swimming.

SHARON: You liked when they looked at you. You liked it that they all wanted you.

PATTY: I was pretending I was Marilyn. You know. Swimming naked in that last movie they never finished because she died?

SHARON: Now there's a great role model for you.

PATTY: Marilyn was very smart.

SHARON: She was on drugs, too.

PATTY: I heard she was murdered.

SHARON: I don't think so.

PATTY: You think she killed herself?

SHARON: No, I think the doctors killed her.

PATTY: Why would her doctors kill her?

SHARON: Because they're doctors. They take an oath. Don't let anybody get out of here alive. That's what doctors are for. To keep the population down. Plus they were men.

PATTY: So?

SHARON: Men worship beauty, but they also want to kill it, because they fear it, because of its power to enslave them.

PATTY: That's kind of dark, Sharon.

SHARON: I'm a dark girl. I tan. You burn.

PATTY: You've thought about this a lot, have you?

SHARON: More than you.

PATTY: You're turning into a very bitter little person.

SHARON: I'm not turning into anything.

PATTY: You're turning into Mrs Cain.

SHARON: I'm not turning into Mrs Cain.

PATTY: I liked Mrs Cain. She was a wonderful lady, and she was always very nice to me, but she was kind of disappointed by life, don't you think?

SHARON: Everybody's disappointed by life.

PATTY: I'm not.

SHARON: You just don't know it yet.

PATTY: I really love it when you patronize me.

SHARON: Mrs Cain hated me.

PATTY: I can see why.

SHARON: I mean it. She did.

PATTY: Mrs Cain didn't hate you.

SHARON: She tried to run me over with her Pontiac.

PATTY: Why would Mrs Cain want to run you over with her Pontiac?

SHARON: She was jealous.

PATTY: Jealous of what?

SHARON: Of me and Ben.

PATTY: Mrs Cain was jealous of you and Ben?

SHARON: Yes. She was.

PATTY: She was old enough to be his grandmother.

SHARON: Age doesn't matter.

PATTY: Yes it does.

SHARON: Not in things like that. Not inside people. Inside people, everybody is between six and fourteen years old permanently.

PATTY: But why on earth would she be jealous about you and Ben?

SHARON: Because he loved me.

PATTY: Oh, I don't think so.

SHARON: It's true. Ben was in love with me.

PATTY: Ben wasn't in love with you. Ben was in love with me.

SHARON: Ben was never in love with you.

PATTY: He used to stand at the other end of the field and watch me in the evening.

SHARON: No he didn't.

PATTY: With the sun going down behind me.

SHARON: He didn't do that.

PATTY: He'd stand there watching me, worshipping me from afar. I can still hear the sounds of children screaming and the ice cream truck going by. The one with that creepy ice cream man. What was that song it played over and over again? It played the same stupid song over and over all summer.

SHARON: I was the one Ben loved.

PATTY: Sharon, I touched him.

SHARON: What do you mean?

PATTY: This one evening, that summer, I touched him.

SHARON: Where did you touch him?

PATTY: Under the pomegranate trees.

SHARON: What do you mean, you touched him?

PATTY: The sun was going down, and it was cool, under the pomegranate trees. And he'd been watching me all day, and we were sitting there, under the pomegranate trees. I was wearing my little yellow sun dress. I looked really nice in that little sun dress. He couldn't take his eyes off me. I could tell he was really aroused.

SHARON: Where was I while this was going on?

PATTY: I don't know. On the other side of the field. Getting some ice cream from the creepy ice cream man or something. What was that song the ice cream truck played? Some really corny, ancient, grandma type song. All that summer. And Ben was just crazy in love with me.

SHARON: You're imagining things.

PATTY: No I'm not. I could see it. I could see how aroused he was. And I was fascinated by it. By the power I had. All this poor guy had to do was just look at me in my little yellow sun dress, and all the blood in his body rushed right to his zipper. He couldn't help it. I felt this tremendous power over him. It was really intoxicating, and also strangely touching. In fact, I was so moved at how much he must have wanted me at that moment, that I just sort of reached out my hand and touched him there.

SHARON: You must have dreamed this, Patty.

PATTY: I didn't dream it. I touched him there. Under the pomegranate trees. And he looked at me while I was touching him, like he thought he was dreaming, and then his eyes closed, sort of like a dog when you scratch its stomach. And I knew he was mine forever.

SHARON: He wasn't yours forever. He wasn't yours at all. He was in love with me.

PATTY: I could tell he'd never forget. As long as he lived, he'd never forget. Being there with me, under the pomegranate trees.

SHARON: Memory is a lie. Memory is an ugly, stupid collection of lies and half truths we tell ourselves to keep from blowing our brains out.

PATTY: Strawberry blonde.

SHARON: What?

PATTY: The song the ice cream man played. It was that really old song about the strawberry blonde. It was playing all the time I was touching him. He's never going to forget. Now that's power.

SHARON: I thought he loved me.

PATTY: Maybe he did, for a while. Men don't have a very long attention span, ordinarily. But I'm the one he'll remember. I'm the strawberry blonde.

(Pause.)

It's getting cooler now.

(Pause.)

It feels nice.

(Pause.)

It gets cool all of a sudden in the desert. You think it's never going to be cool again, and suddenly there it is. It isn't much, but you'll take it. Love is like that. Like the relative coolness of the desert in the night.

(Pause.)

And things come out at night. Snakes and spiders and scorpions and all kinds of awful things. They're just waiting, during the day. During the heat of the day. And then at night they all scuttle out into the dark, to eat things and mate. Some of them mate first and then eat each other. It's really kind of horrible when you think about it.

(Pause.)

Sharon? Are you crying? Did I make you cry? I didn't mean to make you cry. Honest to God I didn't. Please don't cry. I'm always doing that to people who love me, or people I love. But I don't mean to do it. I swear I don't. Sometimes a person just doesn't realize that they have power over people. The power to make them want you. The power to make them suffer. But if you're not used to feeling like you have any power, and then suddenly you discover that you've got it, it's just kind of, exhilarating, you know? But then it makes you sad afterwards. Like sex. It's just like sex.

(Pause. Sound, faintly, in the distance, of an ice cream truck playing "The Band Played On.")

Listen. There's the ice cream truck. Do you want some ice cream? We could get some ice cream, like we used to. We've had a lot of beer, but ice cream is good with beer. Do you want some? Sharon? My treat.

(Pause.)

I could touch you.

(Pause.)

PATTY: (cont.) Would you like me to touch you?

(Pause.)

I could touch you, and then you'd always remember.

(Pause.)

You could close your eyes and remember. And imagine we're under the pomegranate trees.

(Sound of the music. The light fades on them and goes out.)

UNPRIMED

John McKinney

ORIGINAL PRODUCTION
  Theater: WorkShop Theater Company
  Date of Run: Dec. 5-21, 2013

  Directed by Katrin Hilbe

  CAST:
  RUSSELL: Keith Herron
  SARAH: Elizabeth Inghram

CHARACTERS:

RUSSELL: Fifties, smart, attractive, sharp-witted. Drier than a dust martini. An expert at disguising his feelings, perhaps even from himself.

SARAH: Late thirties., smart, attractive, sharp-witted, refined. An appreciator of art, she is more sensitive than Russell, and, consequently, more vulnerable.

SETTING: A large metropolitan art museum. Present day.

An art museum. Afternoon. A single bench is located upstage center. SARAH and RUSSELL enter from opposite sides of the stage, each taking in a different painting. They gradually move around the stage toward each other as they continue to look at paintings hung along the "fourth wall." They notice each other.

SARAH: Russell.

RUSSELL: Hello, Sarah.

SARAH: Well. This is certainly a surprise.

RUSSELL: Is it?

SARAH: What are you doing here?

RUSSELL: Looking at paintings. What are you doing here?

SARAH: You hate museums.

RUSSELL: No I don't.

SARAH: Please.

RUSSELL: Okay, I hate them.

SARAH: I always had to drag you.

RUSSELL: You're right. I remember now. What a drag it was.

SARAH: I thought I could open your mind. My mistake.

RUSSELL: I didn't think you made mistakes.

SARAH: Only one.

(Pause.)

So how are you?

RUSSELL: Angry. How are you?

SARAH: I'm fine, thank you. Especially these last six months.

RUSSELL: Seven. You know, you could have left a note.

SARAH: You're right. *(Beat.)* It was seven. How time flies when—

RUSSELL: When your therapist is going down on you? You should know better than to confide in your sister.

SARAH: On the contrary. I was hoping she'd tell you. It must twist you all up inside that I'm with a woman.

RUSSELL: Yes, it does. I worry about you. Now who are you going to castrate?

SARAH: Why are you here, Russell?

RUSSELL: *(Gesturing to his surroundings.)* To open my mind.

SARAH: You didn't come here looking for me, by any chance?

RUSSELL: And you used to call me a narcissist.

SARAH: Someone else, then?

RUSSELL: You're getting warmer. "Warm," of course being relative.

SARAH: Do I know her?

RUSSELL: How do you know it's a her? Not very open-minded of you.

SARAH: You, with a guy?

(A peel of laughter.)

RUSSELL: I resent that. I'm not sure why, but I resent that.

SARAH: You think I don't know what you're up to? You disappoint me.

RUSSELL: Disappoint. Well, it's a start. When I get to 'devastate' let me know.

SARAH: You were hoping you'd find me so you could parade your new girlfriend in front of me. Really, that's so beneath you.

RUSSELL: You should know. As I recall you were beneath me quite often.

SARAH: I'm amazed you can recall. It was so unmemorable.

RUSSELL: Oh, I disagree. Hard to forget making love to a corpse.

SARAH: If I seemed like a corpse it's only because I was bored stiff. At least one of us was.

RUSSELL: Bored?

SARAH: Stiff.

(Pause.)

RUSSELL: *(Smiles.)* Just like old times.

SARAH: So what time are you supposed to meet her?

RUSSELL: Who?

SARAH: Please.

RUSSELL: Is it so impossible to believe that I came for the art?

SARAH: You have a Day-Glo poster of Michael Jordan hanging in your study.

RUSSELL: Not anymore. I replaced it. With a Matisse.

SARAH: You're kidding.

RUSSELL: Not an original, of course. A print.

SARAH: Which one?

RUSSELL: The dying man drifting in the night? It really speaks to me.

SARAH: Oh yes. The Fall of Icarus.

RUSSELL: Ah. That's why I relate to it. He got burned, too.

(He looks at the painting in front of him.)

This one here I like. The broad, slashing brushstrokes with the rough canvas showing through. Bit of DeKooning influence, don't you think?

SARAH: *(Surprised.)* You know DeKooning?

RUSSELL: Been reading up a bit. I'm taking a course at City College. We're studying the Dadaists, now. What, you think I'm not capable of change? You changed. You left me for lesbianism. How do you like it?

SARAH: Well, if you must know, it's over. It was just an experiment.

RUSSELL: I meant the painting.

SARAH: Oh. I don't know . . . it's a bit . . . raw.

RUSSELL: Raw. Yes. That's how I feel.

(He leans forward to read the title card.)

'Study Number Three on Unprimed Canvas.' You really don't like it? I think it's fascinating. The way the artist purposely lets you see the fabric underneath. No gloss. Nothing covered up. Of course I won't pretend I understand it or that I know what the message is. But then I guess there isn't always a message, is there? Or a note... or a letter . . .

SARAH: Russell—

RUSSELL: Even a 'go fuck yourself' scrawled on the bathroom mirror would have been something.

SARAH: Would saying something now make things any better?

RUSSELL: It might.

SARAH: Alright. Go fuck yourself. Oh, you're right. I do feel better.

RUSSELL: I'm surprised to know you can feel at all.

SARAH: You know what I feel? I feel sorry for you. Cause you blew a good thing and you know it. Or you would know it if you had any blood running through your veins.

RUSSELL: Sorry. You drank it all.

(Pause.)

SARAH: Do you think we could ever just . . .

RUSSELL: Play nice? Where's the fun in that?

SARAH: True. I liked the vampire comeback, by the way.

RUSSELL: Shh. Don't spoil it.

SARAH: Right.

(Pause.)

You know, it's too bad City College doesn't have a course in good taste. Your choice in paintings is atrocious.

RUSSELL: So is my choice in women, but somehow I survive.

SARAH: I would have thought you'd prefer this one, here.

(They step over to the next painting.)

Cold . . . rigid . . . structured . . .

RUSSELL: Is that really how you think of me?

SARAH: Not at all.

(A beat.)

I don't think of you at all.

RUSSELL: I don't believe you.

SARAH: Well maybe sometimes . . . in the morning when I wake up and you're not—

RUSSELL: *(Gesturing to first painting.)* I mean about your not liking this painting. I think you do like it.

SARAH: Oh?

RUSSELL: Yes, I'm sure of it. When you were looking at it earlier, your eyebrows went up. Both of them. When one goes up, you're just curious but both eyebrows . . . ohhh, yeah, this painting's special to you, isn't it?

SARAH: All right! Yes! I think it's brilliant. The way you can see the anger in every brushstroke. The emotions are hanging out there for all to see. It's honest. Refreshing. I can't believe we like the same painting.

RUSSELL: Actually I lied. I hate it.

SARAH: I knew it! It's amazing how opposite we are.

RUSSELL: Oh I don't know. We're both attracted to women.

SARAH: I told you, that's over. Where's this woman you're meeting by the way?

RUSSELL: And I told *you* you shouldn't assume it's a woman.

SARAH: Really! Quick. What's his name?

RUSSELL: Paul.

SARAH: How do you know him?

RUSSELL: My teacher at City College introduced me to him. You know him too, actually.

SARAH: I don't think I know any Pauls. What's his last name?

RUSSELL: Klee.

SARAH: *(Surprised.)* You came for the Klee exhibit?

RUSSELL: You see? Maybe anything *is* possible.

SARAH: Almost anything.

RUSSELL: Things might be different.

SARAH: We both lied about liking that painting. Nothing's changed.

RUSSELL: Yes, something has. The difference is, I *want* to like it. I want to know what it is you see in all that splatter and chaos. I've tried to. God help me I've tried. The classes... the books . . . the audio tours . . . swallowing hour after hour of fucking DeKooning and Pollock disemboweling themselves . . . I keep waiting for it to hit me the way you said it would, but all I ever see is a bunch of spoiled prima donnas vomiting all over the canvas with no more precision or forethought or talent than a two-year-old who spits food all over his high chair and calling it art!

(He moves to the second painting.)

Yes! I like this painting! Yes! Because it's structured! And rigid! I'm sorry! I like it when they paint inside the lines! I like fruit to look like fruit! I like paintings of covered bridges! I like it when it all makes fucking sense!

SARAH: Why? Life doesn't.

RUSSELL: *That's why.*

    (Pause.)

SARAH: I'm sorry about leaving the way I did. I just couldn't play the game anymore.

RUSSELL: But you play so well.

SARAH: That's what scared me. All that dazzling repartee . . . it was like a shiny veneer, not the real thing. I needed to see underneath the gloss now and then. But all those mind games . . .

RUSSELL: So you decided to go lesbo?

SARAH: Case in point.

RUSSELL: *(Realizing her meaning.)* You faked the whole thing.

SARAH: With a little help from my sister.

RUSSELL: You went to a lot of trouble.

SARAH: Not really. I'm used to faking it with you.

RUSSELL: *(Smiles.)* That's my girl.

    (Pause.)

SARAH: I hope you're not thinking what I think you're thinking.

RUSSELL: You mean about you and me . . .

SARAH: Yes.

RUSSELL: . . . and your therapist?

SARAH: What?

RUSSELL: Well. All this time I've been thinking about you two . . . y'know. And now that I know you're not really—

SARAH: In your dreams.

RUSSELL: You really think I'd ask you back?

SARAH: You really think I'd come back?

RUSSELL: I wouldn't give you the satisfaction.

SARAH: As if you ever satisfied me!

RUSSELL: As if you could ever be satisfied!

SARAH: As if you could ever just *be!*

RUSSELL: I draw the line at modern art. Zen, no fucking way!

    (SARAH begins to crack a smile. Perhaps they both do. Pause.)

SARAH: You know it wouldn't work.

RUSSELL: It doesn't work now.

SARAH: We'd only make each other miserable.

RUSSELL: That's why it might work. At least we'd know we're each making the other miserable.

SARAH: Until I couldn't take it anymore. Then I'd run away again.

RUSSELL: I'd find you again.

SARAH: That's crazy.

RUSSELL: Doesn't make sense.

(A beat.)

SARAH: You didn't really come here for the Klee exhibit, did you?

RUSSELL: Well. He was my backup. In case you didn't show.

SARAH: You really like his work?

RUSSELL: Mm. I like his motives.

(A beat. SARAH suppresses a smile.)

SARAH: *Motifs.*

RUSSELL: Motifs. I don't know what I'm talking about.

SARAH: I know. It's wonderful.

(SARAH turns toward the "unprimed" painting.)

You're better off. I'm just like this painting you hate so much. No primer, no gloss. Just the raw me.

RUSSELL: Oh come on. You're not *that* ugly.

(She hits him lightly in the shoulder. He catches her hand, pulling her toward him. They desperately want to kiss, but do not.)

SARAH: Well. I should go.

RUSSELL: Yes, you probably should. Before I get too rigid.

SARAH: It was good for me, too.

(She starts to exit the gallery as RUSSELL watches her. She stops.)

You know, if you like Klee you might want to check out Kandinsky.

RUSSELL: Kandinsky.

SARAH: There's an especially good collection at the Guggenheim. Mondays at five is a good time. The crowds start to thin out around then.

RUSSELL: Mondays at five. I'll keep that in mind.

SARAH: You are trying, Russell. I appreciate that.

RUSSELL: I could never be as trying as you.

(SARAH smiles, shaking her head as she gives him one last look, then turns and exits. RUSSELL watches her un-

til she is gone. He turns and looks back at the "unprimed" painting in front of him. He grimaces. Blackout.)

END OF PLAY.

A WALK IN THE PUBLIC AREA

Greg Kotis

ORIGNAL PRODUCTION:

At the American Globe Theatre in New York City as part of the Turnip Theatre Company's 2001 15-Minute Play Festival.

Directed by Damon Kiely

Cast:
JOHN: Bill Coelius
ROSE: Kim Ima

CHARACTERS:
JOHN: twenties to thirties, an office worker.
ROSE: twenties to thirties, also an office worker.

SETTING: Just after lunch in the public atrium of a big, big office building.

(Just after lunch. John and Rose stroll casually across the public atrium of a big, big office building.)

ROSE: Oh, John, you're such a browny man.
JOHN: Thank you, Rose. That's—very kind of you to say.

(She takes his hand.)

ROSE: A browny, browny, browny man.
JOHN: Thank you.

(She sighs. The two take in the scene around them.)

ROSE: I love the public area this time of day, just after lunch with everyone burpy and sleepy and the table tops still dusted with crumbs.
JOHN: It's a wonderful place to eat one's lunch.
ROSE: Or even one's own.
JOHN: Wha-? I—ah ha ha ha ha ha . . .

(They laugh.)

JOHN: Oh, Rose. I feel so lucky to have you here with me in the public atrium of this big, big office building.
ROSE: I'm the one who's lucky, John.

(They come close to kissing then shyly pull away.)

ROSE: I . . . um . . .
JOHN: I'm sorry, Rose.
ROSE: Don't be sorry, John.
JOHN: I didn't mean to be so forward.
ROSE: I don't mind you being forward.
JOHN: But—

(She puts her hand to his mouth.)

ROSE: I don't mind you being forward at all. I just want us to enjoy our lunchtime together. After all, we only get a half hour.

JOHN: Of course you're right, Rose. Thank you.

(They take in the scene again, resettling a bit after their uncomfortable incident.)

JOHN: A bird was trapped in here the other day.

ROSE: No.

JOHN: True story.

ROSE: A pigeon?

JOHN: Not a pigeon, smaller than a pigeon.

ROSE: Drawn in by the fountain, no doubt.

JOHN: Perhaps.

(Feeling bold, he takes her hand in his, drawing her close to him.)

JOHN: Seeing you here, Rose, by the fountain as you are, I feel —I feel that you are that bird in some small way.

ROSE: Oh, John.

JOHN: Drawn in by the fountain, smaller than a pigeon, beautiful and—flying around.

ROSE: But John, I was drawn in by you.

JOHN: Then, perhaps, I am that fountain.

(They kiss at last, then embrace.)

ROSE: I bet you eat your lunch down here alot, John.

JOHN: Oh yes, I do. Some days I buy from the salad bar—you know the one—and bring it here, to one of these tables to eat it quietly with perhaps only a magazine or a sports section for company. Some days I pack my own lunch and stare silently into the fountain while I savor my thriftiness: peanut butter and jelly, tuna fish salad, ham and swiss on whole wheat. And some days—some days I buy from the kiosk itself, the one over there, the one that maintains these very tables.

ROSE: So expensive.

JOHN: Yes. But on a rainy day . . .

ROSE: I understand entirely.

(They hold each other tight.)

JOHN: Rose?

ROSE: Yes, John?

JOHN: Can I ask you a question?

ROSE: Of course, John, what is it?

JOHN: Earlier—earlier you referred to me as a "browny" man. I'm afraid I don't know what that means.

(She pulls herself away from him a little bit.)

ROSE: Do we have to talk about this now, John?

JOHN: No, of course not, it was only that—

(She pulls away from him entirely, trying desperately to change the subject.)

ROSE: My, it certainly is beautiful here this time of day, don't you think?

JOHN: Yes. I do.

ROSE: I could stay here all day, I really could. Too bad we only get a half hour.

JOHN: I asked you a question, Rose.

ROSE: I know you did, John.

JOHN: Then why don't you—?

ROSE: Can't we just walk and smell the fountain without asking and answering silly questions about words and what they mean? Can't we do that, John? Just for today?

JOHN: Of course we can, Rose. It was just that—

ROSE: John, please! Don't ask me about it again.

(Pause.)

JOHN: Of course you're right, Rose. I didn't mean to press it, I'm sorry.

ROSE: Don't be sorry, John, just—just be with me.

JOHN: I'm here for you.

(They embrace. Then)

ROSE: Oh, look!

JOHN: Yes, Rose?

ROSE: The pigeon! The one you saw, there it is, flying near the fountain.

JOHN: So it is, Rose. So it is.

ROSE: So beautiful.

JOHN: Yes.

ROSE: So free.

JOHN: That too.

ROSE: Do you really think of me as being like that pigeon you saw, just flying around and searching for bits of food left by departing luncheoners and what not.

JOHN: I do, Rose.

ROSE: So beautiful.

JOHN: Like you.

ROSE: Oh John.

JOHN: Rose.

ROSE: Kiss me.

> *(They kiss for a good long time, then embrace, her more warmly than he.)*

JOHN: Although I must say that what I saw was smaller than a pigeon.

ROSE: What's that?

JOHN: The bird that I saw, it was smaller than a pigeon.

ROSE: Smaller than a pigeon?

JOHN: That's right, Rose. Smaller than a pigeon, and therefore not a pigeon.

ROSE: Oh?

JOHN: You said pigeon. I didn't see a pigeon.

ROSE: Well, you saw something.

JOHN: I did see something. It's just that it wasn't a pigeon, it was smaller than a pigeon.

ROSE: What are you after, John?

JOHN: I said it wasn't a pigeon the first time. Why do I have to keep saying it over and over and over and over and over again?

ROSE: Now you're angry with me.

JOHN: I'm not angry, I'm just—well, yes, I suppose I am a little bit irritated.

ROSE: Don't be angry, John. Be happy. We're together now, don't you see? Nothing else matters but that.

> *(They embrace again, if uncertainly. Realizing now what's wrong, Rose backs away.)*

ROSE: You're still thinking about it, aren't you?

JOHN: Thinking about what, Rose?

ROSE: You know what I'm talking about.

JOHN: But what on earth can it mean? "Browny"?

ROSE: And now we're talking about it! How is this supposed to continue, John?

JOHN: Rose, please, relax.

ROSE: You made a promise to me, John.

JOHN: How can I not wonder, Rose? How can I not - How can you ask me not to question? "Browny"?

ROSE: Oh, John, people say things all the time, silly things, meaningless things, what else can people do? You say I said "browny," so I said "browny." What difference does it make?

JOHN: You tell me, Rose, what is the difference that it makes? "Browny"? What on Earth can an expression like that mean?!

ROSE: Oh, John, it means many things to many people.

JOHN: It does?! Other than the cakey treat or the old-timey camera or the little girls' organization, I've never heard the word "Browny" used before in my life! Ever! So you tell me, Rose, what does it mean?! *(Grabbing her now by the shoulders.)* What does it mean to YOU?!

> *(He holds her hard, waiting her response. Then, realizing what he's done, he steps away from her, horrified.)*

ROSE: Actually, I think I'd better go now.

JOHN: No.

ROSE: Yes.

JOHN: Rose, please, don't leave now, not because of this.

ROSE: I'm afraid I'm going to have to.

JOHN: I didn't mean to offend you.

ROSE: Well, you did, John. You offended me a lot, an awful lot.

JOHN: Rose.

ROSE: John, I think we've seen enough of each other for today.

JOHN: Rose, please, you're being unkind.

ROSE: Unkind?

JOHN: Or at least unfair, or perhaps even a little bit—browny?

> *(She slaps him hard across the face.)*

ROSE: *(Hissing)* How dare you.

JOHN: Rose?

ROSE: "Browny"? Me?! Browny?!

> *(She winds up to smack him again then, at the last moment, stops herself. He stares at her, shocked and wounded. Soon she is as shocked with herself as he is.)*

ROSE: Oh, John—

JOHN: Stop. Stay away from me, please.

ROSE: I didn't mean to—

JOHN: I don't care what you meant to do. I don't care about—I think you're right, Rose. Our time together is over.

ROSE: It's just a word, John. It doesn't mean any thing, it just came out. That's all.

JOHN: Oh, it means something, Rose. It means something very much. And it's something I hope I never hear again as long as I live.

ROSE: John.

JOHN: Rose.

ROSE: I hurt you, let me help you.

JOHN: I'd rather that you didn't, actually.

ROSE: John.

(She reaches up to touch his face, he turns his face away.)

ROSE: Well, I suppose this truly is goodbye after all.

JOHN: You're free again, Rose. You should be happy about that.

ROSE: Like that pigeon you saw.

JOHN: Or some other bird.

ROSE: Yes. Some other bird.

(She starts to leave.)

JOHN: And Rose?

ROSE: Yes, John.

JOHN: Don't go back to the salad bar across the street, you know the one. I wouldn't want to bump into you there.

ROSE: No, of course not.

JOHN: Thank you, Rose.

ROSE: Goodbye, John.

JOHN: Goodbye, Rose.

(She exits in tears.)

JOHN: Browny Rose. Browny, browny, browny, browny Rose.

(Lights fade.)

FIN

YOU BELONG TO ME

Daniel Reitz

ORIGINAL PRODUCTION

You Belong To Me was first produced by the HB Playwrights Theatre, New York City, in June 2003. It was directed by Jules Ochoa with the following

CAST:
SUSAN: Dana Reeve
ROBBY: Bruce McCarty

The play was subsequently produced by the Ensemble Studio Theatre in its 34th Marathon, June 2013. Directed by Marcia Jean Kurtz

CAST:
SUSAN: Patricia Randell
ROBBY: Scott Parkinson

The play was broadcast on Playing On Air in July, 2013. Directed by Claudia Catania

CAST:
SUSAN: Amy Ryan
ROBBY: Michael Stuhlbarg

CHARACTERS:
    SUSAN: forty
    ROBBY: forty

SETTING: The New York City Transit #1 Train.

TIME: Spring.

> *The 1 train, traveling uptown. Lights up on Susan, with shopping bags at her feet, staring at Robby. Robby, shabbily dressed, clutching a backpack and with a large, cheap plaid bag at his feet, is in his own world and doesn't notice her.*

SUSAN: *(Softly.)* Robby.

> *(He hears his name called and. He slowly turns his head in Susan's direction. They regard each other for a long moment.)*

ROBBY: Susan.

> *(Silence.)*

SUSAN: God. It *is* you.

ROBBY: Uh. Yes. It's me. In fact. Yup. 'Tis.

SUSAN: Robby. God.

> *(Susan moves to him and hugs him. He's surprised and tentative.)*

ROBBY: Gee. Oh. That's nice. Be careful. I'm…hygienically challenged.

> *(She holds onto him a moment longer, then lets go. She touches his hair.)*

SUSAN: I just…I can't believe it.

ROBBY: I know. It's been…years and days and hours and minutes and months and moments. Hasn't it. In fact. *(Warmly.)* Hi.

SUSAN: Hi.

> *(They both look away. Silence.)*

ROBBY: Where you headed?

SUSAN: *(Quietly.)* Home. *(Firmer.)* Home.

ROBBY: Where's that?

SUSAN: It's uh . . . Eighty . . . uh. *(Laughs.)* Eighty-third. And West End. Yes.

ROBBY: I bet it's very nice.

SUSAN: It's . . . very familiar.

ROBBY: Great. Familiar can be very comforting.

SUSAN: Can be. I guess I don't mean familiar in a comforting way.

ROBBY: Oh. Why not?

SUSAN: Oh, because there was a husband there, now there isn't. Not important anymore. *(Pause.)* But this is…you…you're familiar in a comforting way.

ROBBY: Is that possible?

SUSAN: It is. I've thought about you. A lot.

ROBBY: Same here. I mean, when I'm . . . my head's sometimes . . . were, can be . . . impacted with . . . people. Or the sound of them. But when they empty out sometimes . . . there's grace, rare moments, nostalgia will occur, or I'll be able to read and something will . . . there, for instance, you'll be. Out of nowhere. After all these years. Which is very . . . merciful.

   (Silence.)

SUSAN: Where you headed?

ROBBY: Well funny you should ask, our alma mater.

SUSAN: Oh, you . . . teach?

ROBBY: *(Laughs.)* No.

   (Pause. He laughs again. Silence.)

SUSAN: Because I still go up and attend lectures . . . readings . . .you know . . . Every now and then. Just recently I went to hear Joan Didion. Read. *(Pause.)* So. What do, uh . . . how . . .

   (Pause.)

ROBBY: How am I? What do I do? I've been on disability. For twelve or so years. Off and on. And off . . . so forth.

SUSAN: Oh. Okay.

ROBBY: How about you?

SUSAN: I work for the Public Art Fund. I . . . evaluate applications. For things. Which means I push around paper for a living. For a life. In lieu of.

ROBBY: I would say it's a life devoted to the arts.

SUSAN: Well, that would be kind of you to say. But you've always been kind.

ROBBY: Public art. All those fiberglass cows.

SUSAN: That was me. Us. Everybody liked those dumb cows but me.

ROBBY: And me. *(Laughs.)* They had a nasty habit of commenting whenever I walked by.

SUSAN: *(Laughs uncomfortably.)* So.

    (Pause.)

    So you . . . where are you . . . in the city?

ROBBY: I've been . . . how best to . . . homeless. Transient. In a variety of locations in and around the greater metropolitan area and beyond. But as luck would have it one day around Christmas, last Christmas, I was on the 7 Train —I'd switched from the F to the 7 at 42nd in what I thought was a desperate yet shrewd attempt on my part to give the slip to these two seeming secretary types who had been looking over at me and whispering in what I thought at the time had to do with a larger conspiracy—anyway to make a long story short, as the cliché goes, I jettisoned my plan to go to the 40th Street Public Library to get some reading done and stay warm—pretty accommodating they are there, so long as you don't sleep or at least snore, which isn't much of a problem as I rarely sleep anywhere—I escaped those two girls and was riding somewhere and while I knew I was successful in giving them the slip, so to speak, I was also suddenly feeling quite frankly a little end-of-the-line-like. Because I knew I couldn't go on . . . escaping. And as I said it was Christmas, which only exacerbates the circumstances. But then there was the sign glowing at me, as I rolled along on this train: "Feeling depressed? Free treatment from the Columbia University Depression Evaluation Research Department." I actually laughed. Our alma mater. Reaching out to me. Calling my name as it were. I've been trying to stay on track with the medication they're giving me, gratis. And it looks as if this little studio in Queens might be opening up. Someone at the clinic keeping an eye out for me. And here you suddenly are. My life is complete.

(He accidentally knocks off his glasses, which are held together with tape.)

Whoops.

(He puts on his glasses. She's staring at him again. He looks away, self-conscious.)

SUSAN: You probably never even realized how . . .

(Smiles)

. . . exotic I thought you were.

ROBBY: *(Smiles.)* Hmm. Exotic.

SUSAN: You weren't from Larchmont or the Upper East Side. You didn't go to Dalton.

ROBBY: Nope, oh no. Sure didn't. Nope.

SUSAN: You did it all on your own. That's what so enthralled me about you. You'd already read everything with no guidance from anyone and you carried it all in your head. You had the entire Modern Library in there, Freud and Jung, Vasari's *Lives of the Painters*, the Greeks, Chaucer, Dante, Milton, the Romantics, The American Renaissance, the moderns, the post-moderns. Everything. I just stared in wonder at that head of yours.

ROBBY: *(Laughs.)* Well. And I had more hair, then, too.

SUSAN: I remember I asked you, and you said you came from nothing. I remember thinking how can someone who came from nothing know everything?

ROBBY: Oh it was just information, you know. Just books. It was actually a relief when I discovered everything from Aeschylus on is in Beckett. *(He takes a paperback Samuel Beckett anthology out of his backpack.)* A to B. "Birth was the death of him."

(Laughs.)

So much more portable.

SUSAN: I knew you were a genius.

ROBBY: Susan. Please.

SUSAN: The only genius I ever met. That's why I fell so happily for you. *(Pause.)* Sorry.

(Silence.)

ROBBY: *(Finally, indicating her bags.)* What have you got there?

SUSAN: Oh . . . nothing. Really.

ROBBY: *(Gently.)* Come on.

SUSAN: Oh, well . . . *(Takes out a brightly colored ceramic bowl.)* . . . this bowl.

ROBBY: Very pretty.

SUSAN: Yeah. I'm trying for a Tuscan thing in my kitchen.

ROBBY: So. What else?

SUSAN: *(Embarrassed, taking out a blouse.)* This...top. The color of which I was worried would make me look like I was trying too hard to look...oh, what's the word. Young. And decided it might not. *(Takes out a bottle of wine.)* Bottle of wine that I read about that sounded good. For later tonight. *(Takes out a spray bottle.)* And this...spray. French lilac. And . . . *(Takes out magazine.)* . . . an issue of *House and Home.*

ROBBY: Nice.

SUSAN: *(Looks at the spray in her hands.)* Yeah. *(Pause.)* What's happened to me. I went to Columbia, the Whitney Museum Independent Study Program. Christ, I've become insipid.

ROBBY: What do you mean?

SUSAN: I mean, you carry around Beckett, I have *House and Home.*

ROBBY: You have a home, I don't.

SUSAN: I have an apartment. And I do things and buy things to fill up time. I guess is what I mean.

ROBBY: Sounds like you're just a little lonely is all. *(Pause.)* Besides, you were the one who knew the entire history of art. You taught me more than a few things. It's one thing to have read Vasari, but imagine not knowing the difference between analytical and synthetic cubism.

SUSAN: You knew the difference.

ROBBY: What about your uncanny ability to tell the difference between a Braque and a Picasso? Who else could expound with exactly equal enthusiasm on a Duchamp readymade urinal and a Bellini Madonna? And I certainly never looked the same way at Eva Hesse after I met you. *(Pause.)* And that color top is most definitely not too young for you.

(He smiles. She smiles back. Silence.)

SUSAN: Would you like to come to my place for some of this wine I bought?

(Pause.)

ROBBY: Gee, you know Susan, I haven't touched alcohol in years.

SUSAN: Then just come over.

ROBBY: Well, I have this appointment, you know. Hate to *disappoint.*

(Pause.)

SUSAN: I wondered . . . and wondered . . . what had happened to you since then.

ROBBY: Well. It's been a rough eighteen years.

SUSAN: Is there a way I can reach you? If that's okay?

ROBBY: Well, I'm not really . . . reachable. Kind of here and there, you know.

SUSAN: Well, can I give you my address and phone number?

ROBBY: Oh, okay. Sure. Great. *(He offers his Beckett book.)* Right there. Never leaves me.

(She takes the book, opens it, writes on the inside page.)

SUSAN: Please call me. Will you? Or here. *(She takes out her cell phone.)* Take my cell, just take it . . .

ROBBY: Oh, no.

SUSAN: You can call me whenever you want. Call me if you're in trouble or . . .

ROBBY: No, I can't, it'll, I'll lose it, it'll get stolen. Just, it's okay.

SUSAN: Well here at least . . .

(She goes through her wallet, pulling out bills.)

ROBBY: Susan, *no* . . .

SUSAN: No, I want you to take all the money I have. I have . . . five, six, seven . . . eight. Christ. Fuck fuck fuck.

ROBBY: It's all *right.*

SUSAN: No, it's *not* all right. I'm an idiot. I had all this money today I could've given you, do you know I spent four dollars on a fucking cappuccino and six on a magazine, do you know how much this stupid spray cost? Twenty-two bucks. And thirty on a bottle of wine. I would've given it all to you.

ROBBY: I don't want your money.

SUSAN: Well, what do I do?

ROBBY: Well. Why don't you spray me?

(She looks at him.)

ROBBY: No, I'd like that. Really.

SUSAN: Come to my place, please, you could take a bath.

ROBBY: No, I…just give me a little spritz. Go on.

(Tentatively she sprays some him.)

ROBBY: Mmm.

(Smiles.)

Nice.

(Pause.)

Susan, you know, you don't have to look so sad there.

SUSAN: I don't? Do you know how much you meant?

ROBBY: *(Looks away.)* I think your stop's next.

SUSAN: Look, I'm just not prepared to leave you like this. Okay? I'm just not. So until you…why don't you just stay at my place, I have the room.

ROBBY: Actually, I really like being by myself.

(Pause.)

SUSAN: See, it's funny, but I don't. *(Pause.)* Do you know how far my life has gotten from me?

ROBBY: All too well.

(Pause.)

SUSAN: For a moment there I thought this was…a second chance. Maybe. Being handed to us. Me. You. If I may be so bold. Second chance for what you might ask. *(Pause.)* Eighteen years is a long time, isn't it?

(Sounds of doors opening, then closing.)

ROBBY: That was your stop.

(They ride in silence. After a moment he takes her hand. Lights slowly fade. Blackout.)

END OF PLAY

3 OR MORE ACTORS

ALL AMERICAN

Mayank Keshaviah

ORIGINAL PRODUCTION:

All American was originally produced as part of L.A. Views VI by Company of Angels Theater (Producers Armando Molina, Lui Sánchez, and Amelia Worfolk) in Los Angeles, California, on May 10, 2013. It was directed by Justin Huen; the scenic design was by Art Betanzos; the costume design was by Jackie Gudgel; the lighting design was by Sarah Templeton; the sound design was by Howard Ho; the properties master was Amy Urbina; and the production stage managers were Jennifer Pérez and Adam Gonzalez.

CAST:

KENNEDY KIM: Robert Paterno
JEFFERSON LEWIS: Rufus Burns
YOUNG O'SHEA "ICE CUBE" JACKSON:
        Bruce Lemon
OLDER O'SHEA "ICE CUBE" JACKSON:
        Gregory D. Alexander
LINCOLN THEODORE MONROE ANDREW PERRY:
        Shon Fuller

CHARACTERS:
    KENNEDY KIM: Asian-American, mid thirties.
    JEFFERSON LEWIS: African-American, mid thirties.
    YOUNG O'SHEA "ICE CUBE" JACKSON: African-American, early twenties.
    OLDER O'SHEA "ICE CUBE" JACKSON: African-American, mid forties.
    LINCOLN THEODORE MONROE ANDREW PERRY: African-American, early forties.

PLACE: Hollywood

TIME: Then and now . . .
    . . . but not just now and then

> *NOTE: Public Enemy's song "Burn Hollywood Burn," the inspiration for this play, can be used as pre-show music or as scoring for the play in moments other than the final scene, in which it should play as indicated in the stage directions. Sound effects and other music can also be used to heighten the absurdity of moments such as JEFFERSON's audition, or any other a director might desire to enhance musically.*

> *Outside a casting office at a major Hollywood studio are three chairs in a row next to a door. In one of them sits KENNEDY KIM, a handsome, well-built Asian American. In another, with a chair between them, sits JEFFERSON LEWIS, a handsome, well-built African American.*

> *Both have script sides in hand as they wait. They check their phones, look around the room, and try anything to avoid eye contact. Finally, they catch each other's glances.*

KENNEDY: *(Smiling a lovely "Hollywood" smile.)* So . . .
JEFFERSON: *(Returning the same high-wattage smile.)* Yeah . . .
KENNEDY: Just waiting for my—
JEFFERSON:—callback yeahmetoo.

(Forced "Hollywood" laughter. The following exchange is quickly paced patter, reminiscent of a Mantan More-land-Ben Carter routine.)

JEFFERSON: I really can't imagine that we're up for the same—

KENNEDY: It's a great part. And it would lead to—

JEFFERSON: Wouldn't have to work again for some time. But you can never be too—

KENNEDY: I have a sense about these things.

(A beat.)

Kennedy. Kennedy Kim.

(KENNEDY offers a handshake. JEFFERSON hesitates, but accepts.)

JEFFERSON: Jefferson. Jefferson Lewis.

KENNEDY: That's funny, we're both named after—

JEFFERSON: Very "All American" of our parents. That's why I figured that this role would be perfect for—

KENNEDY: Me too.

(They're wary of each other for a second before switching on their "Hollywood" grins again.)

KENNEDY: I'm just glad they realized I was a man this time.

(Laughing his "Hollywood" laugh, but noticing JEFFERSON's confusion.)

They usually list me as "Kim" comma "Kennedy," you know last name first. But most people see "Kim Kennedy" and expect some white blonde girl to walk through the door.

JEFFERSON: Now that's funny.

(They both laugh until . . .)

KENNEDY: *(Dead serious.)* Not really.

JEFFERSON: *(Recovering.)* Well mine seems to work both ways. Lewis Jefferson is just as black as Jefferson Lewis.

KENNEDY: At least I'm not up against a white guy for a change.

(Their "Hollywood" laughs return, but a bit more knowing this time. They sit for a moment. Then LINCOLN PERRY, in a blonde wig and perhaps even whiteface, opens the door.)

LINCOLN: *(Playing "white.")* Mr. Jefferson, we're ready for you.

> *(Lights shift, leaving KENNEDY sitting in the dark, as JEFFERSON follows LINCOLN, entering the audition through the door. They come downstage. LINCOLN joins OLDER O'SHEA JACKSON, also wearing a blonde wig, as they play white TV producers. They sit with their backs to the audience, perhaps at a table.)*

OLDER JACKSON: Thanks for coming in, Mr. Jefferson.

JEFFERSON: Actually, Jefferson's my first na—

> *(Realizing he's about to correct a producer.)*

Thank you so much for seeing me.

LINCOLN: Of course. We're so excited at the potential of a fall lineup that's, uh . . . representative.

JEFFERSON: So should I start from the top or . . . ?

OLDER JACKSON: Please.

JEFFERSON: *(In character, as John Harris, the sitcom husband.)* Caitlin, honey?

LINCOLN: *(Playing John's wife, with a high-pitched voice and slightly drunk.)* In here!

JEFFERSON: Are you doing what I—? Caitlin, not again! You need to put down the Pinot Noir and the Xanax and turn that off!

LINCOLN: You need to buy better wine, John. This stuff tastes like grape juice.

JEFFERSON: That's because it is. Watching *Steel Magnolias* for the tenth time will not help you, Caitlin Harris. You'll just get sloppy like you do.

LINCOLN: *(Getting weepy because she's drunk.)* But I *love* this movie. It's sooo sad.

JEFFERSON: But it won't help you, honey. Let *me* help you. Let your John-John in.

> *(OLDER JACKSON whispers to LINCOLN, who pauses in his recitation of the lines, leading JEFFERSON to pause as well.)*

OLDER JACKSON: Say, Mr. Jefferson. How would you . . . how would you feel about trying a little something?

JEFFERSON: Sure. Do you want John to be more outraged? More sympathetic?

OLDER JACKSON: Actually, we were wondering if you might read for another role—in addition, of course. But only if you want to.

JEFFERSON: Uh . . . sure. Yeah. That's fine. Do you have the—?

LINCOLN: *(Handing him new script sides.)* Right here. You're Amos. The handyman. He comes over to Caitlin and John's house all the time to fix things, but they're really more like friends.

OLDER JACKSON: Take a minute, read it over, and just let us know whenever you're ready.

JEFFERSON: Okay. Sure. Just a sec.

LINCOLN: Don't be nervous. We know we just sprung it on you. You'll be great.

JEFFERSON: *(Finishing reading and processing it.)* All right. Let's give it a try.

> *(As Amos, but fighting the impulse to launch into broad stereotype.)*

Knockety-knock! Mr. Harris? You there?

LINCOLN: *(Reading along, as John.)* Is that you, Amos, you sly devil?

JEFFERSON: Sho' is. Your wife called me n' said your kitchen sink was a doin' that nasty, funky thang again that it do. That the case?

> *(As JEFFERSON reads, OLDER JACKSON and LIN- COLN non-verbally encourage him to "go for it" and really "black it up.")*

LINCOLN: I'm afraid so. You think you can handle it?

JEFFERSON: *(Full-on "cooning.")* You know I been fixing them thangs since I was just out the crib. No sink ever got the best o' Amos Jefferson. I'm just go'n go out to muh truck and—

OLDER JACKSON: *(Interrupting.)* Oh my God! I just realized you and Amos have the same last name!

JEFFERSON: Well, actually, Jefferson's my first name but—

LINCOLN: How funny is that? And you were great!

OLDER JACKSON: So great!

JEFFERSON: *(Uncomfortable.)* Thanks.

OLDER JACKSON: In fact, and I hope I'm not stepping out of line here, I think I—we—just might be able to offer you the role of Amos.

LINCOLN: You really knocked it out of the park. So what do you think?

JEFFERSON: I mean—that's . . . that's really . . . surprising—and great! But I was wondering, am I still in the running for—

LINCOLN: For John's role? Of course.

OLDER JACKSON: Of course. We just thought we'd offer you . . . more of a sure thing, see if you wanted it. That's all. For John we're still seeing people, but we can't think of anyone who would play Amos better. Isn't that right?

LINCOLN: You really nailed it.

JEFFERSON: Well it's a lot to consider. Do you mind if—could I just call my agent and talk about it with her for a minute?

LINCOLN: Of course, of course. We don't want to rush you. Make your call, take your time, and just let us know. But we really did love you as Amos.

JEFFERSON: Okay. I will. Thank you.

LINCOLN: No. Thank *you*.

(As JEFFERSON leaves.)

And can you send in the Oriental gentleman? I think he's next on the list.

(JEFFERSON goes back out through the door to find KENNEDY waiting.)

JEFFERSON: *(Still reeling.)* I think they're ready to see you.

KENNEDY: *(Looking up from his phone.)* They're ready? Great! Thanks.

(KENNEDY pushes past JEFFERSON and enters the audition room. He disappears from view, as do LINCOLN and OLDER JACKSON.)

(JEFFERSON sits and thinks for a moment. Then he takes out his phone and calls his agent. Lights shift to create an alternate reality.)

JEFFERSON: Hey, Rita? It went . . . it went okay, I think. Actually it was kinda weird. After I read for—

(YOUNG O'SHEA "ICE CUBE" JACKSON enters wearing black jeans, a black hooded jacket, a gold rope chain, and an LA Raiders hat over his curly locks. He has a thin, scruffy beard as well.)

YOUNG JACKSON: Yo Jeff!

(A stunned JEFFERSON stops mid-sentence and stares, mouth agape.)

What, you ain't never seen a *real* black man before?

JEFFERSON: Rita, I'm gonna have to call you back.

(He hangs up on his agent.)

YOUNG JACKSON: I'm fuckin' wichu. If I saw Ice Cube outside my audition, I'd be buggin' out too.

JEFFERSON: You're not really—?

YOUNG JACKSON: The one and only Nigga With Attitude. So why you in there coonin' for these cracker-ass motherfuckers?

JEFFERSON: *(Taken aback.)* It's a major network pilot. And I have a shot at the lead.

YOUNG JACKSON: You think you do. That's why I'm here. Nigga gimme that.

(He grabs the script pages out of JEFFERSON's hand and peruses them.)

YOUNG JACKSON: *(Mockingly, in an exaggerated "white" voice.)* "Caitlin, honey . . . "—Caitlin?! They named a black woman fuckin' Caitlin?

JEFFERSON: She's not black. Well, she might be. The part's not cast yet. It's an All-American family.

YOUNG JACKSON: All-American *bullshit* is what this is.

(YOUNG JACKSON throws down the pages, pulls a Glock out of his waistband and shoots up the script. The noise attracts OLDER O'SHEA "ICE CUBE" JACKSON, who wears a neatly trimmed beard, a V-neck sweater with black jeans, and closely cropped hair.)

OLDER JACKSON: Man, put the motherfucking gun away! You know I don't play that no more!

(YOUNG JACKSON complies, reluctantly.)

I'm trying to finish a Sudoku and I can't have that noise interfering with my "me" time.

(To JEFFERSON.)

Son, you take that handyman part. Make that money. And pay no mind to ignorant-ass thugs like this fool.

YOUNG JACKSON: Fool?? Where d'you think you *came* from nigga?? You useta be me, before you got fat.

(To JEFFERSON.)

Do *not* listen to this fuckin' sell out. How you gonna be O.G. sittin' at home doin' Sudoku on a Friday night? And lookin' like Poindexter in your V-neck sweater and shit. But you take that role and keep coonin' like you did in there, you *will* end up like his ass.

JEFFERSON: *You* ended up like his ass.

YOUNG JACKSON: That's why I'm trying to warn ya! Homey used to say, "Fuck tha police!" Now he *plays* the police!

OLDER JACKSON: *21 Jump Street* grossed over two hundred mil. Yeah, I'm real sad about that.

JEFFERSON: He's got a point.

OLDER JACKSON: And with that money, I create roles for brothers like young Jefferson here. Not the janitor. Not the hoodlum on the corner. Not the fuckin' handyman. I'm talkin' about *real* roles. But first you gotta get the money. Then when you get the money, you get the power. Then when you get the power, then you get the respect. It's evolution, not revolution. But these young'uns talkin' all that gangsta bullshit always lose sight of that. That's why they end up shot, or in jail.

YOUNG JACKSON: You ain't shit! Who respect your ass anymore? And your movies suck! Since *Boyz n the Hood* and *Friday*, every single one of 'em sucks!

OLDER JACKSON: So you've seen 'em?

YOUNG JACKSON: Naw. I ain't down with flicks that exploit the color. And I ain't about to line the pockets of no sellout. But I *know* they suck. You can tell from the billboards.

OLDER JACKSON: *(Sarcastic.)* Somethin' about books and their covers comes to mind.

YOUNG JACKSON: Man, y'all nothing but a buncha sellout coons just waitin' to shuck and jive for the Man, hopin' he throw you a chicken bone. And flashin' them watermelon-eatin' grins while you doin' it too. Like some kinda modern-day Stepin Fechits.

(On cue, Stepin Fechit, aka LINCOLN PERRY, pops in wearing a 19thirties-style suit with suspenders and his trademark newsboy cap on his clean-shaven head.)

LINCOLN: *(With crisp diction.)* You called, young man?

(Off their confused looks.)

Oh, I'm sorry. You were expecting something more like this.

(LINCOLN crumples his cap and puts it back on his head. He slouches, lowers his eyelids to create Fechit's characteristic "sleepy eyes," and starts shuffling along.)

(In a slow, Southern drawl.)

I's suh-pose you was thinkin' I might be talkin' sumpin' like this, huh? Well, as youse can see, I's so lazy dat I can' even move fast as I need tuh. Not even when the massa come a callin' with that paycheck. But I gits dere. Lord, I gits dere somehow.

(Back to his crisp diction.)

And it made me a millionaire. The first black actor in history to do so, by the way.

YOUNG JACKSON: Who the hell are you?

LINCOLN: Lincoln Theodore Monroe Andrew Perry.

(Off JACKSON's confused look, LINCOLN goes back to his slow drawl.)

Buh youse pro'lly knows me bettah as Stepin Fechit!

(A "tah-dah" sound effect accompanied by applause as LINCOLN bows, drops his hat, scrambles to pick it up, and bows again.)

JEFFERSON: Now I'm really confused.

OLDER JACKSON: Then take a lesson from your elders and take that handyman part.

YOUNG JACKSON: I clearly ended up at the wrong party 'cause this is some kinda coon fest. A fuckin' Coon-ceañera, man. Shit. You take that part, you may as well turn in your black card.

JEFFERSON: Says you.

YOUNG JACKSON: Oh, I'm sorry. You wanna keep embarrassing yourself like you did in there, right? Lettin' these crackers make you feel like shit 'cause you a little too dark to be 'All American'?

JEFFERSON: If fools like me don't keep embarrassing ourselves, how's it change?

YOUNG JACKSON: Nigga, change don't come from the inside the cage. You gotta bust that shit open from the outside. Love yourself. Your black self. And never give it up, no matter what kinda coin they shake at you.

JEFFERSON: Well loving my black self would be a lot easier if y'all weren't lurking around every corner yelling "sellout" every time I tried to climb up a rung or two.

YOUNG JACKSON: High class coon ain't no better than a low class one. In fact, he worse, 'cause he know better and he do so anyway. Think on it before you take that part. I'm out!

(Before he goes, he pulls out his lighter and lights it. He looks like he's about to set the place on fire, but instead just walks out with it.)

OLDER JACKSON: The ignorance of youth.

LINCOLN: Pay no mind, young man. Pay no mind.

OLDER JACKSON: *(Bowing slightly, with an "after you" gesture, to LINCOLN.)* Mr. Lincoln.

LINCOLN: *(Returning the bow.)* Mr. Jackson.

OLDER JACKSON and LINCOLN: *(Bowing together at JEFFERSON.)* Mr. Jefferson.

(JEFFERSON, a little confused, half-bows back as OLDER JACKSON and LINCOLN disappear. Lights shift back to "reality" as KENNEDY re-enters through the door from his audition.)

KENNEDY: You're still here?

JEFFERSON: Oh, uh, I was just—I was calling my—

KENNEDY: *(Very self-involved.)* Well, if you must know, I think it went pretty great.

JEFFERSON: Did they, by chance, ask you to play the Korean grocery store owner?

KENNEDY: Wait, how did you—? I read for John, the lead . . . and maybe the Korean store owner. But I'm clearly being considered for both.

(JEFFERSON sighs. Public Enemy's "Burn Hollywood Burn" begins to play as YOUNGER JACKSON re-enters with his lighter still lit.)

JEFFERSON: Wait. You're just a figment of my—

YOUNG JACKSON: Think on it . . .

(LINCOLN, with the blonde wig on, pokes his head out of the door as the producer again.)

LINCOLN: So, what did you decide?

(JEFFERSON remains frozen in tableau, caught between competing voices. The song swells to blackout. End of play.)

AT THE FINISH

Nick Gandiello

ORIGINAL PRODUCTION
        Saloon NYC. April 25th, 2013.

        Directed by Callie Jane Farnsworth

        CAST:
        CASEY: Amy Lynne Berger
        BECCA: Marion Le Coguic
        EDDIE: Matt Ketai

CHARACTERS:
> CASEY: Late twenties.
> BECCA: Late twenties.
> EDDIE: Mid twenties.

PLACE: Boston.

TIME: April 15th, 2013.

Notes: Slashes indicate overlap. Absent punctuation is intention-
al. In the original presentation, a 'VIP' audience member was
involved in the play as part of the festival. If an actor (or audience member) can't perform the VIP role, Eddie can take the
picture himself and the lines from "Hey hi, hey" to "Thank
you so much!" may be cut.

And every day is getting straighter
Time's the Revelator

—Gillian Welch, Revelator

Morning sunlight.

A kettle corn tent at an almost empty market.

*The water is close; if we can't hear segulls and lapping
waves, we can feel them.*

*As we discover them, Becca and Casey are taking plas-
tic shopping bags out of a box, pre-opening them and
stuffing them in a drawer in preparation for the workday,
mid-conversation:*

CASEY: But it's the only thing that can help, it's like—
BECCA: Only?
CASEY: It's like the only response, the only response is // be-
ing kind
BECCA: Only is a big thing, kiddo, it means like // The One Thing.
CASEY: I know, and I know, and it is the one thing we can do: be
kind. All these, these, these horrible, all these awful—
I mean that kid? That kid who got // shot on um,

BECCA: *(Of the bags:)* Ya doing it from the middle again.

CASEY: I know, I got it, but he got shot on um Columbia and Hancock? which is crazy, which is crazy because Eddie runs right by there when he trains like right by there,

BECCA: Casey, the middle

CASEY: And that kid was eighteen. When Eddie was eighteen he hadn't even been diagnosed yet, he hadn't even tried living yet, and this kid died at eighteen? I mean what do we do? I mean I signed up for the Brady Campaign mailing list and I, ya know, I share pertinent stuff on Facebook, which I think is, ya know, contributing, there's a discourse there, but other than that, all I can do is be kind. Like every person who comes up to this counter today, if anybody does show up today, // is to take them as, no I know, okay but

BECCA: What are you talkin about, people are gonna show up.

CASEY: all I can do is take each person as they are, and be patient, and

BECCA: *(Trying to smile)* You know what else you can do is open the bags from the side? Because when you do'em from the middle we still gotta mess with'em with customers on the counter and it slows us down.

People are gonna show up today.

See, there's people right there:

> *(Calling out)*

STEP RIGHT UP, FOLKS! FREE SAMPLES OF ALL OF OUR FLAVORS! FREE KETTLE CORN, FOLKS! HALF-PRICE ON ALL SALES FOR THE BIG DAY!

> *(They wait and watch for a moment, and nothing. Becca flips the bird to the offstage people.)*

BECCA: They ain't ready for this kettle.

> *(They open bags in silence for a moment; the flutter and swish of them.)*

CASEY: You can still listen to me.

BECCA: I can still what now?

CASEY: We have to bring home to work and we have to bring work home, we both knew that starting up, but

BECCA: We can bring work to work, too, we can work at work.

CASEY: But you can't just negate the context of our relationship because you're technically the boss here, you can't just

BECCA: Negate the what? I'm not negating anything!

CASEY: You can still listen to me when I'm feeling something, // you can still—oh, no, okay, go right ahead.

BECCA: STEP RIGHT UP, FOLKS! FREE SAMPLES OF ALL OF OUR FLAVORS! FREE KETTLE CORN, FOLKS! HALF-PRICE ON ALL SALES FOR THE BIG DAY!

(Pause)

Bags.

BECCA: I. Look I just. I have like eight different brains lately and I. I love when you're feeling something. I love what you feel. I can listen.

CASEY: No, I said what I wanted to say.

BECCA: Good, then

CASEY: It's just that what Eddie is doing today got me thinking, ya know, about people helping each other, this whole city is helping each other today and I want to be kind. He should be stopping by any minute. It's almost eight-thirty. Bags.

BECCA: I'm sorry ya can't see him run today.

CASEY: Well, you had to open the tent.

BECCA: I did have to. That twenty grand for the space this season is twenty grand done and done,

CASEY: I know

BECCA: the market keeps our twenty whether we open or not. Can't afford a day off.

CASEY: Guess Mike and Mo can afford a day off.

BECCA: They asked for this day months ago. And they cover for you a lot, with the rehearsals and the auditions, and they're proud of you, doing that. And they don't hold a candle to you on the counter. Sales go up by a grand when you're on the counter, you've seen the spreadsheet. No one does people like you, kiddo.

CASEY: I do people?

BECCA: Oh you do people.

I'm sure ya brother understands.

(Casey shakes her head, looks away.)

BECCA: Hey, he understands.

CASEY: Eddie doesn't understand, because

BECCA: Course he does.

CASEY: He doesn't understand because I didn't tell him.

> *(Beat.)*

BECCA: You didn't tell Eddie ya working today?

CASEY: I was holding out to see if you'd cancel. This run means the world to him.

BECCA: And he thinks you're gonna go watch him today?

> *(Casey nods.)*

BECCA: And he's coming here now.

CASEY: He thinks I'm just helping you pop the first batch.

> *(Becca grits her teeth and picks up another box of bags; she cuts it open it with a key under:)*

CASEY: But I can't leave you here alone, and I didn't wanna fuck up with either of you, and I procrastinated the decision.

BECCA: Here, get another box going.

CASEY: I don't wanna leave you here alone. Let's not start the day like this.

BECCA: Get started with the bags and I'll pop another batch.

CASEY: We don't need three boxes of bags open—

BECCA: The Elite Women's is gonna be done before noon, the First Wave'll be done soon after, and this place is gonna pick up at two o'clock. If we have less bags, we move slower, if we move slower, we make less money.

CASEY: Okay, I'll make // the bags

BECCA: And if I don't pick up sales // this week,

CASEY: I'll make the bags, Becca, god.

BECCA: I won't even break even for the season!

> *(Casey opens bags angrily, rapidly. Becca watches for a moment, then:)*

BECCA: Ya know ya talk a good one about being kind but you're not kind to me.

CASEY: I'm not kind to you?

BECCA: Ya not.

CASEY: Oh I'm sorry, I thought standing here working for you might qualify.

BECCA: You're nice to me, Case. You're considerate. You remember things. On paper, you're great: if I were collecting resumes for girlfriends, you'd get a second interview dumb fast. But you—put me, in front of people.

CASEY: I put you in front of people?

BECCA: Like when that thing happened in Connecticut. You knew I was sad, you knew I was dealing. And I come home from work and you had all our friends over for a 'feeling session.' Who the hell throws feeling sessions?

CASEY: We were interacting with people during a dark time, during

BECCA: I don't feel at the same pace as you, Casey! I was sitting there with Mo, and with Eddie, with all of them while they shared research, and debated policies, and I had to bite my tongue, I had to bite my tongue because I didn't like what I was feeling. And you barely looked at me that whole night while you were being kind.

(Pause)

CASEY: *(Not without compassion)*What is it you bit your tongue on?

BECCA: That it was gonna happen again and none of us could stop it.

(Pause)

CASEY: When the world is ugly, I try to love the people around me more. And I'm sorry if you feel left out but it's all that I can do to help, to

BECCA: See but I don't think kindness is gonna save the world. I don't think feeling and patience is gonna save us. I think working, and trying, and not taking shit from people when they're cruel, I think that might slow things down. But that's the best we can do, kiddo.

CASEY: Enough with that, enough with kiddo.

BECCA: Why?

CASEY: You called me kiddo when we used to be happy so now it just feels like

BECCA: When we were

CASEY: Now it just feels like a mean joke.

(Pause. Stillness.)

BECCA: I'm not

CASEY: God, I didn't

BECCA: I'm not not happy.

CASEY: I didn't mean. I'm not either, I am.

BECCA: You are are happy or you are are not happy?

CASEY: I am happy, I am am, I

BECCA: Because I'm unquestionably, un, unhesitatingly—and you know what I cant believe you just said that to me, what a // fucked up thing for you to say.

CASEY: Becca, I am.

BECCA: You say these things. You say these things from these depths. Every time we get the slightest bit into something you say these things from this, this, this fucking dredge. God, can we not have a disagreement without the fate of humanity coming into it?

CASEY: Dredge is not a place.

BECCA: Dredge is not a what?

CASEY: Dredge is something you do, it's not a from. And it's not the slightest bit.

BECCA: What?

CASEY: We are not the slightest bit into something. This is a fundamental—

BECCA: There's people walking by.

CASEY: Jesus, Becca.

BECCA: Every sale counts, I gotta try. STEP RIGHT UP, FOLKS! FREE SAMPLES // OF ALL OF OUR FLAVORS! FREE . . . fucking . . . HALF-PRICE ON ALL SALES FOR THE BIG DAY!

CASEY: This is a fundamental difference. There is a fundamental difference here.

BECCA: I gotta pop another batch. I gotta get the smell in the air.

(Becca starts putting on popping clothes: overalls over her regular clothes, hat, etc. Casey opens a bag or two, slowly, trembling. Then:)

CASEY: I wanna move back to New York.

BECCA: Pssh. Like I could uproot the business. No way I could go to New York.

CASEY: I know.

(Becca stops changing, looks at Casey.)

BECCA: Are you—? Is this—?

CASEY: I don't know how to be who I am in this city anymore.

BECCA: Case. We have so much set up here. We are doing so much here.

CASEY: I know, and I know I need it in a way. I have never felt more adult than with you, more put together. Everything with the apartment, we fixed a porch together, I mean. I would have never made a spreadsheet of anything. But you are so much more invested in, in moving that way. It's like, god this is gonna sound so stupid, it's like I saw this science thing where if there's one object moving just slower than the speed of light but it's right next to something moving at the speed of light, the second thing is always gonna seem.

BECCA: Casey

CASEY: like it's moving exponentially away from the first object, like forever and forever away

BECCA: Case

CASEY: even if the first object is moving just a little slower, and and and

BECCA: Casey, please, just

CASEY: And I don't think we treat people the same way!

(A long pause)

(Eddie enters, in a running uniform, taking a selfie as he goes.)

EDDIE: I am getting the best moving selfie right now, you have no idea. It's like hashtag motion picture selfie.

(He hugs Casey)

Casey-Facey.

(He hugs Becca)

Hey Becca! How'd the first batch go?

(Becca is trying to smile, but can't stop looking at Casey.)

CASEY: It was good, but, it's kinda slow right now.

EDDIE: Yeah well everyone's heading to Hopkinton. I saw people from like five different countries today already. The world is converging. We should get going. The folks in wheelchairs'll be starting soon, I was hoping to catch some. I know it's like, weird, but I feel this weird like sort of community with them. We should get going to catch them. Oh and Becca I'm sorry you can't come join. I really wanted you there.

BECCA: I

CASEY: Hey, Eddie?

EDDIE: Wow.

CASEY: What?

EDDIE: Wow, you guys are just so present right now. Look at you, you are just so present in this moment.

CASEY: Eddie.

EDDIE: No, I know that sounds like the old me, like hypomanic out the ass? But it's not the old me.

I was walking over here, and I was looking at this day. And I was looking at the water. And now I'm looking at you guys, and I can take you all in.

That's why I wish you could come with us, Bec.

BECCA: I wish I could too. You seem really happy.

EDDIE: Hey I mean. I'm running the biggest run in the world. My kid sister's in love with the best kettle corn chef in New England. And there's this moment. This present moment.

I dunno how much Casey told you, but the anticonvulsants fucked me up for a minute there, but now that I'm good?

It's like I can take in things. Like I saw this video on Facebook of this autistic girl? And she like sees peoples faces as a thousand pictures a second and she hears noises like really intensely, and hey, I'm not saying I know anything about that struggle, but, if there was, if there was a positive of that? That's what I would be feeling right now.

Because I trained to be better. And you guys are working, to be better. And these people. Are all here. Man, I can't wait for that stretch of water in Ashland. And the Scream Tunnel, the kids at Wellesley cheering, 'cause that's like exactly what this day is: that chorus. God, I really sound like the old me right now, but the buildings in Copley, when they catch the sky and reflect it? Like all of that exists. Right now. I know I sound manic but this is the closest I've been to that feeling since the meds. Because of this day.

(A pause.)

BECCA: Well you guys better get going.

(Casey looks at Becca.)

BECCA: If you watch him start then take the car you can wait in Copley.

EDDIE: That's a plan.

(To Casey)

Right?

CASEY: Um.

BECCA: Yeah, you can you can wait for him at the finish.

EDDIE: She won't be able to miss it. Whole world is gonna be looking at that street.

CASEY: Yeah.

(Casey and Becca look at each other.)

EDDIE: Look at you guys looking at each other. You're so fucking present.
I need a picture. I need a picture. Here, let's, lets, try to
No, no we need the tent in the background.
Um.

(To VIP audience)

Hey hi, hey! Hey-o! Could you take a picture of us? Oh my god you're so kind it like radiates.
Okay here we go!

(They all stand together as VIP frames a shot with the I-phone or whatever device. But Becca is just looking at Casey as they huddle together.)

VIP: Hey um. Do you wanna look at the camera, or?

(Becca looks at the camera. VIP takes the picture and gives it back to Eddie.)

EDDIE: Thank you so much!

(He looks at the picture)

Oh my god I gotta instagram that shit. Hashtag no filter, hashtag joy.
God you guys smell like kettle corn.
Okay. Shall we?

(Casey nods.)

EDDIE: Becca, you enjoy the shit out of this day.

BECCA: Take a picture at the finish so I can see.

EDDIE: Uh, trust me, pictures will be taken. Peace, kettle gang-sta.

(He starts to head out.)

(Casey goes to hug Becca goodbye. Becca resists at first, then lets her.)

(She starts to move away.)

CASEY: Just, let me, jesus Becca just let me.

(Becca lets her.)

(They hold each other. A long, long moment.)

(Eddie stands there kinda awkwardly. He snaps a picture of them.)

EDDIE: Hashtag embrace.

(Then he stands there and watches, appreciating it.)

(Casey lets go and moves offstage quickly.)

BECCA: *(To Eddie)* Kay then. Don't fall down, asshole.

EDDIE: Try my best!

(He flashes deuces and heads off. Becca looks outward.)

BECCA: STEP RIGHT UP, FOLKS! FREE SAMPLES OF

(She's breaking:)

FREE

(She pulls herself together)

HALF-PRICE ON ALL SALES FOR THE BIG DAY! STEP RIGHT UP, FOLKS!

Blackout.

BITE ME

Nina Mansfield

ORIGINAL PRODUCTION

Bite Me was originally produced by Ticket2Eternity Productions as part of Disjointed Love Short, New York, New York in September 2011. The production was directed by Adyana De La Torre.

CAST:
ELLEN: Shannon Lower
MARK: Greg Engbrecht
VAMPIRE: Joshua Cameron

Bite Me was produced as part of City Theatre's Summer Shorts Festival 2013, Miami, Florida in June 2013. The production was directed by Margaret Ledford.

CAST:
ELLEN: Vera Varlamov
MARK: Todd Allen Durkin
VAMPIRE: Ken Clement

CHARACTERS:

  ELLEN: An upper-middle class housewife. Mid-twenties
    to mid-thirties.

  MARK: Ellen's husband. Corporate type. Early thirties
    to early forties.

  VAMPIRE: A Vampire. Male.

TIME: The present. October.

PLACE: Ellen and Mark's living room. Expensively decorated.

> *Light swoops into the living room of a modern married
> couple. ELLEN, who is dressed to impress, straightens a
> sheet that covers what appears to be a large animal cage.
> When she hears MARK enter, she smoothes her hair, and
> moves to greet him.*

MARK: Honey, I'm home! The traffic on 95 was insane so I—you
  look nice.

ELLEN: *(Seductive.)* Come here you. How was work?

MARK: *(Setting down his briefcase. Loosening tie.)* The usual. Those idiots still think we're gonna settle. Like they can
  prove we dumped that toxic waste. Why does everyone want
  to blame Big Business for their cancer? What's that smell?
  Are you roasting garlic Ellen? Wait—today isn't our anniversary or something?

ELLEN: I bet you are so sexy when you're crushing the little guy.
  Grrr. Nothing turns me on like a man in a suit.

MARK: *(Remembering.)* June 18th. It is not June. That much I
  know. Contrary to popular belief, not all males forget their
  anniversary.

> *(She kisses him.)*

What was that for? It's October.

ELLEN: I can't kiss you?

MARK: And the outfit?

ELLEN: I can't dress up for my husband?

MARK: *(Suspicious.)* What's going on?

ELLEN: Maybe I was just in the mood.

MARK: Okay, but something put you in the mood, didn't it?

What do you want Ellen? You just got a new Escalade. Bored with it already?

ELLEN: No. I don't want anything. At least not what you think.

MARK: Or does this maybe have something to do with that?

(He points to the large cage with the sheet draped over it.)

ELLEN: Maybe.

MARK: Sweetheart, I told you, a dog is a really big responsibility and—

ELLEN: Just sit.

MARK: Okay, but with my work schedule, I can't be walking—

ELLEN: Shh. You know, how we used to say we wanted to spend all eternity together.

MARK: Yeah. I remember having a conversation like that once. After a lot of tequila.

ELLEN: Do you still feel that way about me?

MARK: Of course I do sweetheart. But a dog is still a really big commitment. They need constant attention. Not to mention the walking, the feeding, the grooming, the chewing of shoes—

ELLEN: Forget about the dog Mark. There is no dog. What I want to know is, do you still want to spend all eternity with me?

MARK: All eternity? Of course I do sweetheart.

ELLEN: And if you could be immortal with me, would you?

MARK: Yeah, sure. Immortal. Whatever you say.

ELLEN: Well, I brought home a little surprise.

MARK: Ah yes. The surprise. Let me a guess. A pit bull.

(She tears the curtain off the cage to reveal VAMPIRE. There are crosses and garlic hung around the cage.)

ELLEN: Voila.

MARK: That's not a dog.

ELLEN: I told you there was no dog. What do you think?

MARK: You've brought home a slave?

ELLEN: He's not a slave darling. He's a vampire.

MARK: A . . . A vampire?

ELLEN: That's what I said. And check this out. He is willing to make us both immortal.

MARK: *(Trying to make sense of the situation.)* He's a vampire?

ELLEN: Sure. Just ask him.

MARK: Uhm . . .

ELLEN: Edward, would you tell him that you're a vampire.

VAMPIRE: My name isn't Edward.

ELLEN: Whatever. Can you explain that I'm not making this up? Because my darling husband doesn't seem to believe me.

VAMPIRE: Yeah, sure. What she said.

ELLEN: *(To Mark.)* He's a little weak right now. All the garlic and crosses.

MARK: How did you . . . where did you find . . .

ELLEN: I was shopping this afternoon, and stupid me thought I'd take a shortcut through that alley in back of Bloomies to get to the lot. You know how they say you shouldn't rifle through your purse looking for your keys because it makes you a target for potential attackers. Well, they're right. Because there I am, digging through my Tory Burch handbag, looking for my keys and suddenly this guy lunges out of nowhere, teeth all pointy and stuff like, *oooo, I'm a vampire* . . .

MARK: I thought they only attacked at night?

ELLEN: Myth. Anyway, luckily, at that exact moment, I got hold of my pepper spray and wham! Got him in the eye.

MARK: Pepper spray keeps vampires away?

ELLEN: Who knew?

VAMPIRE: Do you really have to go into all of this?

ELLEN: *(To Vampire.)* Excuse me. I wasn't talking to you.

> *(To Mark.)*

I think he's a little ashamed.

MARK: About the pepper spray.

ELLEN: About what happened next.

VAMPIRE: Could you please not—?

ELLEN: It's the best part of the story Edward!

VAMPIRE: My name isn't Edward!

ELLEN: So there he is, stunned from the spray. Writhing on the ground like a baby.

VAMPIRE: She's exaggerating.

ELLEN: *(Very physical. She uses Mark to demonstrate.)* When WHAM! Got him in the balls. BAM, I hit him with my handbag, and ZANG, got him again with the pepper spray.

MARK: *(On ground, in some pain.)* Why didn't you just run?

ELLEN: At that point it was like pure adrenaline! I was on fire!

MARK: *(Starting to get up.)* I think I get the picture.

ELLEN: I'm not done yet.

(She continues to demonstrate on Mark.)

Once I had him subdued I realized the emblem on my Tory Burch handbag is totally cross like, so I held it up to his face, and sure enough he was like, *Ahh*, and I was like, "take that you creature of the dark," and he was like, *Ahhh*, and I was like, "that's what you get for attacking women in alleys," and he's like, *please, I can't help it! It's just my nature*, and I'm like, "I don't care if it's just your nature you woman hater," and he's like, *please, I don't hate women, I just want to suck your blood*, and I'm like "ew," and he's like, *you get used to it*, and I'm like "really?" and he's like, *really*, and then he started to lunge for me again, 'cause I'd sort of forgotten to hold up my handbag, but I was like really caffeinated, so my reflexes were on point, so I was like, "take this!" and he was like, *Ahhh*. And then I had this idea.

MARK: You had this idea.

ELLEN: *(Releasing Mark.)* Yes! I thought, why not take lemons and turn them into lemonade.

MARK: Lemonade.

ELLEN: I was like, "you scumbag vampire," and he was like, *I'm really not a scumbag*, and I was like, "Oh yeah?" and he was like, *yeah*, and so I sprayed him with more pepper spray, and made him drape my handbag over his shoulder, which made him loose like all his powers, and then I loaded him into the back of the Escalade and Voila!

MARK: And the cage?

ELLEN: I swung by Petco.

MARK: I see.

ELLEN: So? What do you say?

MARK: To what?

ELLEN: Well, I told him I would let him go if he made us both vampires.

MARK: Made us both—

ELLEN: It would be like a win-win situation. He'd get to drink our blood, and we could spend all eternity together. Wouldn't that be cool!

MARK: You know, eternity is a really long time Ellen.

ELLEN: What are you saying?

MARK: I'm saying do you really want to *never* die?

ELLEN: Well duh? Who wants to die?

MARK: And go around sucking people's blood?

ELLEN: He says you get used to it. Isn't that true Edward?

VAMPIRE: Yeah. You get used to it.

ELLEN: See!

MARK: And you'd have to say goodbye to your Tory Burch handbag.

ELLEN: Yeah. That's the one drawback really. But it would be so worth it to spend eternity with you. I had always imagined growing old with you, sweetie, but this would be like so much better. We would never grow old. You won't grow bald. I'll never start to sag. And I won't have to put you in a nursing home some day or change your diaper the way I'd always imagined. Instead, we could be creatures of the night—or the day apparently—roaming the earth together year after year after year. And then we can curl up in our coffin, all cozy and snug, just waiting for our next adventure.

MARK: We'd have to kill people Ellen.

(To Vampire.)

I mean, that is what you do, isn't?

VAMPIRE: Generally speaking.

ELLEN: I've already thought of that. We would limit ourselves to pedophiles and homeless people.

MARK: I . . . I really need to think about this a little.

ELLEN: What's there to think about?

MARK: It's just that . . . I don't know . . . It's a lot to process and . . .

ELLEN: You are so ungrateful. I go through all the trouble to bring home a vampire, and you need to think about this. What's there to think about? Unless of course you don't want to spend all eternity with me?

MARK: No, honey, it's just that, the blood sucking thing—

ELLEN: You are such a wuss.

MARK: And the killing—

ELLEN: Oh come on. Like *you* actually care about killing people? It's what you do for a living.

MARK: I do not kill people. I represent corporate rights.

ELLEN: The point is, you just don't love me.

MARK: No, that's not it at all.

ELLEN: *(To vampire.)* Wouldn't a guy who really loved his wife become a vampire for her?

VAMPIRE: Whatever you say lady.

ELLEN: See.

MARK: You're gonna listen to him?

ELLEN: He seems to be the only voice of reason around here.

VAMPIRE: Does that mean I can go?

ELLEN: *(To Mark.)* After everything I've done for you! I risked my life to make this happen and you . . . you . . . you don't deserve a woman like me. You don't deserve to spend eternity with me. In fact, you don't even deserve to live.

> *(She begins to unlock the cage.)*

MARK: What are you doing?

VAMPIRE: Sweet.

MARK: Are you crazy? He'll kill us both.

ELLEN: No, just you. He's gonna make me immortal. Isn't that right Edward. Immortal. You and me.

> *(To Mark.)*

Because he understands me. He understands what a woman really needs.

> *(Vampire begins to crawl out of his cage while Mark and Ellen argue.)*

MARK: You just met him.

ELLEN: And what does that say about us?

MARK: I . . . I don't really know.

> *(Vampire composes himself. He creeps up behind Ellen.)*

ELLEN: Exactly. Because you never loved me. Because you never understood me. Because this whole marriage has been a sham. You're . . . you're a selfish monster that's what you—

> *(Vampire bites down on Ellen's neck. She shrieks in pain at first, then pleasure, then fades away.)*

Ahh . . . oooo . . . .ahhhh . . . .

> *(Ellen falls to the floor. Dead.)*

MARK: You . . . you killed her.

VAMPIRE: *(Wiping the blood off his mouth.)* Yeah. You can thank me later.

MARK: Are you . . . are you gonna kill me too?

VAMPIRE: I don't know. Do you really work for some large, evil corporation?

MARK: Well, I wouldn't call it evil. Do you understand the way the world economy works? If we start limiting profit margins, if we put a strangle hold on the way large corporations do business—

VAMPIRE: Yeah I get it. You start doing that, our whole economy could crumble.

MARK: Exactly!

VAMPIRE: It's all about trickle down.

MARK: You know, I'm feeling this synergy here. I know this sounds crazy, but I feel like you really get it.

VAMPIRE: Let me ask you something? Is your company hiring?

MARK: At the moment we're downsizing—shipping a lot of jobs abroad—

VAMPIRE: That's too bad.

MARK: —but I'm sure if you give me your resume. Here, let me give you my card.

(Mark reaches for a card, in a pocket or briefcase. Vampire suddenly grabs and bites him.)

MARK: Wait. I thought . . . I thought we had a connection.

(Mark falls dead to the floor.)

VAMPIRE: Sure you did buddy. And people say I'm evil. Corporate rights my ass.

(Vampire wipes his mouth. Lights fade to black. End of play.)

CAKE

Sherry Kramer

ORIGINAL PRODUCTION
      Source Theatre Festival, Washington, DC
      June, 2013
      Producer of the Source Theatre Festival:
      Cultural DC
      916 G St NW
      Washington, DC 20001

      Directed by Maureen Monterubio

      CAST:
      PACO: Chris Aldrich
      SCOTT: Frank Turner
      LILY: Amie Cazel
      SAMSARA: Mia Branco

      COSTUMES, PROPS: Joni Martin
      SOUND: Elisheba Itoop
      LIGHT: Sean Forsythe
      PRODUCTION STAGE MANAGER: Patrick Magill

CHARACTERS:
  PACO: A long hair Chihuahua.
  SAMSARA: A long hair Chihuahua/miniature Italian greyhound mix.
  LILY: A woman in her late forties
  SCOTT: A man in his late forties

SETTING: The second floor porch of Lily and Scott's house. It's twilight. The light is soft and magical, and slightly dramatic. The sound of crickets—a perfect summer evening.

Scott is sitting in an oversized rattan chair with his feet up on a matching, huge comfy rattan ottoman. Paco is sitting on the ottoman at his feet. Lily is standing. Paco often speaks to the Audience.

PACO: Hello. My name is Paco. And I was made for love.

SCOTT: They're my dogs, I can give them to who ever I want.

PACO: Of all the dogs in the world, only one breed was bred for love.

LILY: What are you talking about, they're my dogs too.

PACO: The Chihuahua.

SCOTT: Nope. I brought them to the marriage, so they're mine.

PACO: *(Samsara, half Chihuahua, half miniature Italian Greyhound, all trouble, walks onto the porch. She is gorgeous and she knows it.)* It is true that Samsara is only half Chihuahua—her father was a dyspeptic miniature Italian greyhound named Peppi—that's who she got her long, exquisite legs and her short temper from, but still. The breeding for love is deeply etched in her blood and bones.

SAMSARA: And there isn't a damn thing I can do about it.

PACO: Darling—don't talk like that.

(Samsara walks past Paco and preens for a bit.)

SAMSARA: I'd rather be made for retrieving. Or sheep herding.

PACO: You hate sheep.

SAMSARA: So? That would probably make me better at it. All I'm saying is—I wish I'd been bred for something productive. Something honest. Something I could be proud of doing, at the end of the day. What do *I* do? I smell the smell of love 24/7. And when I am not busy *smelling* love, I smell *like* love. That's something to be proud of? I wish I'd been bred for anything other than love.

(She walks around the ottoman and back into the house. Paco looks at her long legs with admiration. He sighs.)

PACO: Being bred for love is less convenient that you might imagine.

SCOTT: I'm giving them to my sister. You won't sacrifice enough for them.

LILY: I don't need to sacrifice anything for them, Scott. I love them! When you love someone you don't have to measure what you gave up.

PACO: How is it inconvenient, you ask? Let me count the ways.

LILY: You don't have to measure how much it hurts to prove you love them!

PACO: First, there is no ultimate measure of love. And then there is the way love smells. Which—surprise? Is not always so sweet.

(Sniffs loudly.)

Smell that? Love, when you measure it, stinks. But I have no choice.

LILY: You know I love them as much as you do.

PACO: If love is anywhere, no matter how badly it smells, I must smell it.

(Paco puts his paws over his nose to try to keep from smelling.)

LILY: I might even love them more.

(The smell almost overpowers Paco. He pinches his nose tightly and bravely goes on.)

PACO: Does she or doesn't she love us more, you ask?

(Shrugs)

It's a stupid question. There is no more or less, no as much or as not. It either smells like love, or it doesn't.

LILY: And unlike you, I love them all the time!

SCOTT: I love Paco all the time.

LILY: No you don't, you love him maybe 87 percent of the time.

PACO: *(Paco lets go of his nose.)* Sacrilege! Outrage! Not true! His love for me is eternal, like the stars!

LILY: On a good day, you love him, but when he's bad? When he pees on the oriental?

SAMSARA: *(o.s.)* PACO! NOT AGAIN! Not the oriental.

SCOTT: That's different. That carpet was my grandmother's.

SAMSARA: *(o.s.)* Paco, you promised!

PACO: You know I can't help it! The oriental is lush and dark and unless they catch me at it they can't tell for sure—but he still loves me when I pee on it! Even when he catches me he loves me! I can smell it! I can always smell love.

SAMSARA: *(She walks onto the porch and gets up on the ottoman with Paco.)* And they can smell when you pee on the oriental.

PACO: No, they can't! I have proven that time and time again.

SAMSARA: They try to smell it. They walk on it barefoot to check for wet spots, they crawl on their hands and knees sniffing—

PACO: But the oriental is a true friend. It absorbs everything like a sponge. After all, it's not as if I am a great Dane. I am a Chihuahua—we are talking a delicate rain, not a monsoon. And as for the smell—well, I have a theory—it is something I have given much thought to. It is my theory that they don't smell it because my pee smells like love!

SAMSARA: You have got to be kidding me.

PACO: But how else can you explain it!

SAMSARA: The degree of self delusion here—

PACO: You never give my theories a chance! You just shoot them down! You never once—

SAMSARA: Please! You're just lucky they love you so much. No matter how strong the smell of your pee, their love for you smells stronger. It blocks the pee-smell out.

PACO: That is the conventional wisdom when it comes to peeing in the house. But in my opinion—

SAMSARA: It's the conventional wisdom because in house after house, with dog after dog, all over the world, it has been proven to be the truth.

PACO: You reject the possibility that my pee smells like love.

SAMSARA: Your pee smells like pee. Their love is stronger. End of discussion.

SCOTT: Don't you get tired of him peeing on the oriental all the time?

LILY: Tired, yes.

SCOTT: See!

LILY: Tired is not the same as not loving.

SAMSARA: Don't you ever get tired of it? Of smelling all their love?

PACO: We were made for one thing only—to attach to them and never to be unattached! Stop asking me to betray my DNA!

SCOTT: It's not a crime to hate him when he pees on the oriental! Who wouldn't.

LILY: I don't.

SCOTT: Well, that's because it's not your grandmother's priceless rug.

LILY: I'm the one who has to clean it up, aren't I? And I still don't hate him.

SCOTT: Then why do you hate me?

LILY: I don't hate you.

SCOTT: You do, you hate me. You hate me every time you have to clean up after me. Don't deny it.

LILY: Sweetheart, you're upset about this morning, well don't be, I didn't even notice that—

SCOTT: I'm not talking about that, I'm talking about cleaning up things like--the thing with the IRS.

LILY: Oh. Well, that was hard. When they seized the business for back taxes.

SCOTT: The three times I let my health insurance lapse and didn't tell you.

(Samsara puts her paw over Paco's nose, and he puts his paw over hers.)

LILY: Oh, God, Scott, don't remind me about that. That was bad. Really bad.

PACO: *(But Samsara and Paco are in agony from the smells.)* Hold your breath, my darling, these things never last long.

(They hold their breath.)

SCOTT: The stock tip I gave your mother that—

LILY: Scott, please. My mother—is fine. She didn't need that big house. It really was too much for her. I didn't hate you for any of those things. The only time I hated you—

SCOTT: Ah ha! I knew you hated me!

LILY: —was the time with the cake.

PACO: *(Gasping for air)* Oh, no, not the cake. Why does she bring up the cake!

> *(He tries to stuff tissue, anything into his nose to keep from smelling it.)*

I can't stand the smell of the story of that cake.

SCOTT: I'm sorry about the cake, Lily. I don't know why I did that.

SAMSARA: Oh, no, Paco. Not this time. This time, it's time to grow up.

> *(They struggle, but she removes whatever he has managed to stuff up his nose.)*

You must take the bitter with the sweet! You insist on loving him, on smelling his love--so wake up and smell the cake story, buster. Even though, in my opinion, it is not possible to love a man who has done a thing like this!

PACO: That is the greyhound in you talking! A full blooded Chihuahua would know! I *must* love him! It is not possible to do anything else.

LILY: Valentines Day. You told me to go pick it up at the bakery. You said you'd ordered it special to say "LILY, I LOVE YOU MORE THAN LIFE ITSELF." And then when I got it home and opened the box—

SCOTT: I'm sorry! I've said I'm sorry. You know I'm sorry.

LILY: It said nothing. Nothing at all. It was a blank cake. And you let me call the bakery and scream at them, you stood there and listened to me scream at the counter girl and then you listened to me pry the owner's number out of her and call him and scream at him. Because my cake did not say "Lily, I love you more than life itself', my cake said nothing, and my last Valentines Day had been ruined and by God I was going to make sure that somebody paid! But you'd never ordered it. You'd ordered a plain cake and told me to pick it up. You ordered a cake that did not say I love you and then you told me that it did. I hated you for that. And I still do.

> *(Paco goes over to Scott, and licks his cheek.)*

Oh, Paco, how could he do that?

SAMSARA: Yes, I want to that know too. How could he!

PACO: I don't know. It is not in my blood to know. But the sorrow I feel for him that he *can* do such a thing?

(Paco licks Scott's other cheek, Scott holds him.)

Makes me love him even more.

SAMSARA: Oh, Paco. And that's why *I* love *you.*

(She goes over to Paco, and nuzzles him.)

PACO: You see, Samsara? You don't want to love me for it, but you have no choice. Love. It is hardwired in us both.

SAMSARA: Then why can't he say it? If he loves her--and I admit it, Paco, I can smell it too, he does love her! So why can't he say I love you to her? Why can't he put it on a cake?

PACO: He tried. He tried so hard. He was on the phone to the girl at the bakery and she asked him if he wanted the cake to say something. One minute the words I LOVE YOU LILY MORE THAN LIFE ITSELF were coming out of his mouth. And the next moment—the thought of putting them on a cake made him afraid. And the moment after that he knew that either the cake would say that, or nothing. He could say nothing less. So he said nothing at all. But Samsara, in the end the cake *did* say I love you more than life itself.

SAMSARA: No, it didn't—

PACO: It did. Just not in words. I could smell it then. You can smell it now. He loves her.

SCOTT: Lily?

LILY: Yes.

SCOTT: Of course you get the dogs. You think I'd give them to my sister? The first time Paco peed on her bed, she'd have him put down. She'd make Samsara wear little doggie dresses. No way is she getting the dogs.

(Lily goes to them, they all hold each other. A little buzzer goes off. Lily kisses Scott, then gets a pill box, hands Scott some pills and a glass of water. Paco and Samsara carefully watch him take his pills. There are lots of them.)

SAMSARA: How long?

PACO: *(Sniffs the air carefully)* A week or two. Maybe three.

SAMSARA: You're sure? When I try to smell it—

> *(She sniffs.)*

It seems a hundred years away. It smells—

> *(She sniffs again.)*

As if he isn't sick at all.

> *(She sniffs.)*

It smells—

PACO: You're downwind of her, darling, that's all. The smell of her love is stronger than the truth.

SAMSARA: *(She moves around so she is on Scott's other side. Sniffs. Sadly.)* Oh. Yes. You're right.

> *(She leans tenderly into Scott's side.)*

I admit it, Paco. I act like I'm tired of it, like I don't need it, but the truth is I'll miss it.

PACO: When he isn't here to love us?

SAMSARA: No, when he isn't here for *us* to love *him*.

PACO: Ah. Yes. That is the hardest thing, I know.

SAMSARA: When he dies, where will the smell of all our love for him go?

PACO: Didn't your mother teach you this?

SAMSARA: No, I looked too much like my father, and she held it against me.

PACO: My darling. It is the one convenient thing about being bred for love. The smell of love doesn't go anywhere.

> *(Scott finishes taking his pills. The two dogs and Scott and Lily take deep breaths, inhaling as if trying to take in the scent of the entire world.)*

It never goes away.

> *(Blackout.)*

END OF PLAY

DETECTIVE STORIES

Philip J. Kaplan

ORIGINAL PRODUCTION

DETECTIVE STORIES premiered July, 2013 at 10 by 10 in the Triangle@The ArtsCenter, Carrboro, NC.

Directed by Michael O'Foghludha

FEATURED:
Michael Brocki
Mark Filiaci
Bonnie Roe

CHARACTERS:

> MAN 1: KYLE BUTLER, the Detective; CHAMBERS THE BUTLER, the Suspect; ARTHUR PRENDER-GAST, the Victim; GUINAN, the Detective; DOW, the suspect
>
> MAN 2: CHAUNCEY HOWELL, the Victim; WARREN EARL, the Detective; CARY STUBBS, the Suspect; MR. TURING, the Victim; MUIR, the Detective.
>
> WOMAN: SUSAN BEDLOW, the Suspect; LADY BELVEDERE, the Victim; LINDSAY, the Detective; GRACE, the Suspect; MOTHER, the Victim.

SETTING: A table with a chair, that serves as the resting place for the victim. Nearby are two candlesticks and a bottle.

PRODUCTION NOTES: Should be one continuous play, no blackouts, even as the actors switch roles. New characters should be suggested through changes in mannerism or small clothing changes.

Scene 1

> *Set. A table and a chair. There are two candlesticks, and a bottle of gin. The cast is two men and a woman. They take turns playing the Detective, the Suspect and the Victim. At open MAN2 plays CHAUNCEY HOWELL, the victim. He sits at the desk head down, dead. MAN1 is currently KYLE BUTLER, the Detective. He is talking to WOMAN, currently SUSAN BEDLOW, the Suspect.*

KYLE: Miss Bedlow, at 8 pm your neighbors heard a gunshot.
SUSAN BEDLOW: Yes, I—
KYLE:—And you were upstairs in your bedroom.
SUSAN BEDLOW: No, I was—
KYLE:—Downstairs in your bedroom?
SUSAN BEDLOW: No, My bedroom is up—
KYLE:—And the door to this room, where the body was found, was locked from the inside.
SUSAN BEDLOW: No. The door—

KYLE:—How could you have come upstairs, when your bedroom is downstairs?

SUSAN BEDLOW: I wasn't—

KYLE:—Did Mr. Howell have any enemies?

SUSAN BEDLOW: There were—

KYLE:—Are you trying to hide something

SUSAN BEDLOW: I'm trying to get a word in—

KYLE:—Chauncey Howell was murdered!

SUSAN BEDLOW: Obviously! He has a hole in his—

KYLE:—How do you explain the tomatoes in his refrigerator?

SUSAN BEDLOW: What?

There is a pause. Susan looks like she's about to say something. Just as she opens her mouth.

KYLE: How do you explain the tomatoes—

SUSAN BEDLOW:—Shut up! Shut up! Let me finish one goddamned sentence!

KYLE: Did you kill him?

SUSAN BEDLOW: Yes! I bashed his head in with a candlestick so I could collect his insurance!

(beat)

Oh, crap.

KYLE: Cuff her boys. That wraps up another case by Kyle Butler. The Detective Who Constantly Interrupts.

(They quickly switch positions. The Woman now takes the role of the Victim, in the exact same position, head down on the table. MAN1 is now CHAMBERS THE BUTLER, the Suspect and MAN2 is the Detective, WARREN EARL.)

WARREN EARL: Where did you find the body?

CHAMBERS: I found Lady Belvedere at her table writing a note, and eating a cheese and tom-ah-to sandwich.

WARREN EARL: Hmmmm. Tomatoes.

CHAMBERS: Tom-ah-tos.

WARREN EARL: I see. It's all coming together.

CHAMBERS: How so?

WARREN EARL: Don't you see the connection? Lady Belvedere. Lady Day—that was Billie Holiday's nickname. And today was not a holiday, but it *was* a red letter day! Why? Be-

cause Tomatoes are red. And Lady Belvedere was writing a
letter at the time of her demise. See! Letter! Red! Day!

CHAMBERS: How do you know she was writing a letter?

WARREN EARL: The envelope, the pen, the stationary, you said
she was writing a note, but that's not important.

CHAMBERS: It's very important. She was writing a letter exposing my past.

WARREN EARL: But how does it tie together? Chambers, hand
me that blood stained candlestick.

CHAMBERS: Which one? The one I used to smash her head? Or
the one that was simply splattered when I smashed her head
with the first candlestick?

WARREN EARL: Give me the second one. The candle is signifi-
cant, but why? Candle . . . candle . . . candle, got it! There are
eight letters in the word candle. K is the eighth letter in the al-
phabet if you exclude vowels. Sarah Vowel is a writer of light
hearted historical essays. Essanay was the studio that produced Charlie Chaplin's earliest films. Are you following?

CHAMBERS: No.

WARREN EARL: I know who killed Lady Belvedere!

CHAMBERS: Charlie Chaplin?

WARREN EARL: Close! Not Charlie Chaplin, but . . . . Summers, the local Chaplain. He did it.

CHAMBERS: And your proof?

WARREN EARL: You want more than that? Are you against me
too, Chambers? Or are you just blind to the obvious, like everyone else. I hear them talking. "Another one of Warren's
crazy conspiracy theories." Why don't they believe me?
Ever since I took up numerology and had that head injury, no
one believes me.

CHAMBERS: I do.

WARREN EARL: Thank you Chambers.

CHAMBERS: Thank you Conspiracy Detective Earl.

WARREN EARL: That closes the case I call, "The Moon Landing was faked."

*(They switch positions. The Woman now takes the role of
the detective, LINDSAY. Man1 is ARTHUR PRENDER-
GAST, the Victim. Man2 is the suspect, CARY STUBBS.)*

LINDSAY: According to my notes, Mr. Stubbs, you owed the deceased twenty thousand dollars. In my book, that's called motive. Motive does not equal guilt, but there's sometimes a strong correlation.

(beat)

Well, what do you have to say?

CARY: Lindsay Lohan?

LINDSAY: Yes. Lindsay Lohan, girl detective. What of it?

CARY: I thought you were an actress.

LINDSAY: I am an actress, but in my spare time— when things get too hot—I help the Milwaukee, PD. And this looks like a yarn that the MPD can't unravel. Arthur Prendergast was found in a room locked from the inside with no murder weapon and yet a bullet in his head.

CARY: Well, no—he was—

LINDSAY: Don't be awed by my celebrity. Please, treat me as you would any shamus pounding the beat.

CARY: I loved you in MEAN GIRLS.

LINDSAY: I'll sign autographs after I've cracked this case. What's important is we have a murder victim here.

CARY: I guess your struggles give you an insight into—

LINDSAY: Wait! A clue.

(Lindsay picks up a bottle of gin.)

LINDSAY: This requires more investigation.

(She chugs the bottle and exits.)

(They switch positions. The Woman now takes the role of GRACE the suspect, Man2 is MR. TURING, the Victim, and Man1, GUINAN the Detective.)

(GUINAN is feverishly typing on an iPhone while GRACE stares. After a moment.)

GUINAN: (reading from the phone)
Were you ever . . . in . . . Bulgaria?

GRACE: No.

GUINAN: You're sure?

GRACE: Yes.

GUINAN: Hmmmm.

(Guinan resumes typing.)

GRACE: Don't you want to look at the body?
GUINAN: Shhhh.

(beat)

I notice that you're left handed.
GRACE: I'm right handed.
GUINAN: Oh.

(Guinan resumes typing.)

GRACE: What are you doing?
GUINAN: I'm crowd-sourcing the investigation. I post the facts on my twitter account, and thousands of people help me do research and make suggestions.
GRACE: Is that effective?
GUINAN: When I have a good connection. Oh! According to BABSLOVESPIZZA you recently withdrew 50,000 dollars and bought a one way ticket to Lima Peru. How do you explain that?

(Grace takes out an iPhone and starts typing.)

GUINAN: I asked you a question!
GRACE: I'm just checking in on my support group . . . for advice.

(to herself)

Change the subject.

(to Guinan)

You're quite attractive, Mr. Guinan.
Guinan types something.
GUINAN: *(reading)* You can't dis— dis—

(Shows the phone to Grace.)

GRACE: It's a typo. I think they meant distract.
GUINAN: Of course. You can't distract me!
GRACE: *(loudly, but reading)*
Groupon deal of the day. 50% off flowers.

(beat)

Oh. I mean.

(reading)

I am the real victim here.

GUINAN: How so?

GRACE: *(to herself)* Hmmm. 15 suggestion for Multiple Personality Disorder. 30 for, "It's a frame up!" Oh, look—over 200 suggestions for identify theft. They bump into each other and drop their phones. They pick up the wrong one.

GUINAN: *(reading)* I am the victim of identity theft! You can't pin this on me!

GRACE: *(reading)* You murdered Mr. Turing!

GUINAN: *(reading)* I demand a lawyer!

GRACE: Oh my God! Look at this!

> *(Shows phone to Guinan.)*

GUINAN: That's a kitten stuck in a sock.

GRACE: Yes.

GUINAN: That is so cute!

> *(They switch positions. The Woman is MOTHER, the victim, Man2 is MUIR the Detective and Man1 is DOW, the Suspect.)*

MUIR: I see it now. You didn't go for the quick kill. You did it slowly. You used her, and used her, and took and took.

DOW: I didn't know! You have to believe me! I didn't know!

MUIR: You didn't know your poison would eventually kill her?

DOW: I didn't know it was poison!

MUIR: You expect me to believe that?

DOW: I took the same poison. I've been taking it for years. Would I take poison if I knew it would kill me.

MUIR: Only an insane man would poison himself. And only an insane man would poison her. By killing her, you've doomed yourself. You've doomed us all.

DOW: But I wasn't alone. They helped.

> *(MUIR looks at the audience.)*

MUIR: You're right! They too are to blame—with their cars and their overconsumption.

DOW: And their complacency. They sit and watch.

MUIR: We are victims and killers at the same time.

DOW: We are all to blame in the death of ... Mother Earth.

(The Woman comes to life, slowly stands center stage and says to the audience.)

MOTHER EARTH: Please recycle.

MUIR: *(to Mother Earth)* Is that a general comment? Or a metatextual reference to this play?

MOTHER EARTH: You're the detective. You figure it out.

BLACKOUT

East of the Sun

Regina Taylor

ORIGINAL PRODUCTION

East of the Sun was commissioned and presented by RED BULL THEATER as part of the 2013 SHORT NEW PLAY FESTIVAL (May 13, 2013).

Produced by Craig Baldwin

Directed by Liesl Tommy

CAST:
#1: LINDA POWELL
#2: CHRISTIAN CONN
#3: EDWARD O'BLENIS
#4: JO MEI
#5: HEATHER RAFFO

CHARACTERS:

      #1/MARS Female African-American
      #2 Male White
      #3 Male African American
      #4 Female Asian-American
      #5 Female White

(/ mark means dialogue is overlapped)

Each sit or stand- lined across the stage -or- they are interspersed among the audience. Except for #1 who is MARS—each has i-pad or smart phone into which they are typing.

1: 38 dollars—

2: 38 dollar application fee. Why not—

1: A one way ticket—to Mars—

3: Mars—Named after a Roman-

1&3: god of war—

(We see 1 Shadow Boxing—)

2: If men are from Mars—then I am going home-

4: Cool.

5: Weightless.

(1 stops shadow boxing)

4: Wow—

1: Ten months to get there-

4: Fucking awesome—

2: Step right up—

5: I've always dreamed /of going to Mars.

1: Step right up—step right up—

1&2: Anyone can apply—

5: For thirty eight dollars.

2: Give me your tired, your poor—

1: Anyone 18 or over—

3: Only the fittest—Mental, physical stamina—psychological fortitude—/required—

2: Your huddled masses—

4: Only four chosen the first trip—

3: Men and women—

1: But no couples—

5: -No couples? But I have the best boyfriend on earth-

2: The best on earth—Maybe time to check out another planet-

5: Do they want us to repopulate?

1: The technology doesn't exist yet for you to get back home—

4: We don't exist—Not yet. The first humans to colonize the red planet—

2: Do you see her in that red dress—

3: The first living beings to touch her since—

5: Do you think they want us to fuck—

1: The plan- Two by two- Two men- Two women- to start with-

2: Then more and more of us—will follow—

5: Our bodies would have to acclimate to the planet—

4: Our bodies will change—

3: Forty will be selected for seven years of training—Bootcamp-

2: Booya—

1: At the end of 7 years 4 will be chosen—

4: —To make the ten month flight to Mars.

5: Doesn't even sound possible—

3: There was a time—

1: Once on the way there's no aborting—if anything goes wrong- no turning around—

5: Total commitment—

3: Buzz Aldrin- Armstrong—

4: HOLY SHIT BATMAN! Can you imagine—

2: *(imitating Armstrong—)* One small step for man—

5: What America used to be—

4: Beautiful—

3: Fearless—

1: Of course there has to be informed consent-Weightless environment poses health risks—Along with an increased risk of cancer due to the effects of space radiation. A higher risk for women.—

3: We used to be known for risk taking—It's time to step in front of the line again—

1: The crew would rely on a closed-loop life support system: recycling water urine and sweat—

2: Time to show the world what we're made of—

1: There may be injuries sickness and death—

4: Have to be able to take care of yourself—

1: No emergency rooms up in space-If you make it—

3: When we do—

1&2: Barren—red desert—

1: Carbon dioxide atmosphere—

4: *(delighted)* Spacesuits every time we want to go outside! The live and work spaces—Interconnected inflatable pods on the surface of the planet!

1: The atmosphere not breathable and the temperatures could either freeze you or burn you up.

3: *(game for anything)* We may have to live underground—

4: To be the first! Well worth the sacrifice—

5: Her celestial beauty—

3: Like a regal red boned gal—Billy Holiday—

2: Like Beyonce—

2,3,4&5: —shaking and shimmering in the night sky—

(As #1 SHADOW BOXES)

4: I stare up into heaven- mesmerized—

2: 38 dollars for a chance of a lifetime—I'm down.

(#1 Stops Boxing)

1: The price of the mission—over 6 billion dollars—to be paid by selling the tv rights—

3: Like the Olympics—

1: So the world can watch the selection process, the training, the space travel and the subsequent life on Mars. Viewers would vote on the final 4.

(Each recording themselves on ipads and smartphones—)

2: I work as a supervisor at the Super Kmart in Galveston. Been working there since junior high. Always was a science nerd— Was always the class clown—

3: Where I'm from- moving from block to block is an adventure.

4: I love horror movies and amusement parks—I love the rush of the roller coaster—

3: All my friends are dead.

4: I love bungy jumping- I work in IT. I like helping people solve problems—

5: When I was a little girl I used to sit up in the pecan tree and look up in the sky—thought that I could touch the moon—

2: What weighs more—2 lbs of feathers- or 2 lbs of rocks—

5: Always dreamed of being free-

2: They both weigh 2 lbs—badump!

5: Free of gravity. Free of the burdens of this world-

2: A neutron walks into a bar and the bartender says—"for you- no charge"—ba-dump. I got a million of them- literally—a million /o them—

5: —I'm studying to be a nurse—

2: This is more than anything I can hope to accomplish here.

3: Varsity Football in School—Graduated with a degree in engineering. Always loved Sci Fi—

2: If Iron Man and Silver Surfer got together- they would be-

3 & 2: Alloys!

2: BAdump!

4: And I'm a good person. I think that should count.

(they stop filming themselves)

1&5: Nothing to do now but wait—

2: Have to get out of here.

4: Can't stay here—

3: In under a hundred years we'll be able to travel to Mars in under a month—

5: In under a hundred years we can travel in under a week—

4: Hours

2: then seconds—

3: Mars will be ours—

2: To start clean—

3: Fresh—

5: Pure.

4: I want to be part of the solution.

(All look towards #1)

1: They are coming. I can hear them.

(As lights go down- 2/3/4/5 are lit by their ipads or cell phones—Their heads appear to float bodiless in space— We HEAR MUSIC: "East of the Sun West of the Moon"— As they speak, sing or hum:)

2,3,4&5: East of the sun and west of the moon
   We'll build a dream house of love dear
   Close to the sun in the day
   Near to the moon at night
   We'll live in a lovely way dear
1: They'll be here in the blink of an eye-
   And then—
   What will happen to me then?—
2,3,4&5: Sharing our love in the pale moonlight
   Just you and I, forever and a day
   Love will not die; we'll keep it that way
   Up among the stars we'll find a harmony of life to a lovely
   tune
   East of the sun and west of the moon
1: No—Not without a fight.

   (We see #1/ MARS shadow boxing—)

   Lights out.

   End of Play.

Fully Accessible

Bruce Graham

ORIGINAL PRODUCTION

Produced by Theater Breaking Through Barriers at the Clurman Theatre—Theatre Row June 13-28

Directed by Christina Roussos

CAST:
DONNELLY: Ann Marie Morelli
VICKI: Mary Theresa Archbold
SECURITY: Shawn Randall

SETTING: This theater. Day.

A theatre. Work lights illuminate. The stage is empty except for DONNELLY, a woman in a wheelchair.

DONNELLY is primly dressed, looking very "official." A briefcase sits next to her chair. On her lap is a clipboard with a form on it.

DONNELLY glances at her watch. She has been waiting a few minutes and is not pleased about it.

The door at the back of the house opens and DONNELLY perks up as VICKI CALDWELL enters.

DONNELLY: Ms. Caldwell?

(Vicki is shocked. She did not expect anyone. Vicki is very casually dressed. Sneaker, jeans.)

VICKI: Yes.

DONNELLY: Your assistant said you were down here.

VICKI: Oh.

DONNELLY: But you weren't—were you?

(Vicki moves to the foot of the stage.)

VICKI: Well, I'm sorry, but you're a little early.

DONNELLY: I'm not supposed to be here at all so how could I be early? Little lapse in logic here, Ms. Caldwell.

VICKI: Aren't you with—

DONNELLY: No, I'm not. Agent Donnelly. I'm with MOFA.

(She flips an ID and puts it away.)

VICKI: MOFA?

DONNELLY: The Mayor's Office of Full Accessibility. The office was formed to be in compliance with directive B6092 dash 7 of the Americans with Disabilities Act. This is a surprise site inspection.

(a beat)

Surprise.

VICKI: An inspection?

DONNELLY: A *surprise* inspection. Therefore I can't be early or late because that would imply the visit was scheduled, thus eliminating the surprise.

VICKI: I'm sorry but I'm not familiar with your office.

DONNELLY: That's painfully obvious, Ms. Caldwell.

VICKI: Call me Vicki.

DONNELLY: I prefer professional formality. I'm not a theatre person. Your front door. The automatic one—the disabled accessible door.

VICKI: Yes.

DONNELLY: The one with the international disabled sign. The little bald stick figure with his buttocks encased in a circle indicating a wheelchair.

VICKI: I'm familiar with it.

(Vicki waits. Donnelly says nothing at first.)

DONNELLY: Hate that sign. Incredibly sexist. Little bald stick figure. Obviously a man.

(she lets out a profoundly disgusted sigh)

Anyway . . . your front door.

VICKI: Yes.

DONNELLY: It's incredibly slow. From the time I hit the little wheelchair man button to the time it fully opened—

(consulting form)

Seven-point-one seconds. Now, what if I was running late for a show—

VICKI: That door is designed to open slowly. A lot of people use it and if it just swung open quickly they could get hit.

DONNELLY: Are these people disabled?

VICKI: No, not all of them.

DONNELLY: Then they deserve to get hit. Ridden your elevator lately, Ms. Caldwell?

VICKI: Just now.

DONNELLY: Any trouble reaching the buttons?

VICKI: No.

DONNELLY: 'Course not. I do believe you're . . . standing. What if you had been in my position?

(Donnelly makes an ominous looking note on her clipboard form.)

VICKI: You seem to have gotten here all right.

DONNELLY: And I had to strettttchhh. What if I was a disabled little person?

VICKI: Little person like a midget or something?

DONNELLY: I'll ignore that insensitivity. Picture this scenario. A little person in a wheelchair goes into your elevator. She has short arms and stubby little fingers. The doors close. And what happens? Nothing—because she can't reach the buttons! She's stuck in there screaming—

(She waves her arms like a tyrannosaurus rex and adopts a a voice like a Munchkin on helium.)

DONNELLY: "Help, help! I can't reach the buttons!"

VICKI: Pardon me for saying this but that seems a bit insensitive towards little people.

DONNELLY: Hey, some of my best friends are little people.

(Donnelly watches as Vicki climbs the step unit to the stage)

Nice . . . non-ramp you have there.

VICKI: If a little person in a wheelchair came to a show here one of our employees would have been happy to help him or her with the elevator buttons.

DONNELLY: That's not much help on a Tuesday morning, is it? Unless you have really weird matinees here—

VICKI: Agent Donnelly, this is not a good time. We're expecting a load-in any minute.

DONNELLY: What's the play?

VICKI: *(thrown)* Endgame.

DONNELLY: Love *Endgame*.

(pointedly)

Hamm's in a wheelchair.

VICKI: I know.

DONNELLY: *Man Who Came to Dinner*. That's a good play.

VICKI: Yes.

DONNELLY: And *Little Foxes*. The husband's in a wheelchair. Drops his heart medicine and the new bottle's upstairs. But he can't get to it and he dies. Know why?*(before Vicki can react)* Because his house was not fully accessible.

VICKI: That was also, like, during the Civil War, wasn't it?
DONNELLY: You know what's a really good movie?
VICKI: *(hazarding a guess) Rear Window?*
DONNELLY: Yes! Tell me, is the actor playing Hamm disabled?
VICKI: I don't cast the plays I just rent the theatre.
DONNELLY: I see.

(another note)

Do you hire any disabled here?
VICKI: We have a blind woman who does tele-marketing for us.
DONNELLY: I didn't see her.
VICKI: She didn't see you either.

(realizing)

Oh, no—I meant, she couldn't see you—I mean wouldn't see you—even if she saw—because tele-marketing is upstairs and—
DONNELLY: "Up *stairs*." I see.

(makes note)

Lotta' stairs.
VICKI: We hired a disabled person just last week.
DONNELLY: Really?
VICKI: Just last week.
DONNELLY: What department?
VICKI: I'm . . . not sure.

(Another note.)

DONNELLY: Ms. Caldwell, let me ask you something.

(pointedly)

How could I get onto this stage?
VICKI: Excuse me?
DONNELLY: How could I . . . get on this stage?
VICKI: Audition?

(she begins to laugh)

Get a good agent?

(she laughs harder)

I'm sorry, I'm sorry. I love that joke and I've never gotten to do it. Every time I'm near the park I pray someone asks me, "How do I get to Carnegie Hall?" so I can say, "Practice." So when you asked how you could . . . you know . . . get on the stage . . .

(Donnelly's not enjoying this so Vicki reigns it in and the laughter fades)

I uhh . . . used to do improv.

DONNELLY: O-kay—let me repeat the question. Let's say Hugh Jackman is standing here taking a bow and I'm in the audience and bring him flowers and he motions me to come up there with him. He's straight, you know.

VICKI: Yes, I—

DONNELLY: Just because he does musicals people shouldn't assume he's gay—

VICKI: I didn't say he was.

DONNELLY: All right then. Hugh Jackman motions me to come up on stage with him. How do I get up here?

VICKI: Well, you couldn't. From the house.

DONNELLY: So it's not accessible?

VICKI: It is, just not from down there. You'd have to go out to the lobby and—

DONNELLY: Oh, and in the meantime Hugh Jackman's standing here saying to himself, "Wow, I guess she's not interested." So he calls on some other woman who **can** get up here. One of you Walkies!

VICKI: Walkies?

DONNELLY: So I lose out on meeting Hugh Jackman all because you are not in compliance.

VICKI: Walkie? Is that what you call us?

DONNELLY: Please. Don't act so shocked. As if you never called someone like me a "Wheelie."

VICKI: No, I never have.

DONNELLY: Well, not to our face, I'm sure. I know your type. "Some of my best friends are Wheelies but I wouldn't want my sister to marry one.

VICKI: I don't even have a sister. This is ridiculous.

DONNELLY: Oh sure. Easy for you to say as you're just walkin' around on your . . . your . . . legs.

VICKI: Let's be honest. This is a small theatre. I really doubt someone like Hugh Jackman is ever gonna' do a show here.

DONNELLY: We're hypothesizing. You don't mind, do you—a little hypothesizing?

VICKI: Actually, I don't mean to be rude but no, I don't have time for hypothesizing. This theatre has been inspected and we are in total compliance with the Americans With Disabilities Act of 1990. I have the papers in my office.

DONNELLY: So you're telling me that this theatre is fully accessible to the disabled.

VICKI: You can't get directly on stage to hug Hugh Jackman, no, but everything else—

DONNELLY: *Fully* accessible?

VICKI: Yes.

DONNELLY: I see. And what about your ticket prices?

VICKI: Excuse me?

DONNELLY: Fifty-two dollars for a Wednesday matinee? Plus "handling" charges. You call that accessible?

(Vicki begins to type on her I-Phone.)

VICKI: That's not the "accessible" we're talking about here.

DONNELLY: "Accessible" has many meanings. Have you given any thought - any thought at all—to disabled discounts.

VICKI: Disabled discounts.

DONNELLY: Disabled free tickets would be even better.

VICKI: Are you serious?

DONNELLY: Very serious. And I don't want you to think I'm just picking on your theater. That restaurant next door?

(pointing to clipboard)

They're getting a surprise next. Sixteen dollars for a glass of Merlot. And it's half empty.

VICKI: Wait a minute, wait a minute. It sounds to me as if you're looking for a bribe here.

DONNELLY: You can't bribe a MOFA agent.

VICKI: Because there's no such thing as a MOFA agent!

(showing her the I-Phone)

There is no Mayor's Office of Full Accessibility!

(A beat.)

DONNELLY: We're new.

VICKI: *(into her phone)* I need security in theatre two.

DONNELLY: I wouldn't do that if I were you. I've got a list of violations here—

VICKI: I can't believe this. You want free tickets because you're in a wheelchair. I bend over backwards for you people—

DONNELLY: Whoa—"you people." Careful there.

VICKI: Ramps for you. Audio descriptions for the blind. Signing for the deaf. The trans-gendered people want a third bathroom and the gays want me to get rid of the drapes. It's not really a disability thing—they just don't like the fabric. You know how much of our budget goes to keeping you people — yes, I said it again—you people happy.

DONNELLY: You think it's easy being one of "you people" huh?

VICKI: I'm not saying—

DONNELLY: Well, it's not, lemmie tell you. Stuck in a wheelchair my whole life. Go to get on a bus and everybody hates you because they have to lower the platform. "Oh, one of them. We're never gonna' get there." Having to be one of Jerry's Kids—

VICKI: Jerry Lewis?

DONNELLY: Four years old my parents take me to Vegas. I get put in this room with all these other kids in wheelchairs. They made me hug Liberace! Even at four I knew he was a third rate musician with too much hairspray but I did it. *They made me!* And then we had to gather around Jerry. All these little kids in wheelchairs and we had to just sit there as he sang "You'll Never Walk Alone" to us. Obviously the man doesn't understand irony!

(a deep breath)

Now, knowing all this, you would begrudge me a disabled discount?

(Off stage we hear SECURITY'S VOICE.)

SECURITY: What's the problem here?

(Vicki turns, relieved help is here. Then her face drops as SECURITY enters. He's also in a wheelchair.)

VICKI: You must be the new guy.

SECURITY: Just started. Sorry I took so long. Those buttons in the elevator are rough.

VICKI: I'd like this woman escorted off the property. She does not belong here.

SECURITY: You heard her, let's go.

DONNELLY: No.

> *(Security starts forward; she goes backward. He goes left; she goes right. Vicki just stands there in mild shock watching this whole thing.)*

SECURITY: We can do it the easy way or we can do it the hard way.

DONNELLY: The hard way.

> *(Security pursues her; Donnelly keeps away from him. They begin to drive in a circle with Vicki in the middle.)*

VICKI: Why don't you call some back up?

SECURITY: All under control, ma'am. I don't need a Walkie here to help me.

VICKI: Stop calling us that!

SECURITY: Okay, I'm gettin' out the pepper spray!

VICKI: No pepper spray!

DONNELLY: It's my right as a disabled person to free or vastly-discounted theater tickets!

SECURITY: Okay, you asked for it.

> *(He shoots the pepper spray. Because he's in a fast moving wheelchair, however, it blows back in his face. He lets out a painful scream.)*

SECURITY: Goddamn it! I do that every time!

> *(as he heads off stage)*

Gotta' go the men's room.

> *(to Donnelly)*

I'll be back lady!

> *(He exits. Silence. Finally Vicki turns to Donnelly, who looks very proud of herself.)*

VICKI: I have a show loading in here in five minutes.

DONNELLY: Then you have a problem.

VICKI: Okay . . . okay. If I put you on the comp list will you just get the hell out of my theater?

DONNELLY: Sure.

VICKI: Then please go. Now.

(As Donnelly heads out.)

DONNELLY: Could you make it for two? I hate goin' to the theatre alone.

THE LIGHTS FADE

I Love You I Love You

Josh Levine

ORIGINAL PRODUCTION:
    Produced July 15-23, 2013 at The Kraine Theater, 85 East
    4th Street, New York, NY in Shorts: A Happening.

    Directed by Amy Ashton

    CAST:
    LEEZA: Sarah Randall Hunt
    RALPHIE: Patrick McAndrew
    KATIE: Meg McCrossen
    SHAUN: Brian Patrick Murphy

CHARACTERS:
>   RALPHIE (m): mid twenties, graduate student. Feeling
>   warm.
>   SHAUN (m): mid twenties, graduate student. Feeling
>   cold.
>   KATIE (f): mid twenties, graduate student. Feeling sick.
>   LEEZA (f): mid twenties, graduate student. Feeling
>   REAL good.

THE TIME: Way past their bedtime.

THE PLACE: a disheveled shared living space in an apartment
near campus.

> *At rise: a disheveled shared living space in a college
> dorm. There's a beaten-up old couch, a coffee table with
> one leg being balanced on dvd cases, and a very plain
> desk, as well as two doors that lead off to the two bed-
> rooms. Four young people sit on the ground around an
> almost empty bottle of tequila and a messy pile of play-
> ing cards. RALPHIE sits next to SHAUN who sits next
> to KATIE who sits next to LEEZA who is sitting next to
> RALPHIE. It's way past their bedtime, but they are in the
> middle of a tense card game.*

> *After a moment of concentrated silence:*

LEEZA: Go fish!

KATIE: Shit. I have to take another shot?

SHAUN: That's how we play the game.

RALPHIE: Tequila is not my friend.

LEEZA: It might be tonight!

KATIE: If I throw up, y'all. I have to grade those fools papers tomorrow.

SHAUN: You're not gonna get sick.

> *(Katie takes a card from the pile and pours herself a shot,
> which she downs in one gulp.)*

LEEZA: I am feeling REAL good. Just so everyone knows.

RALPHIE: What'd she say?

LEEZA: She's drunk.

RALPHIE: Is it my turn?

LEEZA: No it's my turn.

RALPHIE: Oh. I wanted it to be my turn.

LEEZA: Ralphie, do you have any jacks?

RALPHIE: No! Go Fish!

LEEZA: My. Pleasure.

> *(Leeza takes a card from the pile and pours herself a shot, which she downs in one gulp.)*

RALPHIE: Shaun, do you have any hearts?

SHAUN: Go fish.

RALPHIE: Fuck. Here we go!

> *(Ralphie takes a card from the pile and pours himself a shot, which he downs in one gulp.)*

SHAUN: Katie, any diamonds?

KATIE: Yes! Thank god.

> *(Katie hands Shaun two cards.)*

RALPHIE: It makes my belly so warm.

SHAUN: I'm freezing.

RALPHIE: You want to wear my hoodie?

LEEZA: It's good though, right?

SHAUN: It's Katie's turn.

RALPHIE: When's it gonna be my turn?

LEEZA: Soon.

KATIE: *(to Leeza)* And I can ask for anything?

SHAUN: Anything you want.

LEEZA: Anything at all.

KATIE: *(after a moment)* Leeza, will you kiss me?

LEEZA: What?

KATIE: I mean, what. I mean, do you have any twos?

LEEZA: Go fish.

> *(Katie takes a card from the pile and pours herself a shot, which she downs in one gulp.)*

KATIE: This game sucks.

SHAUN: Leeza, your turn.

LEEZA: Ralphie, do you want to have a threesome?

RALPHIE: Excuse me?

LEEZA: Do you have any threes?

RALPHIE: Go Fish.

LEEZA: Alright!

(Leeza takes a card from the pile and pours herself a shot, which she downs in one gulp.)

RALPHIE: Shaun, will you give me your heart?

SHAUN: What?

RALPHIE: Do you have any hearts?

SHAUN: Go fish.

RALPHIE: Fuck.

(Ralphie takes a card, pours a shot, and downs it.)

SHAUN: Katie, can I shower you in diamonds?

KATIE: Excuse me?

SHAUN: Diamonds. Do you have any diamonds?

KATIE: Go fish, bitch.

(Shaun takes a card, pours a shot, and downs it.)

RALPHIE: This game is hard.

SHAUN: You just need to know what to ask for.

LEEZA: Katie's turn!

KATIE: Leeza, do you want me to?

LEEZA: Do I have any twos?

KATIE: Sure. Do you have any twos?

LEEZA: Just one.

(Katie reluctantly takes the card.)

My turn!

Ralphie, do you know that I lie awake every night in my bed and dream that the pillow next to me is you?

RALPHIE: *(addressing his cards)* Let me see.

LEEZA: That your skin is soft like my jersey sheets and your hair smells like my laundry detergent?

RALPHIE: Go fish.

(Leeza pours a shot, and maybe takes a card.)

Shaun, do you know that I lie awake every night in my bed waiting for you to find the porn site I left open on my computer in hopes that you'd get curious and take a peek?

SHAUN: *(addressing his cards)* I don't think so.

RALPHIE: Hoping to find that it does give you a boner to see two guys twisted up like tumbleweeds?

SHAUN: Go fish.

(Ralphie pours, and maybe takes a card.)

Katie, do you know that I lie awake in my bed every night with my eyes fixated on your sheets in the hopes that I might will them to slowly slip off your body and onto the floor?

KATIE: *(addressing his cards)* I doubt it.

SHAUN: Letting the moonlight reveal your gorgeous skin floating in the air over your bed like an angel who's fallen from the sky?

KATIE: Go fish.

(Shaun pours, and maybe a card.)

Leeza, do you know that I lie awake in my bed every night listening to you whimper and squeak like a puppy?

LEEZA: *(addressing his cards)* Maybe.

KATIE: Imagining you running through a nightmare with no way out but through the open protection of my arms?

LEEZA: Go fish.

(Katie pours, and maybe a card.)

SHAUN: *(to Katie)* I wash my hair with Leeza's shampoo to smell like her for you.

(Shaun downs his shot.)

KATIE: Go fish.

LEEZA: *(to Ralphie)* I wear Shaun's dirty undershirts beneath my clothes to smell like him for you.

(Leeza downs her shot.)

RALPHIE: Go fish.

KATIE: *(to Leeza)* I use Ralphie's Old Spice deodorant to smell like him for you.

(Katie downs her shot.)

LEEZA: Go fish.

RALPHIE: *(to Shaun)* I sneak into Katie's room and douse myself in her perfume to smell like her for you.

SHAUN: Go fish.

(Ralphie downs his shot.)

KATIE: And the only reason I cut my hair short was so that if you were to squint hard enough like you're looking into an eclipse you'd see me as a man.

SHAUN: And the only reason why I shave my face twice a day is to be softer, more rounded, more gentle for you to touch.

RALPHIE: And the only reason I burn myself in those stale smelling tanning beds till my skin peels off is so that I resemble something darker and less ghostly for you.

LEEZA: And the only reason I had my breasts filleted down like pieces of chicken in a Martha Stewart magazine was to be less of a woman for you.

KATIE: But it hasn't even phased you.

RALPHIE: And you never look my way.

LEEZA: It was obviously for nothing.

SHAUN: Cause you'll never ever touch me.

KATIE: And you haven't even noticed but my hair grew back.

RALPHIE: And you haven't even noticed but my skin grew back.

SHAUN: And you haven't even noticed but my beard grew back.

LEEZA: And you haven't even noticed but my tits grew back.

KATIE: Cause all you do is think of him.

LEEZA: And think of him.

RALPHIE: And think of her.

SHAUN: And think of her.

(A moment. They all look at their cards.)

RALPHIE: Who's turn is it?

KATIE: I don't know.

LEEZA: I don't want another turn.

SHAUN: What time is it?

RALPHIE: My head hurts.

LEEZA: I'm getting hungry.

SHAUN: I have to be at the copy center by 9am.

KATIE: I don't know when I'm gonna grade all those damn papers.

(A moment.)

LEEZA: You want me to get you some Advil, Ralphie?

RALPHIE: I'll just drink some water. You need a ride to work in the morning, Shaun?

SHAUN: I'll walk, should be nice out tomorrow. Let me know if you need any help with your papers, Katie. I flew through mine last semester.

KATIE: It's really not that many. You want some of that caramel popcorn my mom sent, Leeza?

LEEZA: I've got a luna bar in my room.

KATIE: Alright.

RALPHIE: Okay.

LEEZA: Yeah.

SHAUN: I think for the next game night we should just play Sorry.

(They all get up.)

(Someone goes to a door. Someone goes to the desk. Someone rests of the couch. Someone goes to the other door.)

(And then:)

RALPHIE: I love you.

SHAUN: I love you.

KATIE: I love you.

LEEZA: I love you.

(They all turn back around.)

(They are wide awake.)

End of play.

INTERVENTION

C.J. Ehrlich

ORIGINAL PRODUCTION

Produced May 10 2013 by Touch Me Philly Productions LLC, for "Normal . . .?" (a night of original shorts questioning our perception of normality) at The Adrienne Theater, Philadelphia, PA.

Directed by Nathen Wurzel

CAST:
LEON: Cris Welti
SASHA: Amanda Sylvester
WOODY: Glenn Booker
SYD: Jesse PO
MARLENE: Darcie Moloshok

Producers: Alyson Rodriguez Orenstein and Amanda Sylvester of Touch Me Philly Productions LLC.

CHARACTERS:

> MARLENE: female, twenties, Women's Studies major at NYU
>
> SASHA: female, thirties to forties, a university librarian, whose right and left brains are in constant conflict. Wears a fashionable scarf around her neck. Her hair is bound up in stereotypical librarian fashion.
>
> WOODY: male, thirties to fifties, youthful outlook, Leon's dentist
>
> SYD: male, mid to late twenties, a stoner, dropout and campus hanger-on, deli delivery boy, drug dealer and all-round nice guy
>
> LEON: male, ageless, perpetual sophomore, Film major at NYU, youthful, not handsome but possessing a dark, seering charisma. Also he's a vampire.

All characters can be of any ethnicity.

TIME: Tuesday evening, Spring.

SETTING: Marlene and Leon's cheap off-campus apartment in the very East Village.

SYNOPSIS: A diverse group of acquaintances meet to confront Leon with his problem, but nobody agrees on what the problem IS.

UP ON (OPTIONAL): RED LIGHT. A pile of bodies moan and writhe as a police siren wails. Or not.

UP ON: *MARLENE, SASHA, SYD and WOODY sit in a circle of mismatched chairs in Marlene and Leon's shared apartment.*

MARLENE: Just tell him how he, his actions—make you feel.

SASHA: Use "I" not "you" statements. "You make me feel bad when"—

MARLENE: I *said* that. First we support him. Work up to it. Then we shame and break him. Careful - he's got a wicked temper.

SYD: We be in some serious dudu with wacked-out juju.

WOODY: Whoa-ho. Don't want to be here when Leon gets mad.

SASHA: Will he lash out with righteous rage?

MARLENE: Better throw in lots of compliments. But don't drag it out. I have a Semiotics midterm tomorrow.

(she rolls her eyes)

"Cinema of Horror: The Female as Victim".

SASHA: *(using "air quotes")* I'm not here in any "official capacity". But we must support Leon, and his "life choices".

MARLENE: *(growling)* Not all of them!

SASHA: May I remind you that NYU has a "24/7" policy of "tolerance" for our students, be they—

MARLENE: *They're* not students. Syd?

SYD: I'm phly, playa. Woods?

WOODY: I'm down. Solid. We'll straighten him out.

SASHA: Can't we avoid judgmental terms like "straight"!

MARLENE: Sasha, chill. Now it'll be very in-your-face, all of us here—

SASHA: From the diverse quadrants of his complex life—

MARLENE: He may freak. Like if Syd ran into say, Robert Pattison, at the deli.

WOODY: Or, uh, Steven Hawking at the Bowl-o-Rama.

SYD: Don't diss the Hawkman, dude. He can bowl. He can waterski if he so choose. Don't define him by the wheelchair, brah.

SASHA: Judge not what we are or have been, but what we can be. Heleman 7: 6. Just because a man or woman or a—ah—

(she glances at Marlene)

—is differently—ah, abled—what do you prefer to be called?

MARLENE: "Ah"— Marlene.

SASHA: Tell me Marlene. What's Leon like, here in his nest? Does he put on his proverbial pants one leg at a time?

MARLENE: And, his actual pants.

SASHA: Not that you care about his pants—I mean—do you—

MARLENE: Sasha could you possibly keep it in the box? If you must know, Leon and I have a very traditional non-traditional roommate situation. Which includes a lot of—debate.

SYD: Game set match. Steven Hawking rocks.

(SYD and WOODY tap fingers. They will do this often, in a variety of styles.)

SASHA: Where does Leon hide the . . . evidence?

MARLENE: Ugh. He spreads it around everywhere.

WOODY: Be like running into the Pope . . . at the Crusades!

SYD: Homie. The Pope was, like, King of the Crusades.

SASHA: You studied the Crusades? Seen photos of the Crusades.

MARLENE: Why are we talking about this!

SYD: Crusader dudes weren't allowed to take pictures! Homeland Security was tight!

SASHA: The Pope dispatched men to the Crusades. He delegated. Imagine what the infidels would do to the Pope!

MARLENE: *(with a little howl)* People. Look into my not-happy eyes. We are WAY off topic.

(academic)

Furthermore, women were completely marginalized in the Crusades. Men write the history books. And speaking of the Crusades—Nobody speak of the Crusades. It was a bad time for Leon. He lost, uh, a lot of family.

SASHA: How exotic. He's Maltese?

MARLENE: He's a . . . genealogist.

SYD: Why does he get to examine women's bodies?

WOODY: It's Leon. Think the ladies ask to see his diplomas?

(SYD and WOODY high five.)

MARLENE: Quick intros. Woody is Leon's dentist.

WOODY: Lemme tell you, that's one challenging set of cuspids—

MARLENE: And Syd here is Leon's, uh—

SYD: Friend. We're just friends. Special friends. We get high together. Damn! I say that last part outloud?

SASHA: *(lusty)* And I'm Leon's . . . librarian.

MARLENE: And—? His—

SYD: Technically she's everyone's librarian.

SASHA: *(tart and sweet)* Well no, not yours Syd. Not since you dropped out to chase your fortune as a delivery boy.

SYD: Says the village bicycle of librarians.

SASHA: Quiet, you! Don't think I haven't noticed *The Anarchists Cookbook* is exactly nine years overdue!

SYD: Those records were deleted!

SASHA: Shh! Yet. Despite Leon's horrible, shameful weakness—

MARLENE: Don't say weakness. It implies weakness.

WOODY: It's a rocky life, for sure. What's the hardest thing I ever did? Put braces on the Tyler twins?

SASHA: Despite the tacks he throws under his tires—Leon's brilliant! First NYU student ever to attempt a combined Film/Engineering major.

(EVERYONE gasps, impressed.)

He must fly between classes. And when he's not dissecting cats and crafting edgy film scripts, Leon reads like a shark! You should see him in the stacks, diving into the 909s, churning through the 619s, gobbling the chum of the 157.8s—

(off their looks)

Modern torture, abnormal psychology, experimental medicine.

MARLENE: Ha! Physician heal thyself.

SASHA: But how can he get A's in Visual *and* Fluid Dynamics, yet miss the painfully obvious—?

MARLENE: He skims.

SASHA: And why don't I ever see him at happy hour at McSorley's?

WOODY: She doesn't know—?

MARLENE: We all have parts of our life we try to . . . deny.

SASHA: *I* am an open book.

MARLENE: Sasha. Think. Have you had an actual conversation with Leon?

SASHA: Not exactly—but we're almost a couple, really, as yet to breach the barriers of borrower-lender, student-mentor, victim-stalker—

SYD: So you're saying, there's nothing between you.

WOODY: Except the checkout desk.

SYD: Very smoove, very smoove—

MARLENE: That's Leon for ya. Sash, wouldn't be an intervention without you.

(MARLENE sniffs the air and growls.)

LEON: *(OFF)* MARL?

SASHA: He's coming . . . I feel him. He's very close.

> *(mopping her brow dizzily)*

Oh. Every atom in this rattrap throbs with his presence!

WOODY: We shall overcome!

MARLENE: Act nonchalant! Start with a joke! Speak from the heart—

SYD: You got it, pretzel queen.

SASHA: *(overlapping)* My heart burns to speak!

> *(LEON enters. Does a double take. EVERYONE looks very nonchalant. Then, confused, all rise, except Marlene, to start a slow handclap. MARLENE smacks her head.)*

LEON: This is study group? We're discussing Moby Dick?

MARLENE: *(applauding lightly)* And what an epic it is.

LEON: Sorry. Couldn't get past chapter two. He got it so wrong.

SYD: I only read the reviews.

MARLENE: Spark Notes.

SYD: Movie rocked!

WOODY: They was robbed at the Oscars!

SYD: Remember that sexed-age-anarian, did the one-hand push-ups?

SASHA: Oh I read Moby Dick! But I prefer books about the *Crusades*. Yes, Leon. I know all about your love of the Crusades.

> *(MARLENE smacks her head.)*

LEON: You do? Well she was not a witch! Dumb ass Crusaders.

> *(beat)*

Funny how I know you all—Not you! Who are you? I am Leon.

SASHA: You see me every day, Leon. I'm—

> *(SASHA poses like a librarian.)*

LEON: I don't take judo . . . . Hey, I'm hungry. Get me a drink, Marl. I'll take a Zombie. A Bloody Mary. Or . . . something stronger.

MARLENE: Always thirsty!

SASHA: No! Resist!

SYD: Sha-wing! A joke! A vampire, an axe murderer, a guy with a hockey mask and a rabbi walk into a blood bank—

LEON: This is more than weird. And how come nobody has a copy of Moby Dick? Yeah. So, I have this date under the High Line with this cute marketing major—

(LEON tries to leave. SASHA springs up.)

SASHA: Cancel that date! Think of your liver! I . . . compel you—

(LEON puts SASHA in a trance. After this she is very dreamy. MARLENE gestures, emphatically. Completely confused, EVERYONE slowly shouts:)

ALL: SUR . . . PRISE . . . ?

LEON: Is it my birthday? *Again.*

MARLENE: It's your intervention!

LEON: The hell?

MARLENE: We, your nearest and dearest, or the next best thing, are here to tell you. Leon. We like you just the way you are. But your choices suck!

LEON: It's an experimental film. Fine! I'll cut the eyeball scene!

MARLENE: Leon, it's the goddamn 21st century!

(They ALL nod their heads. Pause.)

LEON: Damn it Marlene! You OUTED me? To my dentist, drug dealer and the judo coach? . . . Great! Get out the Ajax, I have to kill em all.

MARLENE: That is such a defense mechanism.

LEON: Now I have to change my name and transfer again. Princeton better have smarter professors than they did in 1832.

SYD: We're your buds, Count Chocula.

WOODY: I already know! You always tell me you hate yourself, the morning after.

LEON: I do? Geez. What's in that nitrous?

SYD: Think we could go on a vision quest, without you unburdening your immortal soul?

LEON: Syd, you still get high with me. Woody, you clean my teeth—

WOODY: They're kind of a tip-off.

LEON: Wow. It's been building up inside me for so long, this craving for real connection. After 900 years of mystery I finally spilled my guts. And you like me. You really like me.

WOODY: So, you're an immortal blood-sucking demon. My second wife was twenty-eight years younger.

MARLENE: What are you all talking about? We're here to confront Leon's rampant sexism! And his knee-jerk opposition to gay marriage.

SYD: Bigotry? Uncool, bloodman!

WOODY: Really . . .? Not the vampire thing?

MARLENE: Well if you want to go with that—! Leon you're a misogynist caveman, a homophobe, an undead blood-sucking demon, and your films are inaccessible. It's wrong wrong wrong.

LEON: I gotta be me.

MARLENE: You *use* women! Look at her.

> *(SASHA takes off her scarf, revealing two bloody puncture wounds on her neck.)*

SASHA: *(dreamily)* I love you, Leon. But you seducing me over and over, sucking my blood 'til I black out then wiping my memory and leaving me to wallow in my loneliness and borderline alcoholism—well sometimes I think it's about your own pleasure.

MARLENE: This is who you want to be?

LEON: Like you have nothing to hide. What's that I hear? Credence Clearwater singing "Bad Moon Rising"? Oh, are we out of Nair again? Folks, you'll be shocked to learn that my roommate is a very hormonally challenged moon-chasing woo—

SYD: A woof? A woolly mammoth.

WOODY: A Wookie! How many syllables?

MARLENE: Whoa! Not my intervention! And not that you'd notice, I haven't attacked a human since I met Kiki, Spring break in the Yukon. If I can change, so can you.

LEON: I have it totally under control—trust me. She likes it.

> *(LEON bites Sasha's neck, erotically.)*

MARLENE: Complete denial. And this is like, every night. Plus he never does the dishes.

LEON: A few hobos, a couple vagrants, now and then a freshman pre-law! I'm like a public service.

SYD: Heartless murder? Super uncool, bloodman.

LEON: I don't kill them all. Usually I just put irrational fear into their hearts and they transfer to a nice safe place, like the Army.

MARLENE: Wait'l you get staked through the heart, Mr. Public Service—

WOODY: Can we talk abstinence?

SASHA: Abstinence . . . Is like a drug . . .

WOODY: How do you like small animals?

SASHA: They are . . . very cute . . .

LEON: I drank only pigs' blood from Oliver Cromwell to frigging Calvin Coolidge. Barnyards get old after 300 years!

SYD: Meditation, yoga and herbal remedies? Also I have some kick butt quay-yays.

WOODY: Synthetic plasma gets "bloodier" every day.

LEON: But the aftertaste—!

MARLENE: Try to adapt. For us? One day at a time.

(SASHA nods through her trance.)

LEON: I can cut down . . . She's a near perfect vessel. With just a hint of creme de menthe.

SASHA: We'll be . . . exclusive?

LEON: Just you. And now and then a few politicians. So, who wants to play the uptight librarian meets the insatiable vampire?

(LEON gathers SASHA into his arms.)

MARLENE: And? *And*—?

LEON: And . . .

(he sighs)

Who wants to see the Twilight marathon, after.

SASHA: And go out for gelato? Oh, Leon.

MARLENE: *(howling)* Woo HOOOOOO!

SYD: Dude, I love interventions!

END OF PLAY

Lost in Thought

Christopher Lockheardt

Original Production
Simple Machine
Boston, MA
857-574-0550

May 12, 2013

Directed by Adrienne Boris
Fight Choreographer: Meron Langsner

Cast:
MAN: Stephen Libby
WOMAN: Anna Waldron
TOM: Tim Hoover

CHARACTERS:
    MAN: any age
    WOMAN: similar age
    TOM: male, similar age

SETTING: The play is set within the memories and imagination of a man washing dishes.

AT RISE:

(At center stage, a MAN is washing dishes, lost in thought. A WOMAN enters right. She takes a few steps towards the man. He does not look at her.)

WOMAN: There's something extraordinary about you.

(The man freezes for a moment and then returns to his dishes. The woman crosses the stage to stand on the other side of the man, but a half-step closer.)

Do you like this spot? I drive up here all the time when I need some quiet . . . and privacy.

(The man continues washing dishes, but a grin sneaks onto his face. The woman moves to a new spot, a half-step closer.)

Excuse me? I know this sounds weak and helpless, but . . . I can't reach that box of cereal. Would you mind? I must be the only one who buys that brand because the store always puts it on the top shelf.

(The grin widens. The woman moves to a new spot, a half-step closer.)

Oh my God. That was . . . AMAZING. I can't . . . I can't even breathe. How did you ever learn to do that? Did you take a class or something?

(The grin breaks open into a smile. The woman moves to a new spot, a half-step closer.)

It's always the same. Every time you have a choice, you never choose me. Never.

(The grin falters. The woman moves to a new spot, a half-step closer.)

What are you doing here? What could you possibly want? How simple do I have to make this for you before you understand?

(The grin fades. The woman moves to a new spot, a half-step closer.)

There's something extraordinary about you.

(The grin disappears. The woman moves to a new spot, a half-step closer. The woman's lines come quicker and quicker as she spirals in closer to the man. His reactions to them become more and more stony.)

WOMAN: You know what I miss? I miss feeling pretty. I used to feel so pretty around you. You used to make me feel beautiful.

(Move.)

This is where I always want to be. Curled up with you, my head on your shoulder. I never want to leave this spot. I want to stay here forever.

(Move.)

Don't say that. Of course I miss you. I miss you every day. But missing you has nothing to do with it. You know that, right? Right?

(Move.)

You remember me? The short girl with the inconvenient taste in cereal? I don't usually do this. I mean, I absolutely never do this, but . . . . Would you like to . . . Would you be free sometime to . . .?

(Move.)

Don't look like that. You knew this was coming. You wanted it to come.

(She is now leaning on his shoulder, her mouth whispering in his ear.)

There's something extraordinary about you.

(He grabs her. For a moment they lock eyes. Then he spins her around and gently but forcefully marches her offstage. Once she is gone, he returns to his dishes. He

stands over the sink, his head bent. Then he takes a big breath and thrusts his hands back into the water.)

(The woman returns. She enters, takes a few steps toward him, and stops, frozen.)

(He sneaks a glance at her and then returns to his dishes. He sneaks another glance. And another. He turns and looks at her. He walks over to her.)

(He stands in front of her. She remains frozen. He takes her wrist and raises her arm, stretching it out above and in front of her. Her arm remains in that position. He then adjusts her other limbs until she appears to be straining towards something out of her reach. He walks behind her.)

MAN: Still hungry for the hard-to-reach stuff, eh?

    (Pause.)

    Still craving what you can't get, eh?

    (Pause.)

    Still have a taste for the inconvenient, eh?

    (Pause.)

    Need a hand, stranger?

    (She unfreezes and spins around.)

WOMAN: Oh. Hi.

MAN: Hi.

WOMAN: How are you?

MAN: Miserable. Heart-broken. Lost.

    (She freezes. He rethinks. She unfreezes.)

WOMAN: Oh. Hi.

MAN: Hi.

WOMAN: How are you?

MAN: Better. Slowly. But . . . you know . . . surely. Mostly, that is.

    (She freezes. He rethinks. She unfreezes.)

WOMAN: Oh. Hi.

MAN: Hi.

WOMAN: How are you?

MAN: Good. Good. How are you?

WOMAN: Good. You heard about me and Tom, I assume.

> *(She freezes. He stares at her. He then returns to the dishes. He stands over the sink, his head bent. Then he takes a deep breath and walks back to the woman. He adjusts her frozen limbs until she appears to be straining towards something out of her reach. He walks behind her.)*

MAN: I thought you were settling for the bottom-shelf brands now?

> *(She unfreezes and spins around.)*

WOMAN: What is that supposed to mean?

MAN: I heard about you and Tom. Congrats.

WOMAN: You're such an arrogant prick, you know that?

MAN: No, really. Well done. He sounds like an extraordinary guy.

WOMAN: I can't believe you. I don't see you in months and suddenly you're sneaking up behind me in the grocery store and—

MAN: Months? It hasn't been months! Years! I haven't seen you in almost two years!

WOMAN:—sneaking up behind me and abusing me about—

MAN: You call this abuse! I tell you what abuse is! Abuse is me showing up at your door and you . . . and you . . .

> *(She freezes. He stares at her. He then returns to the dishes. He stands over the sink, his head bent. Then he takes a deep breath and walks back to the woman. He adjusts her frozen limbs until she appears to be straining towards something out of her reach. He walks behind her.)*

Need a hand, stranger?

> *(She unfreezes and spins around.)*

WOMAN: Oh. Hi.

MAN: Hi.

WOMAN: How are you?

MAN: Good. Good. How are you?

WOMAN: Good. You heard about me and Tom, I assume.

MAN: Yeah, that's . . . great. Tom's great. He's really . . . I've heard he's a really nice guy.

WOMAN: He is.

MAN: That's good, because . . . because you deserve a nice guy. You know? You really do.

WOMAN: Thanks. Listen . . . I'll see you around, okay?

MAN: Yeah. Okay.

(She exits. He watches her go. Then he returns to the dishes. He stands over the sink, his head bent. Then he takes a big breath and thrusts his hands back into the water.)

(The woman returns. With her is TOM. They are holding hands. They enter, take a few steps toward him, and stop. They begin slow dancing.)

(The man sneaks a glance at them and returns to his dishes.)

(The woman begins running her hands through Tom's hair and caressing his cheeks. The man sneaks another glance at them. He returns to his dishes.)

(The woman begins passionately kissing Tom. The man sneaks another glance at them. He returns to his dishes.)

(The woman whispers in Tom's ear.)

WOMAN: Do you like this spot? I drive up here all the time when I need some quiet . . . and privacy.

(The man does not look up from the dishes. The woman whispers in Tom's ear.)

Oh my God. That was . . . AMAZING. I can't . . . I can't even breathe. How did you ever learn to do that? Did you take a class or something?

(The man does not look up from the dishes. The woman whispers in Tom's ear.)

You know what I like? I like feeling pretty. I feel so pretty around you. You make me feel beautiful.

(The man does not look up from the dishes. The woman whispers in Tom's ear.)

WOMAN: There's something extraordinary about you.

(The man rushes the couple in a rage. He knocks Tom to the ground and begins punching and kicking him. The woman watches silently. The man pummels Tom until he is too exhausted to continue. He looks at the woman. She stares back at him expressionless. He stumbles, sick with shame, back to the sink. The woman helps Tom to his feet. They begin slow dancing again.)

TOM: Darling?

WOMAN: Yes, love?

TOM: Do you . . . do you ever think of him?

WOMAN: Who?

TOM: You know.

WOMAN: Oh. No, never. Why?

TOM: I just thought maybe . . .

WOMAN: No. There's no point in thinking about him.

TOM: Why is that?

WOMAN: Because I can't imagine him ever thinking about me.

BLACKOUT

MOTHRA VS THE CASTING DIRECTOR: AN ALLEGORY

David Bar Katz

ORIGINAL PRODUCTION
> City Theatre
> John Manzelli, Artistic Director
> Susan Westfall, Literary Director & Co-Founder

Directed by Margaret Ledford

CAST:
HOWARD: Todd Allen Durkin
LAURA: Renata Eastlick
MOTHRA: Ken Clement
SHOBSHIN : Irene Adjan

WINNER—National Award for Short Playwriting, 2013

Summer Shorts Festival 2013
Presented by City Theatre and the Adrienne Arsht Center
Carnival Studio Theater (at the Ziff Ballet Opera House)
Miami, FL
June 7 - 30, 2013

CHARACTERS:

    HOWARD: male, Casting Director, thirties to fifties.
    LAURA: female, audition reader, twenties to thirties.
    MOTHRA: male, thirties to fifties.
    SHOBSHIN: female, twenties to thirties.

SETTING:

    A casting director's cramped office. The small space is littered with show biz memorabilia.

AUTHOR'S NOTE:

    However outlandish the situation, actors should approach the material as realistically as possible. The casting session is real, as is Mothra and the desperation of his circumstances. He's a struggling, out-of-work (fictional) monster; find those moments when he's willing to do whatever it takes to get the job, then finally snaps.

    Howard, the casting director sits at his desk. Laura, the reader, has just shown someone out. On top of the desk is a miniature of the set-design for a haunted house.

HOWARD: *(yelling to off-stage)* Thanks, Hellraiser! Great audition.

LAURA: Yeah, really scary.

HOWARD: People are going to shit themselves when the real Hellraiser jumps out at them. Great guy.

LAURA: This is going to be the best haunted house, like, ever. *(off of haunted house model)* So many great places for monsters to hide in there.

HOWARD: Who's up next?

    (Laura hands Howard a headshot.)

LAURA: Mothra.

HOWARD: THE Mothra?

LAURA: Yeah. He sent his reel.

HOWARD: Shit.

(Laura pushes a button on a remote and footage of Mothra fighting Godzilla plays on the monitor.)

Enough. I know his work. Just bring him in.

(Laura gets up and opens the door into the hallway.)

Last time Mothra auditioned for me he smelled like bourbon and pussy.

LAURA: *(into hallway)* Mothra?

(Mothra enters. He's a guy with moth antennas, large reflecting sunglasses and huge moth wings. But the conceit is that this is in fact the real Mothra.)

MOTHRA: Howard! How the hell have you been?

HOWARD: Good, Mothra. How are you?

MOTHRA: You know how it is.

HOWARD: Working much?

MOTHRA: Well, they were going to do another Godzilla film. I was set to co-star, then they went with King Ghidora instead.

HOWARD: The three-headed monster?

MOTHRA: Yeah.

HOWARD: Tough break.

MOTHRA: It's okay. I played a judge on an episode of Law and Order last week.

HOWARD: So what are you going to do for us today?

MOTHRA: I've prepared a scene from Alien.

HOWARD: You know this is a hunted house gig?

MOTHRA: What is the ship in Alien but a haunted house in space?

HOWARD: Okay, great.

(Mothra hands pages to Laura.)

MOTHRA: *(to Laura)* Stay with me on this, honey. I never know where it's gonna take me. This is when Sigourney Weaver's character interrogates the decapitated android.

(Mothra gathers himself. He notices how far the reader is from him.)

Move in, honey.

(She moves her chair closer and keeps going per Mothra's instructions.)

Closer. Closer. *(beat)* Closer.

HOWARD: Enough.

(Mothra cues Laura to read.)

LAURA: *(reading)* How do we kill it, Ash? There's gotta be a way of killing it? How? How do we do it?

MOTHRA: *(reading)* You can't.

LAURA: *(reading)* That's bullshit!

MOTHRA: *(reading)* You still don't understand what you're dealing with, do you? Perfect organism. Its structural perfection is matched only by its hostility.

LAURA: *(reading)* You admire it.

(Mothra does the rest from memory.)

MOTHRA: I admire its purity. A survivor . . . unclouded by conscience, remorse, or delusions of morality.

HOWARD: Mothra, let me just stop you there. That was really good. But we need scary, jump out of the dark and freak someone out kind of acting.

MOTHRA: I've freaked out whole cities, Howard. I think I know how to spook jittery children.

HOWARD: Okay, well, let's see some of that then.

MOTHRA: I hear you.

HOWARD: You do?

MOTHRA: Look, Howard, after I leave here I'm auditioning for a non-traditional casting production of Annie and I think what I've prepared for them might be a little bit more in line with what you're looking for.

HOWARD: Mothra, as scary as musical theater is, it's not the genre we're really . . .

(Mothra goes to the door and motions someone else to come in.)

MOTHRA: Shobshin, come in here.

(Mothra yells into the hall in Japanese.)

(An Asian woman enters. She is holding a sleeping bag. Mothra yells at her in Japanese.)

SHOBSHIN: Mister, I told you I don't speak Japanese.

(Mothra barks more instructions at her in Japanese.)

I don't understand. I'm Korean!

HOWARD: *(re. the sleeping bag)* What's that for?

MOTHRA: I need to simulate my pupae stage for this. Gimme a second.

> *(Mothra climbs into the sleeping bag and is entirely encased in it, standing up, with only his face showing. Shobshin hands the sides to Laura.)*

> *(to Laura)*

When Shobshin begins singing my theme song we will begin the scene. Got it?

LAURA: Sure.

> *(Mothra takes a moment to get into character.)*

MOTHRA: This is from Raging Bull.

> *(Shobshin begins the sing the Mothra theme song in Japanese. [The actual fully produced song is played back through the theater and Shobshin lip-synchs to it.])*

> *(Mothra begins the following scene from Raging Bull.)*

Do me a favour.

LAURA: What?

MOTHRA: Hit me in the face.

LAURA: What?

MOTHRA: Hit me in the face!

> *(Shobshin starts dancing around Mothra as she continues his song.)*

LAURA: Forget about it.

MOTHRA: I want you to. Go ahead.

LAURA: I said forget about it.

MOTHRA: We have fights all the time. Go ahead.

LAURA: No!

MOTHRA: You afraid? Come on, hit me.

LAURA: I ain't hittin' you.

MOTHRA: Mothra silk!!

> *(Mothra sprays Laura in the face with silly string which he shoots out so it looks like it's coming from his mouth.)*

Hit me with everything you got!

(Laura hits Mothra.)

Harder!

(She hits him again. Mothra falls to the floor. Shobshin dances around copying their fight movements in her dance.)

You throw a punch like you take it up the ass. Harder!

(Laura's now kicking the shit out of Mothra who's down on the ground.)

Harder! Harder!

HOWARD: Okay, enough.

(Shobshin stops singing.)

MOTHRA: *(from the floor)* What? Too scary?

HOWARD: I'm sorry, Mothra. Shobshin. Out.

(Shobshin exits. Mothra writhes in anguish on the floor.)

MOTHRA: *(desperate)* I need this one, Howard.

(Mothra starts sobbing. He takes some yarn out and starts chewing on it for comfort.)

HOWARD: I'm sorry.

MOTHRA: You're sorry? City destroying giant monsters aren't scary anymore. How does that make any sense? Everyone tells me "Mothra, you have to anthropomorphize. Mothra, you have to anthropomorphize." So here I am looking half-human like a fucking pussy. I'm a giant moth, for christ sakes! People should be shitting themselves!

HOWARD: Look, I'll call you back in for a Time Warner Cable commercial I'm doing next week.

MOTHRA: I'm an actor, Howard. Not a prop. Fucking Mega-Godzilla is playing Richard III uptown!

HOWARD: He's got the training for that kind of thing. Look, you're over-qualified for this. And frankly, moths aren't scary.

MOTHRA: Oh, yeah? Then why in Annie Hall does Woody Allen talk about being creeped out in the country by the moths caught, you know, in a screen door. Remember that?!

HOWARD: That's a joke. It's meant to be funny.

MOTHRA: What the fuck's funny about moth carcasses!?

HOWARD: Look, giant bugs don't scare people anymore. Back in the day you were an allegory for Japanese anxiety over the A-bomb. It just doesn't play anymore.

MOTHRA: If bugs aren't scary why's everyone so freaked out by a big centipede in that indie film?

LAURA: It's a human centipede.

MOTHRA: A human centipede? That's not scary, it's ridiculous.

LAURA: A bunch of people are sewn together mouth to anus to mouth to anus to mouth to anus.

MOTHRA: Okay, so what the hell's that an allegory for?

LAURA: I think it's an allegory for how in our society people sometimes get sewn together mouth to anus to mouth to anus to mouth to anus.

MOTHRA: Well, I just hope the first guy's hungry.

HOWARD: You can't compete with that kind of horror.

MOTHRA: Look, I defeated fucking Godzilla! That's gotta count for something.

HOWARD: This is a haunted house gig. In your most threatening form you're like a block long, right?

MOTHRA: Two. Two blocks.

HOWARD: Mothra, you won't even fit in the building.

MOTHRA: I can stay in pupae form . . . ?

HOWARD: Moth pupae is not scary. Only people wearing cashmere will scream. And I have to mention it . . . You smell like booze.

MOTHRA: Booze? I don't drink. I was working a birthday party and some bitch nanny threw moth balls at me. Let's see you get the smell of naphthalene outta your antennae!

HOWARD: Mothra, you need to go. I have some actually scary monsters waiting to get in here.

> (Mothra's quiet for a moment. He picks up his resume off the desk.)

MOTHRA: Did you see under 'special skills' I horseback ride and . . . ?

HOWARD: Out!

> (Mothra starts desperately tap-dancing.)

What's that? You're tapping? Get the hell out!! You're a joke.

MOTHRA: That's it. I'll show you who's scary.

(Godzilla theme music plays. Lights dim and pulsate. Mothra bursts out of the sleeping bag. Everyone cowers. Sound effects of Mothra attacking fill the theater.)

(Mothra grabs his wings and pulls them back and forth creating a wind that throws Laura and Howard to the ground.)

(Mothra, picks up the model of the haunted house then, squawking and flapping his wings, he stomps on it.)

I'm fucking Mothra!!! I'm still an allegory!!

(Lights dim as he keeps stamping and terrifying Howard and Laura.)

(As the theater darkens a candle appears from far stage-right held by Shobshin. A Japanese cover of "I Don't Know How to Love Him" from Jesus Christ Superstar plays. Mothra calms down and quietly sings along as he is drawn towards the light.)

(singing)

He's just a Mothra. Just a Mothra . . .
Gracefully dancing Mothra follows Shobshin and the candle out of the theater.

Blackout.

Fini

MOVING DAY

Kathryn O'Sullivan

ORIGINAL PRODUCTION
Originally produced on April 26, 2013 in Washington, DC as part of The Theatre Lab's third annual Dramathon at Theatre J. Dramathon producers: Buzz Mauro and Deb Gottesman.

Directed by Lee Mikeska

CAST:
LINDA KELLEHER: Kim Schraf
TOM KELLEHER: Steve Malone
JENNIFER: Kathleen Alvania
MICHAEL KELLEHER: Chris Sell
FUNERAL DIRECTOR: Alisha Johnson

CHARACTERS:

LINDA KELLEHER: Early fifties.

TOM KELLEHER: Fifties, Linda's husband of thirty years

JENNIFER: Mid-twenties to late thirties, Linda's book club friend.

MICHAEL KELLEHER: Mid-twenties, Linda's son.

FUNERAL DIRECTOR: Mid-twenties or older, male or female.

PLACE: A funeral home viewing room.

TIME: The present.

SCENE: A funeral home viewing room.

> *AT RISE: TOM, JENNIFER, and MICHAEL stand at a distance from one another gathered near a casket. Inside lies . . .*
>
> *LINDA, arms crossed over chest, eyes closed.*
>
> *FUNERAL DIRECTOR stands to one side.*
>
> *The room is silent a moment and then Funeral Director steps forward.*

FUNERAL DIRECTOR: *(to audience)* We're gathered here today to honor the life of Linda Kelleher, a beloved wife . . .

> *(Gestures to TOM; he sniffles.)*

. . . mother . . .

> *(Gestures to MICHAEL; he chokes back a sob.)*

. . . and fellow book club enthusiast. *(Nods to Jennifer; she wails uncontrollably.)*
Linda's passing was unexpected, most especially to Linda. That is, after all, the nature of an accident. Nothing can change that. All we can do is move forward. So move on, we must . . . all of us. And that's what I'm here for. To help people move on.

(FUNERAL DIRECTOR retreats. A brief moment of silent prayer and then TOM, JENNIFER, and MICHAEL sigh in unison.)

MICHAEL: I can't believe mom's gone.

TOM: Me either, son.

JENNIFER: Book club won't be the same without her.

(TOM and MICHAEL look at JENNIFER.)

I'm sorry. That sounded stupid. I never know what to say at these things, I mean viewings. See, there I go again.

TOM: It's fine.

JENNIFER: I'm Jennifer by the way. Linda was in my book club.

(TOM smiles.)

TOM: So I gathered. I'm Tom, Linda's husband. This is Michael.

(MICHAEL forces a smile. An awkward pause follows. JENNIFER steals a glance at LINDA inside the casket.)

JENNIFER: She looks so, so . . .

(She wrinkles her nose, sees TOM and MICHAEL looking at her expectantly, and fakes a smile.)

. . . peaceful?

(LINDA's eyes pop open.)

LINDA: Peaceful?

(Sits up.)

Fuck peaceful.

(TOM, MICHAEL, and JENNIFER freeze. LINDA emerges from the casket, stretches, and surveys the room.)

Why are funeral homes always so dark? It's not like the dead are light sensitive. Someone care to explain that?

(She turns to the group for an answer; sees TOM, MICHAEL and JENNIFER, frozen.)

Oh. Right. You can't hear me. I'm

(using air quotes)

dead.

(She sighs, irritated, and turns to the audience.)

I'm supposed to be on the sunny beaches of Hawaii right now, sipping daiquiris, and discussing *Fifty Shades of Grey.* Now that's peaceful. This

(Looks around.)

. . . this ain't peaceful. A word of advice to you lucky folks I hear breathing out there ... Never, ever, trust your GPS. I'm serious. You think that little device with the firm, yet seductive voice is interested in helping you get where you wanna be? You think I was aiming to end up here? I should have followed my instincts instead of that stupid gadget. Gone left instead of right. Gone to the airport instead of off a bridge. That's always been my problem . . . not following my instincts. That's how I ended up with Tom.

(TOM, MICHAEL, and JENNIFER unfreeze.)

TOM: Linda was looking forward to getting away; said the trip would be a fresh start after . . .

MICHAEL: After what?

LINDA: After I told your father I was leaving.

TOM: It's not important now.

LINDA: *(to audience)* But it is important . . . was important.

JENNIFER: I picked out a new Patricia Cornwell novel for our trip. Linda liked those Kay Scarpetta stories. We were going to read on the plane and discuss it when we got to Hawaii.

(TOM looks at JENNIFER, puzzled.)

TOM: Linda was going to Hawaii with the book club?

JENNIFER: No. It was just Linda and me. She said she had a big surprise and didn't want the others around.

LINDA: Here it comes.

MICHAEL: I didn't know mom was going to Hawaii. Dad, why weren't you?

TOM: Your mother told me she wanted to be alone. To be honest, for months I suspected there was someone else. But now . . . well, apparently she was going with a friend.

MICHAEL: Why would you think mom was cheating?

LINDA: I wasn't cheating, not really.

(TOM paces, piecing together bits of information from his memory.)

TOM: It was something about the way she was carrying on. I hadn't seen that look in years. And, I found receipts.

MICHAEL: For what?

TOM: Dinner at the Palm.

JENNIFER: Oh, that was me. Linda and I met up after work one day and she insisted on paying.

LINDA: Just two friends getting together. Nothing unusual about that.

TOM: And tickets to the Joffrey Ballet.

JENNIFER: That was me again. A surprise for my birthday. So sweet.

LINDA: A birthday gift. Perfectly natural.

TOM: And a red teddy from Victoria's Secret. Don't tell me that was for you, too.

> *(LINDA looks heavenward, feigning innocence, and hums.)*

JENNIFER: Maybe the teddy was for you.

TOM: Don't be ridiculous. I haven't seen Linda in lingerie for years.

MICHAEL: *(covering his ears)* Lalalalalalala.

TOM: Oh, Michael, grow up.

LINDA: *(to audience)* He never could handle us talking about sex.

> *(JENNIFER and TOM look off into the distance, lost in thought . . . then, as they put two and two together, slowly turn and stare at one another. An awkward tension fills the air.)*

JENNIFER: So. That was the big surprise.

> *(Pause)*

TOM: So.

> *(Gives JENNIFER the once-over.)*

You're the other man.

MICHAEL: What are you guys saying?

LINDA: Come on, Mikey. You can figure it out.

> *(MICHAEL crosses to and looks in the casket. To Audience)*

What dear Tom can't explain to our son is that years ago, I took a wrong turn

(Gestures to TOM.)

and had finally had the courage to take the right one.

(Indicates JENNIFER.)

(MICHAEL looks at TOM and JENNIFER.)

MICHAEL: Mom's a les . . . a les . . . Mom's gay?

LINDA: Ah, there's my boy. He may not be Einstein, but he's mine.

TOM: Apparently your mother felt there was someone else she'd rather spend her life with. Evidently, that someone was Jennifer.

JENNIFER: But I'm not . . .

TOM: It's okay. I understand.

JENNIFER: No. Really. I'm not gay.

MICHAEL: Mom's a lesbian? Really?

LINDA/TOM/JENNIFER: Yes.

(MICHAEL quiets.)

JENNIFER: Okay. There was one time in college but that's it. Linda and I were friends. Good friends. But nothing more.

(JENNIFER, TOM, and MICHAEL freeze. Their poses should be exaggerated but not overly so.)

LINDA: What do you mean nothing more? What about that female romance novel you chose for the club? What was that if not a sign? And after the ballet? You kissed me on the cheek. I felt that kiss for hours. What was that?

(She moves away from the group.)

Oh, gees, the trip. What if I hadn't died? What if I had ended up in Hawaii with Jennifer? There I would've been, half-naked in a red teddy on an island declaring my love to someone who didn't love me. I would've made a fool of myself.

(FUNERAL DIRECTOR crosses to LINDA and taps her gently on the shoulder. To FUNERAL DIRECTOR)

Yeah, yeah, just a minute.

(to herself)

Thank goodness for the GPS. If I hadn't listened to those directions I'd still be alive, humiliating myself.

(FUNERAL DIRECTOR taps LINDA.)

Just a minute, I said.

(FUNERAL DIRECTOR taps again.)

FUNERAL DIRECTOR: Linda.

(LINDA is startled.)

LINDA: How . . . how long have you been able to hear me?
FUNERAL DIRECTOR: Since you opened that mouth of yours.
LINDA: Hey. Show some respect for the dead.

(FUNERAL DIRECTOR smiles.)

FUNERAL DIRECTOR: It's time.
LINDA: Time? For what?
FUNERAL DIRECTOR: To move on.
LINDA: I hate to break it to you, but I've already moved on.
FUNERAL DIRECTOR: Not completely.

(LINDA eyes FUNERAL DIRECTOR.)

LINDA: You're not a funeral director, are you?
FUNERAL DIRECTOR: Think of me as your new and improved
    GPS.
LINDA: In case you hadn't noticed, me and GPS don't exactly
    have a great track record.
FUNERAL DIRECTOR: I'm different.

> *(LINDA paces then spots MICHAEL, TOM, and JENNI-*
> *FER in their frozen tableau.)*

LINDA: But what about my son?
FUNERAL DIRECTOR: Your son will be fine.
LINDA: And my husband. Look how heartbroken he is.

> *(LINDA and FUNERAL DIRECTOR look at TOM. His*
> *pose is anything but heartbroken. TOM, JENNIFER, and*
> *MICHAEL unfreeze.)*

JENNIFER: *(to TOM)* Listen. I didn't come here to cause any
    trouble. I really had no idea how Linda felt. I told you, I'm
    not good at these things.
TOM: That's true.

(A pause, and then JENNIFER and TOM smile.)

JENNIFER: I know we didn't start out on the right foot, but maybe you and Michael would like to join me for a bite to eat at the diner?

TOM: That would be nice.

MICHAEL: I am kinda hungry.

> *(LINDA watches TOM, JENNIFER, and MICHAEL pause at her coffin.)*

Mom was gay.

> *(with a shrug)*

Hm.

> *(They exit. LINDA crosses to her coffin, looks in, and then moves away.)*

LINDA: You know what it's like to live without being able to fully express who you are?

> *(Glances at FUNERAL DIRECTOR.)*

No. Of course, you don't. It's difficult in the beginning. But each day, little by little, it gets easier until one day you find yourself married to a decent man with a loving son and you have no idea who you are. Then someone like Jennifer comes along, young and beautiful and easy, and you rediscover emotions you hadn't felt in decades. A cloud has been lifted. You're alive and free. You plan a trip to Hawaii, to live the life you know you were always meant to, and just when you're at the brink of finding happiness, you take a wrong turn and drive off a bridge.

> *(Looks at FUNERAL DIRECTOR.)*

I'm afraid.

FUNERAL DIRECTOR: Of what?

LINDA: Getting lost. Going in the wrong direction again. If I make a wrong turn here …

> *(Gestures as if toward Hell, whispers.)*

… who knows where I'll end up.

> *(FUNERAL DIRECTOR holds out his hand.)*

FUNERAL DIRECTOR: So trust your instincts.

(LINDA hesitates, crosses to FUNERAL DIRECTOR, nods, and sighs heavily.)

LINDA: I really wanted to go to Hawaii.

FUNERAL DIRECTOR: Believe me; this is going to be way better than Hawaii.

(LINDA smiles, takes FUNERAL DIRECTOR's hand.)

(Lights fade)

END OF PLAY

My Body

Rachel Bublitz

ORIGINAL PRODUCTION

My Body was produced with Subversive Theatre Collective in Buffalo, New York. It ran from June 13th - July 7th, 2013, with other short political plays.

Directed by Gary Earl Ross

CAST:
LAURA: Deborah Krygier
PATRICK: Kevin Dennis
SALLY: Kevin Dennis

CHARACTERS:
> LAURA: Female, thirty-five to fifty-five, any race, has
> an authoritative presence.
> PATRICK: Male, twenty-eight to thirty-five, any race.
> SALLY: Female, twenty to thirty, any race.

SETTING: An office.

TIME: The future.

> *We are in a LAURA's government office. LAURA is on
> stage. LAURA presses the button on her intercom.*

LAURA: Sally, please send in my next appointment.

> *(PATRICK enters. PATRICK wears a robotic looking col-
> lar around his neck.)*

Good afternoon, my name is Laura Goodman. I'll be review-
ing your case today.

PATRICK: Good afternoon.

LAURA: You want approval for the permanent removal of your
collar, correct?

PATRICK: Yes ma'am.

LAURA: And you have all of your paperwork in order?

PATRICK: Yes ma'am, it's all there.

LAURA: Please sit down. It's nice to see such a young man with
his priorities straight. Well, hand over your paperwork.

> *(PATRICK hands LAURA a thick questionnaire. LAURA
> begins to read.)*

PATRICK: I've included three letters of recommendation, instead
the minimum of two.

LAURA: I see, very nice. Patrick Hill, is it?

PATRICK: Yes.

LAURA: This is very well organized. I can tell that you took the
time. You'd be amazed at how many botched applications I
get in here every day.

PATRICK: I can only imagine.

> *(LAURA turns the first page and begins to read the sec-
> ond page.)*

LAURA: Steady income, you've been teaching for seven years?

PATRICK: That's correct.

LAURA: What grade do you teach?

PATRICK: Second grade.

LAURA: Like the little ones, do you?

PATRICK: I do.

LAURA: That's nice. And I see you passed all of the disease screenings.

PATRICK: There were a lot of tests.

LAURA: We're very serious about what we do here.

PATRICK: I can see that.

(LAURA turns to the next page in the paperwork.)

LAURA: Oh, there seems to be a mistake here.

PATRICK: There is?

LAURA: Are you married?

PATRICK: No.

LAURA: Engaged?

PATRICK: No.

LAURA: Are you homosexual?

PATRICK: No.

(Pause.)

LAURA: Is this some sort of practical joke?

PATRICK: I'm sorry?

LAURA: Did Sally put you up to this?

PATRICK: Sally?

LAURA: My assistant. She thinks she has a great sense of humor.

PATRICK: Sally has nothing to do with this. I'm here to have my collar removed.

LAURA: Do you not understand what we do here, Mr. Hill?

PATRICK: I know perfectly well.

LAURA: Then I don't see how you thought you could just waltz in here without a marriage certificate and think that we'd approve your application.

(LAURA opens a drawer to retrieve a "rejected" stamp and proceeds to stamp his application.)

PATRICK: I just thought—

LAURA: (*Interrupting*) That your three letters of recommendation would sway me? You obviously underestimated how serious we take collar removal. Please take your application and leave my office. I have serious applications I need to review.

PATRICK: It's not right.

LAURA: What did you just say?

PATRICK: The collars. It's not fair.

LAURA: Fair? You're talking to me about fair? Are you familiar with our figures Mr. Hill? Since collars have been implemented, we've eradicated sexually transmitted disease. Rape and sexual abuse is down 99%, and there aren't any repeat offenders. Molestation is down 98%. These collars make the world a better place.

PATRICK: But at what cost?

LAURA: What cost? Nothing is more important than the safety of the women and children in this country. You should understand that, being a teacher.

PATRICK: I agree that sexual abuse is wrong, but can you really punish the masses for the mistakes of the few?

LAURA: You categorize rape merely as a mistake?

PATRICK: I think rape is wrong, obviously, and—

LAURA: (*Interrupting*) And child molestation? Is that just another mistake to you? What grade do you teach again?

PATRICK: Second. But I would never—

LAURA: (*Interrupting*) I know you wouldn't. You can't. For the good of us all.

PATRICK: But I have rights!

LAURA: James 1:14, "But every man is tempted, when he is drawn away of his own lust, and enticed. Then when lust has conceived, it brings forth sin: and sin, when it is finished, brings forth death." Giving into your lust and self satisfying is a sin. Besides, abandoning your seed is an abomination! Child abandonment.

PATRICK: It's not a child, it's just . . . It's just biological waste.

LAURA: It's a potential child. Do you know how many unwanted children are born every year in this country?

PATRICK: None.

LAURA: That's right. Zero. The only country in the world. Children today are born into families that have the resources to care for them. The high school drop out rate is nonexistent, and we are at 100% literacy. A far cry from the archaic ways of our past.

PATRICK: But it's my body! Don't I have a say in the matter?

LAURA: Now I know this is a joke. Your body? Are you serious with this rhetoric?

PATRICK: Very serious. It is my body, I have the right to do whatever I want with it.

LAURA: Oh Mr. Hill, it's much too important a choice for us to let you decide it on your own. I mean, every day, day in and out, it's just too much of a temptation for men.

PATRICK: (*Losing his temper*) I'm an adult! I vote, this is my body! Mine! You can't tell me what I can and cannot do with it. I demand that you remove my collar. Remove it now! Right now! I can make good choices, I will make good choices. But it's my body, let me make my own choices!

LAURA: Oh you poor dear. The government has decided that you don't have the mental capacity to make to follow the correct path on your own, and rightly so. We had to take charge. It's for your own good.

PATRICK: But—

LAURA: (*Interrupting*) No buts. Just listen. You have been rejected for collar removal today. Unless you want me to call security, I recommend you leave my office. You should know if I do call security I will stamp your application with my "permanently rejected" stamp. Which will make you ineligible for collar removal.

PATRICK: You have the power to permanently reject me?

LAURA: Oh yes, we also have much more permanent methods for containment.

PATRICK: What would . . . No, you couldn't.

LAURA: It's not pretty Patrick. Go on, get out of here. Go and meet a nice girl, come back when you're settled. You are an excellent candidate, your application was very well organized and we appreciate that. With a wife I'm sure you'll be approved.

PATRICK: Alright.

LAURA: There's a good boy. I'm sure a fine looking man such as yourself won't have a hard time finding a woman.

PATRICK: What? Oh, right. Thanks. (*Pause*) It's torture, what you're doing. You're torturing half of the population.

LAURA: I would love to chat, but I really need to get to my next appointment. Thank you for your time.

PATRICK: But—

LAURA: (*Interrupting*) Remember your manners.

PATRICK: I'm sorry for wasting your time. It was nice to meet you too.

    He exits. LAURA pushes the button on her intercom.

LAURA: Sally once you see Mr. Hill out please step into my office.

    (SALLY enters.)

SALLY: Yes?

LAURA: Did Mr. Hill give you any trouble on the way out?

SALLY: No, he just wandered off. He was rejected?

LAURA: He isn't married, not even engaged.

SALLY: You're kidding.

LAURA: I thought it was your job to review these applications and weed out the bozos.

SALLY: Laura, they're men, they're all bozos.

LAURA: In the future, I expect more professionalism on your part. That application never should have reached my desk.

SALLY: You're absolutely right, it won't happen again.

LAURA: You'll be out of a job if it does, do you hear me?

SALLY: Yes ma'am.

LAURA: Real uppity piece of work that one. Self righteous, you know? He said he wanted control over his body. Like it was his right or something. As if we can trust men to function in society with a working penis.

SALLY: He can't help it Laura. After all, he's only a man.

    SALLY exits. End of play.

ONE LIFE

Mark Cornell

ORIGINAL PRODUCTION

One Life was originally produced by Theatre Three,
Jeffrey Sanzel, Executive Artistic Director.
March 3, 2013.

It ran March 3-April 6, 2013

Directed by Jeffrey Sanzel

CAST:
LUKE: Brian Smith
ACTION: James D. Schultz
THOUGHT: Odell Cureton
FEELING: Tamralynn Dorsa

CHARACTERS:
>   LUKE: male, thirties
>   ACTION: male, forties
>   THOUGHT: male, sixties
>   FEELING: female, twenties

SETTING: The world.

TIME: The course of a lifetime.

NOTE: The character of LUKE should mime all of his action (except for one moment at the end). There should be no props. The chorus, whenever necessary, should represent the characters they describe in their narration, or simply convey, in a broad sense, that those characters are present. They should not stand and talk. They should be active. The play, then, becomes very fluid, almost like a choreographed dance.

>   *A bare stage. A man, LUKE, lies in a fetal position. Around him are ACTION, THOUGHT, and FEELING.*

ACTION: You are born on September 16, 1964 in a hospital on a hill in Fairfield, California.

>   *(LUKE sits up, dizzy and cold.)*

ACTION: *(cont'd)* You arrive two minutes after your identical twin brother. You are disoriented, cold, and your umbilical cord is wrapped around your neck.

>   *(LUKE chokes.)*

FEELING: This is highly upsetting. So you cry. For 12 straight days.

>   *(LUKE cries.)*

ACTION: Your mother names you Luke, and your brother, John. You are baptized in a beautiful, but morose Catholic Church.

>   *(LUKE looks a little frightened.)*

FEELING: The ceremony gives you strange feelings of guilt.

ACTION: You crap a lot.

 (LUKE grimaces.)

FEELING: You enjoy crapping.

 (LUKE smiles, then rises to his feet.)

THOUGHT: Your mother is obsessive-compulsive and likes to dress you and your brother in matching clothes.

 (LUKE looks down at his clothes. "Mom?!")

FEELING: You hate this. So does your brother. It makes you both feel like you have no individual identity.

ACTION: School is mostly a bore, but you're a good athlete, especially in baseball and basketball.

 (LUKE mimes playing baseball and basketball.)

FEELING: It gives you feelings of self-worth . . .

 (LUKE puffs out his chest.)

ACTION: . . . even though your father pushes you, and belittles you, and humiliates you to win at all costs.

 (LUKE deflates.)

THOUGHT: From Catholicism, you learn how to stifle yourself and, at the same time, be judgemental of others.

 (LUKE wags a finger.)

FEELINGS: Your eyes open for the first time when a pony-tailed girl in the third grade calls you a "stuck up turd."

THOUGHT: From your brother, you learn to laugh.

 (LUKE "laughs.")

ACTION: You show an interest in writing. Your brother in painting. These artistic pursuits completely baffle your parents.

FEELING: Your mother just wants you to be a good Catholic boy. Your father wants you to "be a man."

 (LUKE clasps him hands in prayer. Then makes two strong fists.)

ACTION: As you grow up, no one can tell you and your brother apart. People ask questions like "when you wake up in the morning, do you know who you are?"

 (LUKE folds his arms, annoyed.)

THOUGHT: You begin to realize that being a twin can sometimes make others seem very stupid.

ACTION: Your father is a mechanic in the Air Force and the
family moves wherever he is stationed. Ohio, Kansas, Ken-
tucky, Thailand, and back to California.

(LUKE makes like a plane.)

ACTION: *(cont'd)* You make friends, you lose friends.

(LUKE mouths "hello," then waves "goodbye.")

FEELING: You feel your only true friend is your brother.

ACTION: No one comes between you and your brother. Not
even girls.

LUKE puts up a hand, as if to say "stop."

ACTION: *(cont'd)* When you are 16, your father is dishonor-
ably discharged for assaulting a superior officer. Lost, and
full of drink, he deserts the family.

LUKE looks for his father. Then stops.

THOUGHT: You never think of him again.

ACTION: You go to four different colleges before graduating
from UCLA with a degree in English. You're the only one
in your family to graduate from college.

LUKE walks up to get his "diploma."

THOUGHT: You are proud of yourself, but you think all the
other students are smarter than you.

ACTION: Your first real job is in a library. Most of your co-
workers are sociopaths.

LUKE shelves "books," looking worried.

ACTION: *(cont'd)* You marry a half-Japanese financial analyst
when you are 26. She is a pit bull in heels.

(LUKE runs for cover.)

ACTION: *(cont'd)* You divorce within three years.

FEELING: The most hurtful thing she says to you is the last
thing she says, which is "Luke, you were a disappointment."

ACTION: You move back in with your mother, who now lives
in San Francisco. She is good to you . . .

(LUKE slings a "bag" over his shoulder and walks, as if travelling.)

FEELING: . . . but it takes you one solid year to feel like you can breathe.

(LUKE takes a deep breath.)

ACTION: You get a job writing high school sports for a small, North Bay paper.

(LUKE takes notes as if doing an interview.)

THOUGHT: You're inspired by young dreamers with big dreams.

ACTION: You write your first play at 30-years old. It's about baseball.

(LUKE types, excited.)

FEELING: It's the most exciting thing you've experienced in years.

ACTION: Theater people like it.

(LUKE accepts congratulations.)

THOUGHT: But you know it is limited. Because you are limited.

ACTION: It never gets produced.

(LUKE is disappointed.)

FEELING: Still, you feel you are at the beginning of something new and amazing.

ACTION: You go back to UCLA for graduate school in playwriting. Your artistic output is staggering. But success dodges you.

(LUKE writes furiously.)

FEELING: You do not lose hope, though. Writing gives you a purpose.

ACTION: You get a job in marketing at a major regional theatre in L.A.

(LUKE introduces a "marquee sign.")

FEELING: But being so close to the action, without participating, is both a blessing, and a curse.

(LUKE pines.)

FEELING: *(cont'd)* You fall in love with a Quaker girl from Swarthmore, Pennsylvania.

(LUKE touches his heart.)

THOUGHT: She is red-headed and beautiful and smart, but you mistakenly believe you can make her happy.

ACTION: But you really, really try. You get married in Maine and the two of you dream of one day living there.

(LUKE smiles, walks down the "aisle.")

ACTION: *(cont'd)* You move, instead, to Chapel Hill, North Carolina, when she is offered a faculty position at UNC.

(LUKE starts a new life.)

ACTION: *(cont'd)* You have your first and only child at the age of 36. It's a boy. He craps a lot.

(LUKE beats his chest like Tarzan.)

THOUGHT: He seems to like to crap a lot.

ACTION: You stay home with him.

(LUKE paces, rocking a "child.")

FEELING: It overwhelms you.

ACTION: Your son won't eat or sleep. He gets very sick. He looks like he's going to die. But he rallies.

(LUKE frets, then rejoices.)

THOUGHT: And it briefly restores your faith in all things.

ACTION: But he is forever delayed, and out of sync.

FEELING: Still, you treasure his innocence.

(LUKE marvels.)

THOUGHT: Your son has no idea what the words "war" and "gun" mean. He doesn't know about swear words, or loneliness, or heartache. Even at nine-years old, he still believes in Santa Claus with all his heart.

ACTION: So much so that your family celebrates Christmas all year long.

FEELING: Sometimes you feel he is the luckiest kid in the world.

(LUKE smiles.)

ACTION: You write a great play just after your mother passes. The play is about her.

THOUGHT: For the first time as a playwright, you tell the truth.

ACTION: The play goes to New York and gets a spectacular review in the *New York Times*.

> *(LUKE is in awe of New York City.)*

THOUGHT: At 48 years old, you think you have finally arrived.
FEELING: You are beaming.
ACTION: But you never write another great play, because the truth, for you, is elusive.

> *(LUKE turns away, into "obscurity.")*

ACTION: *(cont'd)* Your son drifts through life. He has few friends. He gets into drugs. One day, he falls asleep at the wheel on a back-country road. And dies. He is only 19 years old.

> *(LUKE covers his face.)*

FEELING: The grief is paralyzing.
ACTION: Your fifties are a blur.
THOUGHT: You and your wife spend years in denial.

> *(LUKE wanders, like a zombie.)*

FEELING: When you come out of it, indefinable regrets haunt you. You begin to miss your brother.

> *(LUKE turns towards his "brother.")*

THOUGHT: And at the age of 61, you realize the two of you have not lived in the same state in 35 years.
ACTION: You go to visit him in Florida. He is a massively successful realist painter.
FEELING: There is not, and has never been, any jealousy between the two of you.
ACTION: You play a lot of really bad golf together.

> *(LUKE "golfs." Badly.)*

THOUGHT: You discover how to laugh again.

> *(LUKE "laughs.")*

ACTION: You come home to find your wife in the hospital after a breakdown. You stay by her side for three years. One October night, she tells you you were the love of her life. The next morning, she does not wake up.

> *(After getting to his knees, as if at her bedside, LUKE stands, in shock.)*

FEELING: Her death leaves you numb.

THOUGHT: You don't know what to feel. Hoping to fill the emptiness . . .

ACTION: . . . you move to Maine.

(LUKE drives a "truck.")

FEELING: It is an old dream, and you are an old man, and you feel lost and alone there.

(LUKE turns in many directions.)

ACTION: You move to Florida and live with your brother. Sunshine, everywhere!

(LUKE arrives in Florida. Sunshine, everywhere!)

ACTION: *(cont'd)* One day you run into an old UCLA professor in a cafe and he says he saw your play in New York and it changed his life.

(Listening, LUKE smiles, stunned.)

THOUGHT: But as he pontificates, you realize he's talking about someone else's play.

(LUKE loses the smile.)

ACTION: You go back to church after a long, long time away.

(Now old, LUKE slowly gets on his knees.)

FEELING: It is strangely comforting.

THOUGHT: You think a lot about your mother.

(LUKE clasps his hands and looks up.)

THOUGHT: *(cont'd)* Only now can you appreciate her complete devotion to you and your brother.

ACTION: You start a new play. You want to chronicle your entire life.

(Rising, LUKE writes.)

FEELING: You try to write the truth, but this time you discover you can't write about what hurts.

ACTION: So you don't finish the play.

(LUKE pushes the "play" away.)

ACTION: *(cont'd)* You engulf yourself in your brother's life.

(LUKE meets and greets.)

ACTION: *(cont'd)* But this is his life, and not yours.

> *(LUKE is sad.)*

THOUGHT: And no matter how close you two may be, you are not the same person. You wonder a lot about your life, and what it all means. You wonder "what if?" You think about your innocent little boy. And that beautiful red head from Swarthmore, Pennsylvania.

FEELING: And it crushes you.

ACTION: And then you and your brother go play golf. Badly.

> *(LUKE plays "golf." Badly.)*

FEELING: And you're happy again.

> *(LUKE "laughs" and "laughs.")*

FEELING: *(cont'd)* Until . . .

ACTION: . . . at 81, you have a massive stroke. It doesn't kill you, but you are rendered nearly incapacitated.

> *(LUKE seizes up, then goes still.)*

ACTION: *(cont'd)* On your birthday, your brother gets you both matching baseball uniforms, as a joke.

> *(LUKE "laughs.")*

ACTION: *(cont'd)* You are wearing yours when a second stroke kills you on the back porch of his house.

> *(LUKE lies down.)*

FEELING: You feel no pain. You only feel your brother's hand on yours.

THOUGHT: You're not even aware when it's not there anymore.

ACTION: A light comes.

FEELING: You laugh at the cliché.

> *(LUKE makes an audible laugh. He reaches and reaches for the light.)*

ACTION: Something compels you to reach towards the light.

THOUGHT: And you don't know what that something is.

FEELING: And you hope, above all hopes, that wherever you're going, that one day, your brother . . .

THOUGHT: . . . and your mom . . .

FEELING: . . . and your son . . .

THOUGHT: . . . and that beautiful red head . . .
ALL: . . . will all be there, too.

> *(LUKE lies back, clasps his hands.)*

> *(Lights fade.)*

> *The End*

THE ORIGIN STORY OF LEWIS HACKETT

Ron Burch

ORIGINAL PRODUCTION
   The play was first produced in the 2013 Shorts Festival
   by The Red Brick Road Theatre Company,
   Los Angeles, CA. June 27 - 30, 2013.

   Directed by Emily Mae Heller

   CAST:
   LEWIS: Michael Heiman
   NANCY: Casey Semple
   POLLY: Meggan Taylor
   MIKA (MIKE): Rebecca Kahn
   ADAM: Jarrett Kaufman

CHARACTERS:

    MIKE: a man in his twenties to thirties. Any race.
    ADAM: a man in his twenties to thirties. Any race.
    POLLY: a woman in her twenties to thirties. Any race.
    LEWIS: a man in his thirties to forties. Any race.
    NANCY: a woman in her thirties to forties. Any race.

LOCATION: An office

TIME: Now, kind of

NOTE: In regards to set, five chairs will do the job. Lewis and his boss, Nancy, enact all the stories the workers tell so they change from one thing to the next quickly and seamlessly. Any props may be used but aren't necessarily needed.

> *An office. Two simple locations. On one side of the stage—a desk with a chair or two. On the other side, two chairs. Around the desk stand two men and a woman: MIKE, ADAM, and POLLY. They're all holding coffee mugs.*

ADAM: . . . I still can't believe Lewis Hackett got the promotion. Where'd that guy come from?

POLLY: He worked in sales. What about all of us? We're more qualified.

MIKE: I can't believe Nancy gave it to him.

POLLY: I was next in line. Instead she gives it to that guy.

MIKE: Yeah.

ADAM: I like him.

> *(They look at him.)*

ADAM: What?

MIKE: You know what I heard? I heard they met in a bar.

> *(LEWIS enters followed by NANCY. They cross to the two chairs.)*

LEWIS: Could I buy you a drink?

NANCY: Okay.

LEWIS: Want to fuck?

NANCY: Sure!

LEWIS: But just so you know: I need a job.

NANCY: Don't worry. If you're good, you're getting the promotion.

POLLY: I heard it was a restaurant.

LEWIS: Could I buy you an entree?

NANCY: Sure.

LEWIS: Would you like . . .

> *(sexily)*

. . . dessert?

NANCY: If it's good, you're getting the promotion.

MIKE: No, no, no. Stop being petty, you guys. I heard it was nepotism. They're related or something.

LEWIS: Hey, aren't you my fourth cousin on my mother's side?

NANCY: Is your Mom Betty Lou Susie Angelena Orndorf?

LEWIS: Yeah, I heard there was a promotion up for grabs.

NANCY: Are you even qualified to work in package design?

LEWIS: No, but my mother once saved your father's sister's life while she was at an Italian restaurant and there was a hit on a mobster in there and my mother dove across the table, tackling your father's sister and saving her life before my mom took out the hit man with a plate of linguini.

NANCY: Oh yeah! You're hired.

ADAM: That's the dumbest thing I've ever heard.

MIKE: Really?

ADAM: It was rigatoni.

POLLY: I heard they served together in the military.

MIKE: Nancy was in the military?

POLLY: Yeah I hear she's got a skull and crossbones tattoo on the left cheek of her ass.

> *(Lewis and Nancy get on the floor in sniper positions. They freeze and talk quietly.)*

NANCY: How long have we been here?

LEWIS: Three days.

NANCY: Any sign of the target?

LEWIS: Negatory. Wait a second.

NANCY: See him?

LEWIS: No, I just went number one.

ADAM: I heard they were on the German side in World War II.

LEWIS: Strudel?

NANCY: Yah.

MIKE: They're not old enough for that, you idiot. It must've been the Middle East.

LEWIS: Falafel?

NANCY: Yeah.

(He slowly gives her a piece. She eats it and chokes.)

ADAM: Well, I heard she died over there.

(Mike and Polly stare at him.)

POLLY: Adam, if she died, how could she be our boss?

(Lewis hits her on the back. She coughs.)

NANCY: You saved my life.

LEWIS: Remember that if you ever have a promotion to give.

NANCY: *(emotionally)*You got it, Sarge!

POLLY: It wasn't the military, it was the CIA.

ADAM: Nancy was in the CIA?

POLLY: Yeah, she has that classified tattoo on her ass.

(Nancy sits in the chair and pretends to smoke. Lewis, also with pretend cigarette, comes up behind her. Both are in "spy" mode.)

LEWIS: Excuse me, did you see the black dog howl at the red door?

NANCY: Yes. The dish ran away with the spoon.

(Lewis sits.)

MIKE: No, actually it was the Post Office.

(Lewis stands.)

LEWIS: Excuse me, did you see the black dog howl at the red door?

NANCY: Yes. I maced it.

MIKE: No, wait, actually, now that I think about it, it was the IRS.

(Lewis sits.)

LEWIS: You're going to be audited.

Nancy sobs loud and long until—

NANCY: I'll give you a promotion in my company if you don't.
LEWIS: Okay.

> *Polly checks her cellphone.*

POLLY: Megan on Five just sent me a text. She says they've known each other since they were kids.

> *(Lewis and Nancy become five years old. They're both shy and a little embarrassed.)*

LEWIS: You want to see my penis?
NANCY: Yuck.
LEWIS: I like you.
NANCY: Really?
LEWIS: Will you be my girlfriend?
NANCY: Okay.
LEWIS: If you ever have a promotion to give, can I have it?
NANCY: Yeah.
LEWIS: Are you sure you don't want to see my penis?

> *(Nancy thinks about it.)*

MIKE: Polly, I don't buy it.
ADAM: Wait, Mike, did she look at his penis?
MIKE: Who cares? Megan on 5 believes in UFOs. You can't believe anything she says. I mean, who is *he* really? I think it's where he went to school. I heard Harvard.

> *(Lewis puts a pipe in his mouth and becomes a Harvard student.)*

LEWIS: "Don't pahk the cah in Hahvahd yahd."
ADAM: No, I heard state school.

> *(Lewis takes the pipe out of his mouth and takes out a beer. He's now drunk.)*

LEWIS: Man, I'm so wasted.
POLLY: I heard it was a California school.

> *(Lewis keeps the beer and takes out a joint.)*

LEWIS: Dude, what's school?
MIKE: No matter what school he went to, he must have a secret we don't know about.

> *(Lewis sits with Nancy a la an interview.)*

LEWIS: Well, I'm interested in the promotion because I'm a genetically enhanced mutant with an IQ of 2000. I come from a planet in the Orion Nebulae, landing here in a spaceship when I was a tiny boy, escaping from a hostile race of aliens who were threatening my world. I can also move objects with my mind and can bench press a car. Under my fake human head, I look like an insect.

ADAM: She probably is too.

NANCY: Welcome to Earth, fellow Orion.

(As greetings, they make insect noises.)

MIKE: *(to Adam)* Adam, were you like born stupid or what?

ADAM: Yeah, probably.

MIKE: I meant maybe he has something on Nancy.

LEWIS: *(threateningly)* I know your great grandfather slept with Calvin Coolidge and if you don't give me the promotion, I'll reveal it to the world.

NANCY: *(distraught)* I knew it'd come out some day!

POLLY: Mike, I just thought of something.

MIKE: What?

POLLY: What if he's just really smart and qualified for the job?

NANCY: So tell me something about yourself.

LEWIS: I started my own company when I was in high school and I sold it for a good profit to a large corporation but I became interested in product design and feel I need to work my way up. I graduated from an Ivy League university, did several internships, and designed a new fabrication process for the industry. I'm single with no kids and no hobbies except my love of work. I'll probably work every weekend just because I like to work and my references include a former President of the United States.

NANCY: Hmm, well, I guess you're qualified for the promotion.

(Mike, Adam, and Polly think about this.)

ALL THREE: Yeah/Probably/Crap.

(Lewis and Nancy cross over to Mike, Adam, and Polly.)

LEWIS: Hey, guys, how're you doing today?

MIKE: Congrats on the promotion.

POLLY: Yeah, you were the obvious choice.

ADAM: *(to Lewis)* Some day I want to be you.

NANCY: So you're all okay with it?

MIKE: Oh yeah.

POLLY: Absolutely.

ADAM: *(to Lewis)* Seriously. Some day I want to be you.

LEWIS: Thanks, Adam. That's really nice. And thank you all for being happy for me.

MIKE: No problem, Lewis. Well, we should get to work.

> *(Mike, Polly, and Adam exit.)*

LEWIS: Sometimes this human head really squashes my antennae.

NANCY: You're telling me.

> *(They adjust their "heads" and speak in "insect talk" as the lights fade.)*

> *END OF PLAY*

Parting Gifts

Joe Calarco

ORIGINAL PRODUCTION

Presented by The Theater Lab in Washington DC for their Dramathon, 10 minute play festival, April 26, 2013.

If you are performing this play please check with the author's agent, Beth Blickers of Abrams Artists Agency beth.blickers@abramsartny) to confirm you have the most current draft.

CHARACTERS:

CHARLIE: Late thirties. Good looking. A guys, guy.

STEPHANIE: Late thirties. Pretty. Smart. A bright, fresh energy. Slightly neurotic.

CODY: Mid to late twenties. From Utah. Very good looking. Corn fed. A jock.

STEVEN: forty year old. Smart. Dry sense of humor. Hopeful.

NATALIE: Late sixties. Stephanie and Steven's mother. Has money and carries it well. A great hostess. The Queen Bee.

A summer home in the Berkshires. Very comfortable. Idyllic. Out upstage windows we can see a lakefront. A wedding bouquet is on the couch. CHARLIE, a good looking man in his late 30s stands up from behind the couch pulling his pants up. He holds his hand out and STEPHANIE grabs it and stands up from behind the couch as well. She is a very attractive woman in her late 30s and is in a full wedding gown with veil. She is rumpled. They have just had sex.

STEPHANIE: That was great.

CHARLIE: *(kissing her)* Mmmm . . . .

STEPHANIE: I mean really, really great.

CHARLIE: *(laughing and kissing her again)* MmHm.

STEPHANIE: Let's do it again.

CHARLIE: The guys are waiting. I was just supposed to be grabbing some beers. We gotta finish setting up outside.

(STEPHANIE tries to pull him back down to the floor.)

STEPHANIE: They'll understand.

CHARLIE: And isn't this like sacrilegious or something. I mean I'm not even supposed to see you in the dress, let alone fuck you in it. Won't we turn to salt or something?

STEPHANIE: Doesn't count 'cause we've both been through it before. It doesn't matter the second time, only the first time.

CHARLIE: Well that sounds very, very convenient.

STEPHANIE: I'm resourceful that way.

(CHARLIE pulls her down behind the couch again. After a moment CODY, a very attractive guy in his mid to late 20s enters.)

CODY: Hello?

STEPHANIE: *(screams)*

CHARLIE: Shit!

(STEPHANIE pops up from behind the couch.)

STEPHANIE: Hi!

CODY: Oh. Hey. Wow. So you must be like the bride.

STEPHANIE: Uh. Yeah. Exactly.

(CHARLIE remains hidden behind the couch.)

CHARLIE: I'll be with you in a sec. Just waiting for things to . . . calm down over here.

CODY: The bride. Wow. That means you gotta be Susan-Stacy-Sarah—

STEPHANIE: *(holding out her hand to shake)* Stephanie. And you're?

CODY: Cody.

STEPHANIE: Of course you are.

(CHARLIE pops up from behind the couch and sticks his hand out.)

CHARLIE: Sorry about that. Hi.

CODY: Hot.

STEPHANIE: This is Cody.

CODY: Hey.

CHARLIE: Hi.

CODY: Sorry about the hot thing.

STEPHANIE: Oh it's fine.

CHARLIE: No worries.

CODY: It was for both of you really. The hot thing. I mean, he's really hot yeah, but then my mind went to him *with* you and that was even hotter, cause well you are too. Hot, I mean.

STEPHANIE: Oh that's sweet. Isn't that sweet sweetie?

CHARLIE: Adorable. And you're?

CODY: Cody.

CHARLIE: Yeah, yeah, we got that. What are you doing here?

CODY: Oh! Oh, oh, oh, I'm with—

(STEVEN enters through the front door. He is in a suit and sunglasses.)

STEVEN: Me.

(STEPHANIE screams and runs across the room into his arms.)

STEPHANIE: Stevie!!

STEVEN: Hey sis, great dress, its bad luck, you're doomed. Hi Charlie, your fly is open. Sorry for junior here. He hasn't a manner in the world. *(to Cody)* Did you knock?

CODY: Well . . .

STEVEN: You didn't knock?

CODY: No

STEVEN: I said knock.

CODY: The door was unlocked.

STEVEN: Maybe in Utah people enter unlocked houses on a regular basis, but here in civilization it means you're probably entering a crime scene either during or right after the bloodletting has occurred. Either way, entry is not advised. *(to Stephanie)* So. As much as I approve of pre-conjugal, conjugal visits, aren't there things to be done?

CHARLIE: Exactly.

STEVEN: Guests arriving.

STEPHANIE: No, you're just insanely early.

STEVEN: I'm not the only one.

STEPHANIE: What are you talking about?

STEVEN: I think Dad and Mom are just behind us.

STEPHANIE: What?!

CHARLIE: You think or you saw?

STEVEN: I saw Dad's Mercedes in the rearview mirror.

CODY: He did. He sped the rest of the way here to warn you.

STEVEN: And you say I'm a bad brother.

STEPHANIE: This can't be. This cannot be.

CODY: What's the big deal? It's just your—

(NATALIE sweeps through the door.)

STEPHANIE: Mom!

(NATALIE looks up and down at her daughter's wedding dress.)

NATALIE: This is the dress?

STEPHANIE: Yes Mom.

NATALIE: It's not what I would have picked, but then again I wasn't asked. Hi Charlie, you're fly is open. *(noticing Cody)* And who are you?

CODY: I'm Cody.

STEVEN: He's with me Mom.

NATALIE: For how long?

STEVEN: Long enough.

NATALIE: Long enough for marriage?

CODY: Whoa.

STEVEN: Not quite yet.

NATALIE: But there's the possibility?

STEVEN: There's always the possibility Mom.

CODY: Whoa, whoa, whoa, we just met. Like, on Thursday.

(MOM and STEPHANIE and CHARLIE just look at STEVEN.)

STEVEN: You sent me a plus one invitation okay? You can't just come alone when you get a plus one invitation. And I haven't had a plus one to bring to anything for like three years okay? And Mom you keep sending me these gay You-Tube wedding videos, and they're really beautiful, I mean really fucking beautiful, and it's just depressing okay, and so I'm standing in line at Shake Shack, yes, Charlie, I was standing in line at Shake Shack, and I have never, and I mean *never* gone to Shake Shack in my life, but Thursday night after watching my third gay YouTube wedding video of the day, thank you very much Mother, I just felt the need for some reckless dietary behavior. So I'm standing there in that god awful, inexplicably long line, waiting for an average burger, and a syrupy, shake, with a side of worse than Ore Ida frozen potato French Fries and suddenly my foot feels like it's being stabbed by dozens of freezing pin pricks. And I look down and I see that a snow cone has fallen on my foot.

CODY: I got stung by a bee.

STEVEN: He had been standing behind me holding a snow cone. A red, white, and blue snow cone when—

CODY: BZZZZ!

STEVEN: Plop.

CODY: It fell right over.

STEVEN: Right onto my foot.

CHARLIE: "By dozens of freezing pin pricks?"

STEVEN: Exactly. It was romantic!

NATALIE: As charming as that story is, it doesn't quite rank with the greatest love stories ever told, and my heart is fragile, so I'm sorry Cody but I may keep my distance for a bit. My daughter hasn't let me take part in the planning of either of her weddings, so my attachment to her partners has always been a little, how shall I put this, abstract though thanks to her father her first wedding wasn't really much of an affair. And though I admire dearest Charlie here even though he possesses the inability to zip up his fly properly when that embarrassing fact is brought to his attention—

(CHARLIE finally zips his fly up all the way.)

—he is his own man. Tradition means nothing to him. They planned this wedding together without my input so . . . though I will love him as a son in law should be loved, there is a small, chasm between us I'm sad to say because of my lack of input in the most important day of their mildly charmed life together so far. But Stevie has always promised me that he and I would plan his wedding together, so his relationships have always been much more personal for me. If I see real possibility there, my mind goes toward place settings and centerpieces and parting gifts, and so if this little liaison were to be only that, a passing fancy, my heart might break from the disappointment of not being able to see what could possibly be the perfect wedding through to the end. So please forgive me if I keep myself somewhat guarded when it comes to you. But I wish you good luck and God's speed. I really do. And if all goes well, I see a custom made Tom Ford tuxedo in your future.

CODY: Whoa.

STEVEN: I'm going to go sit with Dad in the car.

NATALIE: He's not in the car.

STEPHANIE: Where is he?

NATALIE: He's not here.

STEPHANIE: What do you mean he's not here?

NATALIE: As free-thinking and loving as a three hour car ride with your ex up to the Berkshires for your daughter's wedding may sound to all of you, in reality it's barbarous.

STEPHANIE: Fine, fine, I can see that. I understand, but where is he?

STEVEN: He lent you his car?

NATALIE: He wasn't using it.

STEPHANIE: How is he getting here then?

NATALIE: I can't answer that.

STEVEN: What is going on?

(STEPHANIE grabs her phone.)

NATALIE: What are you doing?

STEPHANIE: I'm calling him.

NATALIE: Don't do that.

STEPHANIE: What are you—?

NATALIE: I'm telling you darling, let this go.

(NATALIE grabs the phone from STEPHANIE.)

STEPHANIE: Mother!

CHARLIE: What is going on here Natalie?

STEPHANIE: Give me the phone!

NATALIE: I will smash this! I swear it! I will pulverize it! Do you think I don't understand violence?! Do you think I don't understand despair?!

STEVEN: Mom, what the hell is going on?

NATALIE: He's dead okay, he's dead.

(Beat)

CODY: Whoa.

STEVEN: What are you talking about?

NATALIE: Your father is dead.

CHARLIE: Jesus Christ.

STEPHANIE: This is crazy.

STEVEN: This isn't possible.

CHARLIE: When did this happen?

NATALIE: When he didn't arrive to pick me up this morning, I went over to his place, and the doorman rang up to let him know I was there and there was no answer. Management let us in and, well, there he was. Dead. I figured he wouldn't be using the car so . . . Here I am. Don't worry I handled all the arrangements on speakerphone on the way here. The funeral is on Wednesday. Calling hours are Monday and Tuesday five to seven.

STEPHANIE: Mother!

STEVEN: Don't you think this is all a little monstrous?

NATALIE: I did what needed to be done! I took care of things so that your sister could have the day she is entitled to.

STEPHANIE: Oh God, what are we gonna do about today?

CHARLIE: Postpone. We'll just postpone.

NATALIE: No! This is your wedding day! Oh, this is soooo like him. Getting in the way of everything good. Well he's not going to get away with it this time. That man is not going to be the reason you have a second horrible wedding!

STEPHANIE: No. No, he's going to be the reason I don't have a second horrible wedding.

CHARLIE: What?

STEPHANIE: This is a sign. This wedding shouldn't happen. That's what this means.

CHARLIE: Babe, come on.

STEPHANIE: No, no, really . . .

NATALIE: Darling. You're talking nonsense.

STEPHANIE: No Mom. You said, you said you didn't have any part in the planning. Maybe that means something too. Maybe I've gone about this all wrong. And Charlie, even you said it. You said we would turn into salt.

STEVEN: What?

STEPHANIE: We fucked right there behind the couch with me in my wedding gown.

CODY: Hot.

NATALIE: Now, really darling, did we have to?

STEPHANIE: And Stevie—the first thing you said when you walked in, you said we were doomed 'cause Charlie saw me in my wedding dress.

NATALIE: Steven, really! Why must you say things like that?!

STEPHANIE goes up to CHARLIE and kisses him.

STEPHANIE: I love you I do. I think I really do. But . . . Can't you see? This is a sign. It's— . . . It's impossible.

(STEPHANIE takes off her veil and runs out the front door. CHARLIE runs after her.)

CHARLIE: Babe!

NATALIE: *(to Steven)* Well, are you going to just stand there? Go get her!

(STEVE breaks down crying. During the following CODY looks in the mirror and puts on the veil and picks up the bouquet.)

NATALIE: She'll be back. This wedding is going to happen. And it'll be beautiful even without my input. It'll be gorgeous. But I do think after all that's happened today, I may end up having to sit on the groom's side of the aisle.

(Beat. CODY looks at himself in the mirror with the veil on and holding the bouquet)

CODY: Who's Tom Ford?

End of play.

PINK, GREY, MAROON

Jenny Lyn Bader

ORIGINAL PRODUCTION
The play was commissioned by Half Moon Theatre in Poughkeepsie, NY and was first presented in their Annual Ten-Minute Play Festival in May 2013.

Curated by Darrah Cloud and David Simpatico.
Produced by Patricia Wineapple.

Directed by Nancy Saklad.

CAST:
TILDA: Alexas Orcutt
STEVE: John Summerford
DIANE: Kathleen Saumure

DEDICATION:
Jenny Lyn Bader dedicates Pink, Grey, Maroon *to her mother, Loti Stein, who attended Vassar College and speaks lovingly of its reunions.*

CHARACTERS:

TILDA, STEVE, DIANE: Alumni of the same college class. They can be played by actors in their mid-forties to fifties, or beyond. But the characters attended school together and should all be the same age.

SETTING: Vassar College campus, Poughkeepsie, NY

TIME: A "big" reunion—say, twenty-five or thirty years after graduation.

AUTHOR'S NOTE: While the play can be performed in different ways, it strikes the author that the clues could emerge lightly and quickly, giving the audience a few opportunities to glean what is happening, but not putting major emphasis or significance on any one clue so that the entire audience doesn't figure the ending out all at once too early.

(TILDA stands in the corner of a large room, uncomfortable, wearing a nametag, holding a drink. STEVE walks toward her. She looks at his shirt and then back at him.)

TILDA: Steve!

STEVE: Yes.

TILDA: I'm terrible with faces. But I can read your nametag. You have excellent handwriting.

STEVE: Thank you.

TILDA: I'm Tilda. Tilda Hart.

STEVE: Of course you are.

TILDA: What's awful is I still think of myself as being 17. And then coming back to campus . . . They let *children* go to college now!

STEVE: No!

TILDA: Yes! They're younger now. They are.

STEVE: But that's not—

TILDA: Okay, I realize they're actually older, with all the "gap years" and all the internship tracks and all the leaving back boys in the younger grades. No offense to boys.

STEVE: None taken.

TILDA: But they don't look like we did then. They look younger.

STEVE: Good thing you've found this entire roomful of grown-ups.

TILDA: Sure, but it's shocking. Oh! And have you heard?—They've changed the school colors to make them more manly.

STEVE: Yep. No more pink.

TILDA: There were complaints. What did they expect, letting men in here? No offense to men!

STEVE: None taken.

TILDA: It's probably so shocking because I waited too long to come back. I shouldn't have waited so many years.

STEVE: I waited too. Waiting is good.

TILDA: But now look. No one is 17, the way they are in my head. Some of them have died. And some aren't even in my head. *(confidentially)* My head is not what it was.

STEVE: Who's died?

TILDA: Chris Fenton. Allie Hatch. Vivi Glauber.

STEVE: *(shocked)* Vivi?

TILDA: Cancer. Two months ago. They're supposed to announce it at the dinner tonight.

STEVE: I thought she'd be here today.

TILDA: Yeah, she thought so too. She filled in her whole page in the reunion book. It went to press just before — You know, she didn't even mention the cancer. She thought it would be in remission by now and she wouldn't have to talk about it. Her page is very upbeat—all children, and gardening, and—

STEVE:—and painting classes, and a pet rabbit named Isaac, and yoga, and watermelon salad.

TILDA: Yes!

STEVE: I read it. The reunion book.

TILDA: The whole thing?

> *(STEVE nods.)*

Wow, I could never do that. I found it . . . a little hard to take.

> *(beat.)*

Do you remember what happened to Patsy Merrill?

STEVE: Married an insurance agent, moved to Chicago. Four children.

TILDA: What about Joan Sully?

STEVE: Interior decorator. Two divorces, three husbands. Two of whom were named Zack.

TILDA: That does not surprise me.

STEVE: That it does not surprise you, does not surprise me.

TILDA: Faye Wheeler?

STEVE: Married a woman. Lives in Vermont. Teaches fourth grade.

TILDA: You memorized it! I couldn't even bring myself to read it. Except for the dead people.

STEVE: That's macabre!

TILDA: I just figured they wouldn't be here to catch up.

STEVE: Right, of course. Actually that's the one part I skipped.

TILDA: How could you skip the dead people?

STEVE: I thought I could visit with them later. But before coming here, I wanted to check in on the living.

TILDA: Now that I'm here, I see that your way is better.

STEVE: It's not better, it's—

TILDA: Yes it's better. Don't contradict me!

STEVE: I wasn't.

TILDA: I am simply not well-prepared for this event. Only up to date on the dead. Not fully briefed on the living. Terrible with faces to begin with. Do you recognize any of the people in this room?

STEVE: Yes I recognize all of them, actually.

(DIANE approaches them. TILDA has no idea who she is.)

DIANE: Tilda! Oh my goodness. Oh my goodness.

(throws herself into Tilda's arms, embraces her)

I was just talking about you. And the time our chemistry professor taught us how to make malt liquor the same day Nina Axelrod taught us to play poker. And that crazy play we did where we had to wear bedsheets. We wore bedsheets. It's all so vivid, all of a sudden, I'd forgotten about it all and looking at you now, I see you in a bedsheet. I see you talking about Jean-Paul Sartre in your pajamas in the corridor. I see us at breakfast trying to add layers of butter to the insides of muffins. What were we thinking? They were already so buttery. Deeply, deeply buttery.

TILDA: Have you . . . met . . . Steve?

DIANE: Hi.

STEVE: Hello.

> *(TILDA is trying to figure out who Diane is, but STEVE is not taking the hint.)*

TILDA: Steve recognizes everyone here.

DIANE: You're kidding!

TILDA: And I hate to admit it, but I don't.

DIANE: Oh yeah, who don't you know?

> *(A beat where no one comes to the rescue.)*

TILDA: *(to Diane)* I'm sorry, who are you?

DIANE: Tilda! It's me. The one you stayed up with all night studying for the art history final and making cartoons of the great masterworks on graph paper.

TILDA: Diane!

> *(They embrace again.)*

DIANE: Ah, that's better. The hug of recognition.

TILDA: I'm awful with faces. And these days.

DIANE: Oh please, it has nothing to do with these days. You were terrible with faces when we were 19!

TILDA: *(suddenly cheering up as she remembers)* I was, wasn't I?

DIANE: Unless the faces were in an art history book.

TILDA: Mmm—did you guys take a tour of the new facilities?

STEVE: No, just wandered about. The Shakespeare garden, the library . . .

TILDA: *(to Diane)* Have you seen the new facilities?

DIANE: Of course I have.

STEVE: Diane teaches here now.

TILDA: Really.

DIANE: How did you know that?

STEVE: Iz—

TILDA: This guy memorized the frickin' reunion book.

STEVE: I did not. But I did read it.

TILDA: And he did the right thing. I messed up. I'm out of touch with these people. I don't know them. I'm spending all my time talking to someone I don't know. No offense.

STEVE: None taken. But—

DIANE: *(interrupting Steve, rapidly, as if trying to remember:)* Whose husband are you?

STEVE: *(quick and casual:)* Oh, I'm not anyone's husband, I . . .

TILDA: *(off-handed, interrupting:)* He's in our class. Right?

STEVE: I am.

DIANE: *(bemused)* Wow, I must be starting to slip after all these years. I thought I knew all the men in our class. There weren't that many.

TILDA: You're telling me?

DIANE: I hear the college is almost 50-50 now.

STEVE: Yes, it does look a bit more — balanced.

DIANE: *(quick aside)* Don't remember there being a Steve…

STEVE: *(rapidly)* Oh, I didn't go by "Steve," I…

TILDA: *(cuts off Steve equally rapidly as she turns to Diane)* What do you teach?

STEVE & DIANE: Biopsychology.

TILDA: So that explains why you're here.

STEVE: Biopsychology explains why we're all here.

TILDA: No, I mean — you teach here, that explains you being at the reunion. Otherwise you might not be the type to show. The reunion type.

DIANE: Yeah, I only had to walk about 20 feet to get here. What's your excuse?

TILDA: Vivi was my link to this place. She always told me about the reunions. I always said one day I'd come here with her. Then when she dropped dead, I realized I say that a lot. "One day." One day we'll have lunch. One day I'll travel to the Middle East. One day I'll come back to campus. But then suddenly everyone you were going to have lunch with is gone, and you haven't ever been to the Middle East, and they're having another war there anyway, and what seemed so possible isn't even likely, and all the little things you mean to do turn into nothing. But the campus is still here so I thought I better show up.

DIANE: Good for you.

TILDA: Yeah good for me. Except it didn't work. There are still people in this class… I'm totally out of touch with, like Stephanie Perkins. Are you in touch with her?

STEVE: *(casual)* Actually…

DIANE: *(interrupting, to Tilda)* No. Not at all.

STEVE: *(to Diane)* So you didn't read the book either?

DIANE: I wanted to read the book but the end of term is so crazy. Half the kids are flipping out about exams and half of them are drowning their sorrows in beer.

STEVE: They can't help that. It's part of the legend. The college was founded with brewery money.

DIANE: Yes, where would all of be without beer? So I've been reading exams. Much more depressing than any reunion book.

TILDA: It is depressing isn't it? But at least I'm here! At least if I never see some of these people again I'll know it wasn't just because I was hiding at home during the party.

DIANE: You enjoy hiding at home?

TILDA: Oh, that could be the title of my memoir. "Hiding at home." Parties make me nervous. I need to force myself to circulate. Actually I should do that instead of staying in this little corner of avoidance and lurking.

STEVE: What do you mean?

TILDA: Talking to you guys. Which is great. I mean,

> *(to DIANE:)*

you remember what we used to do, and

> *(to STEVE:)*

you remember what we're doing now. Still, I gotta circle around the room or else I'll wish I had. But before I go, I must know, what's your secret?

STEVE: My secret? How would you—

TILDA: How do you get yourself to pay attention to that book? Classmates sending photos of themselves meeting royalty, winning awards, draped in glory, and then on the next page, heart attacks, bankruptcies, remorse. And all the people I know in it, they lie, they exaggerate, they omit. They make their lives sound like candy. Why did you read it?

STEVE: I read it because I wrote something in it I hoped everyone would read. Do unto others and all that.

TILDA: Ah.

STEVE: And then, I hoped if they had read it, when I got here, I wouldn't have to explain.

DIANE: I was swamped with grading of course, but I did hear that there was something interesting in the book about oh.

(realizing:)
Oh!

TILDA: Explain what?

STEVE: Honey, you don't have to stop talking to me to go look for Stephanie Perkins. I am Stephanie Perkins.

(Beat.)

TILDA: What?

STEVE: I had a sex-change operation after college. That's why I fell out of touch with all of you. I'm Steve Perkins now.

(A moment. TILDA is overwhelmed. Looks at Diane. Looks back at Steve.)

TILDA: Stephanie!

(hugs STEVE)

I don't believe it! . . . You haven't changed.

STEVE: I have. I'm a man now.

TILDA: Besides that. It's always so much fun to talk to you. And it is again.

STEVE: You certainly have not changed, Tildy. Disagreeing with everybody, lurking in the corner with us, making us laugh. It's good to see you.

DIANE: *(hugs Steve)* Let me give you the hug of recognition. Nice to meet you. Again. I told you I knew all the men in the class!

TILDA: I'm so relieved I don't have to go looking for Stephanie!

STEVE: Yeah, she never shows up at these things.

CURTAIN

THE PROXY

Philip J. Kaplan

ORIGINAL PRODUCTION

The Proxy was performed at the Driftwood Players Theatre, Edmonds, Washington, at their 4th Annual Festival of Shorts, July 2013.

Directed by Chrystian Shepperd

CAST:
ISABELLE: Rita Baxter
DR. WILKINSON: Cindy French
STAN: Theo Asimakopoulos

CHARACTERS:

    ISABELLE: High strung woman, mid thirties to forties.
    DR. WILKINSON: Authoritative. Can be Man or Woman, forties to sixties.
    STAN: Brash when conscious. Isabelle's husband. Man thirties to forties.

SETTING: A hospital room with a bed. Today.

Scene One

    A hospital room, one bed.

    STAN lies in bed motionless. ISABELLE, his wife, enters the room. She looks at him, tenderly touches his face, then takes his pillow. She places the pillow over Stan's face. Stan reacts and struggles slightly.

    DR WILKINSON enters.

DR. WILKINSON: Hey! Stop that!

    (Dr. Wilkinson rushes over to stop Isabelle. She keeps one hand on the pillow and shoves a piece of paper at the Dr.)

DR. WILKINSON: What's this?

ISABELLE: It's a health care proxy for my husband Stan.

    (Dr. Wilkinson tries to take the pillow away from Isabelle.)

ISABELLE: I'm exercising it.

DR. WILKINSON: This doesn't mean—

ISABELLE: Can we have this discussion after I've fully invoked this legal and binding document.

DR. WILKINSON: No!

ISABELLE: What is the problem here? I'm Isabelle, this is my husband, I am merely carrying out his health care wishes.

DR. WILKINSON: And what wish is that?

ISABELLE: We had many conversations about this, Stan and I, and Stan agreed that if he ever had a heart attack while having sex with a woman other than his wife he would not want to be kept alive by artificial or any other means. So if you'll excuse me.

DR. WILKINSON: NO! You're not going to kill anyone at my hospital.

ISABELLE: I'm so sorry. I've violated hospital protocol. *You* want to do the honor.

DR. WILKINSON: Never.

ISABELLE: Oh, I've stepped it in again, haven't I. I've insulted you and kept you from other more worthy patients.

DR. WILKINSON: Right on both counts. I have eight other patients on this floor alone.

ISABELLE: What a burden. I assume you're overworked and understaffed here. That's the fate of the medical profession these days, am I right?

DR. WILKINSON: Sadly true.

ISABELLE: Bureaucrats second guessing you at every turn. Don't you long for the good old days. You charge what you want. No one looking over your shoulder. I wish I could help, but I'm just a civilian. Wait, I see a solution. If I snuff Stan, you have one less patient to worry about. Pillow please?

DR. WILKINSON: Thanks for your concern. But I take pride in my work.

ISABELLE: And I take pride in the law. You, Doctor, are infringing on my New York State rights. See this! It's a notary stamp. It doesn't get any more legal than that! Now out of my way.

DR. WILKINSON: This does not give you the right to murder my patient!

ISABELLE: Well, aren't we judgmental? All Doctors kill someone sooner or later, and I don't label you a murderer. How about this, I'll call you a Doctor, instead of a killer, and you call me an End of Life Coach. That works, doesn't it?

DR. WILKINSON: Do I really need to answer that?

ISABELLE: I concede the point. Your goal is not to kill the patients. When someone dies it's a rounding error. This is an excellent hospital.

DR. WILKINSON: There's a tight budget. We do our best under the circumstances.

ISABELLE: That's quite clear. Let me ask you a question? Do you see my beloved husband Stan here as a collection of symptoms? Or as a whole person?

DR. WILKINSON: Somewhere in the middle. He hasn't been conscious since he arrived. I wish I could spend more time with him.

ISABELLE: Then let me introduce you to Stan.

(Isabelle picks up Stan's hand and makes a Hello gesture to the Doctor. The Doctor returns the gesture.)

ISABELLE: Stan is a lowlife who can't keep it in his pants. He is a man who would entrust me to look after his best interests and then cheat on me with a Barista. Are you getting a sense of him?

DR. WILKINSON: I think so.

ISABELLE: Wonderful. It's important to treat the whole patient, rather than a symptom, don't you think?

DR. WILKINSON: Yes I do.

ISABELLE: Then we're on the same page.

(Isabelle grabs the pillow and pushes it over Stan's face.)

(Dr. Wilkinson grabs it back.)

DR. WILKINSON: What are you doing!

ISABELLE: I am treating the whole patient with the respect he deserves.

DR. WILKINSON: Mrs.—

(quickly looks at the chart)

—Knoll. Let's go outside. You're obviously stressed.

ISABELLE: Thank you for thinking of me. You have compassion, Doctor. You weren't drawn to medicine for money, you did it to help.

DR. WILKINSON: That's true. The money's not that good, and I like to help.

ISABELLE: Then help me! Help me kill this worthless parasite! Are you concerned about lawsuits? I'll only sue if Stan lives to philander again. Do you want his organs? Take 'em. Take 'em all!

DR. WILKINSON: You're insane.

ISABELLE: I want a second opinion.

DR. WILKINSON: I'm calling security!

ISABELLE: I wouldn't. Our insurance does not cover that. You'll be stuck with the bill.

(Stan groans.)

ISABELLE: Shut up Stan! You see what your rush to action has done? He's getting better, and that's all your fault! He sounds like he's in excruciating pain, doesn't he. You don't want my husband to remain in excruciating pain, do you?

DR. WILKINSON: You're not going to convince me. No matter what Stan has done to you—

ISABELLE: —and his children. Think of the children, Doctor.

DR. WILKINSON: —he does not deserve to die.

There is a long pause. Isabelle composes herself.

ISABELLE: Please excuse me. I was obviously out of my mind. The intense rage that comes over you when you discover a gross betrayal such as this may cause rash action. Thank you Dr—

(looks at the Doctor's badge)

—Wilkinson, for making me see the light. Now, I need some time alone with my husband to apologize. No wonder he cheated on me. I'm a terrible person.

(beat)

Why aren't you going? You can scoot now. Continue your rounds. Attend to patients who *want* your help. And when you're gone I won't smother my husband with the pillow. Scouts honor.

DR. WILKINSON: How can I believe you?

ISABELLE: You doubt the powers of your own persuasion? You convinced me with your confident bedside manner and your logical authority. I know when I'm beaten.

DR. WILKINSON: Alright then.

ISABELLE: I will not suffocate my husband with this hospital pillow.

DR. WILKINSON: Good.

ISABELLE: Not when there are so many other legal ways to exterminate his vile existence. I will have Stan transferred to another facility. I know— Mersa Managed Care! They have an appallingly high mortality rate. I trust you'll draw up the necessary paperwork.

DR. WILKINSON: Not Mersa!

ISABELLE: You have a problem with the competition?

DR. WILKINSON: Mersa is an insult to the medical profession. A Medicare Mill!

ISABELLE: Potato Po-tah-oh. I'll order the ambulance.

DR. WILKINSON: He's staying right here!

ISABELLE: Am I to take it my husband is a prisoner here?

DR. WILKINSON: Of course not. But he's in no condition to move. It might kill him.

ISABELLE: I'm not hearing a downside. So it's settled then. As proxy I hereby authorize this move.

DR. WILKINSON: Please reconsider.

ISABELLE: I don't want to have to resort to lawyers.

DR. WILKINSON: No lawyers.

ISABELLE: So where's the gurney.

DR. WILKINSON: We have to stabilize him first.

ISABELLE: I don't understand your medical jargon. I'll take the head, you take the feet.

DR. WILKINSON: No! He stays! I don't care how you threaten me! Mr. Knoll leaves this room on his own two feet or not at all.

ISABELLE: Please listen to reason. Consider Stan's quality of life.

DR. WILKINSON: What are you talking about? He has an excellent chance for recovery.

ISABELLE: I'm talking about the quality of life he will experience if he returns home alive and I am his caregiver. It will be *Whatever Happened To Baby Jane* unpleasant. Have you seen *Misery? Silence Of The Lambs?* He will beg for death. You wouldn't want that for him, would you?

DR. WILKINSON: I've had enough—

ISABELLE: What if I told you Stan was a Christian Scientist?

DR. WILKINSON: I wouldn't treat him, but I wouldn't kill him.

ISABELLE: A malpractice lawyer?

DR. WILKINSON: Is he one?

ISABELLE: No, but he constantly talked about going back to law school.

(Stan sits up groggily.)

STAN: Where am I?

ISABELLE: Back to sleep, honey.

STAN: Isabelle. I can explain.

ISABELLE: So can I.

STAN: *(to Dr. Wilkinson)* Where am I?

ISABELLE: You're lucky to be alive. Very lucky.

DR. WILKINSON: You're in a hospital. You've had a serious—

STAN: A hospital! Not Mersa! Tell me it's not Mersa!

DR. WILKINSON: Don't worry, you're at St. Jerome's.

STAN: St. Jerome's. Have they had the cut backs yet?

DR. WILKINSON: What cutbacks?

STAN: Never mind.

DR. WILKINSON: We're bare boned as it is.

STAN: I'm delusional. Forget I said anything.

DR. WILKINSON: What is he talking about?

ISABELLE: Why Stan, surely you're not bashful about your work.

STAN: Do we have to go into this now?

DR. WILKINSON: What the hell are you talking about?

ISABELLE: Oh, didn't I mention? Stan works for a health insurance company.

DR. WILKINSON: Really.

ISABELLE: Yes. He's in charge of reimbursement claim rates.

DR. WILKINSON: You should have mentioned that sooner.

> *Dr Wilkinson picks up the pillow and begins suffocating Stan.*

ISABELLE: One more question. As I'm now single, are you doing anything after work, tonight?

> *BLACKOUT.*

RISE

Crystal Skillman

ORIGINAL PRODUCTION

Rise was produced as part of THE BEACH PLAYS which were commissioned and produced by Rising Phoenix Rep (Artistic Director, Daniel Talbott) and Kid Brooklyn Productions (Artistic Director, Evan F. Caccioppoli) on July 13-14, 2013, Ocean Beach in San Francisco, CA.

Directed by Evan F. Caccioppoli

CAST:
JAIME: Sam Soule
JOY: Addie Johnson
ANA: Jelena Stupljanin
SALLY: Lila Coley

CRYSTAL SKILLMAN is the award winning author of *Geek* (Produced by Obie Award Winning Vampire Cowboys, earning a NY Times and TONY Critics Pick); *Cut* (The Management, NY Times Critic's Pick; Apollinaire Theatre, Boston); *Vigil Or The Guided Cradle* (ITG/Brick; New York Innovative Theatre Award for Outstanding Full-Length Script*); Birthday & Nobody* (Rising Phoenix Rep in NYC; U.K Premiere with Kibo Productions; Chicago Premiere with Side Project); and WILD, also with director Evan F. Caccioppoli (Chicago Premiere with Kid Brooklyn Productions, NYC Premiere with Sanguine Theatre Company). Crystal's work is published by Samuel French, Applause, Smith and Kraus and available on indietheatre.com

CHARACTERS:

> (*Ages for the three ladies can be open but they would be at least late twenties. Diversity in casting is encouraged.*)
> ANA
> JAMIE
> JOY

TIME: Now.

PLACE: A beach in San Francisco.

NOTE: The moment with the small girl coming in can be cut if desired. In that case Jamie would set up the chairs on her own.

> *Ana runs onto a beach. She is wearing a flowing green dress. Her enthusiasm is infectious. She kicks up sand as she runs. She stops near the water. Dances a bit.*

ANA: Yes! Yes! Yes!

> (*She plays, takes out her phone. Attaches some portable speakers. She puts on Pink's album* The Truth About Love. *She dances around in a circle even more excited. She runs takes her stick and draws in the sand. She creates two sections of lots of little circles. Then between them, one line, then the other. She faces the water. She walks down this "sand asile." She reaches out—pretending her partner is there to go down the asile with her. She goes down once. Shakes her head she isn't sure. Then runs back and starts over. She keeps practicing, but it's never right. Too bratty, or fast or slow but she is enjoying trying. Jamie appears. She watches this for a while. She looks hot and sweaty and has a huge roll-y bag and is holding wilted flowers. Ana finally spots her is this who she thinks she is?*)

ANA: Hey.

JOY: Hi. Is this—I'm looking for a wedding . . . a reception . . .

ANA: Joy?

JOY: Yes.

ANA: This is . . .

(Ana runs up to Joy and kisses her.)

JOY: Yes. Okay! Thanks!

ANA: Jamie is gonna love this.

JOY: Where is . . .

ANA: Parking the car. The traffic getting here. Of course always traffic. Everyone decided to get married today. Isn't that crazy??

JOY: Right. *(Holds out wilted flowers.)* These are for you. The two of you. I got them before I got on the plane—I wasn't thinking. They died on the way. I don't think that means anything.

ANA: Hey. Don't be nervous.

JOY: I'm not.

ANA: All exs are scared to see each other.

JAMIE: Ok.

ANA: Jamie wanted you here. You know what that means? I want you here.

> *(Jamie, a woman wearing sunglasses, comes over the hill.)*

JAMIE: *(Running to Joy)* Joy? Ahhhhhhhhhhhhhh!!!! No way?! You came!!!

JOY: I came!

> *(Joy gives Jamie a hug.)*

JOY: Thin!! You are too thin!

JAMIE: Me? You're . . . are you eating?

ANA: She eats like a horse.

> *(Jamie runs to Ana, scoops her up.)*

JAMIE: Monkey!

ANA: Monkey? I'm a mermaid. That's the theme. We spent months picking out the theme. I am the goddamn theme!

JAMIE: My wife. Excuse me, I love saying that!

> *(Jamie and Ana kiss. Joy stands there.)*

It's just you . . . ? No Sherry?

> *(Joy shakes head "no.")*

Tina? How old is she now . . . ? She must be . . .

JOY: Yeah. I am sorry I didn't RSVP.

JAMIE: You are here! Forget it. You still look twenty-five—like you'd down a thousand fries at the Crispy Critter Hut.

JAMIE AND JOY: U-Ha!!

ANA: What was that again?

JAMIE: University of Hartford—Connecticut where we went for undergrad, told you a thousand times honey.

ANA: Cold. Connecticut.

JAMIE: Only around Christmas.

JOY: The summers get hot.

(Beat)

JAMIE: Joy. You should have seen—at the Clerk's office—all afternoon—everyone in tuxes, dresses, flowers, flowers!

ANA: The flowers.

JAMIE: Jonathan is bringing them. Monica's getting here with the chairs. Terry's bringing some food. We have—like 7 minutes—and then we will be descended upon! "Renegade Beach No Permit Jamie and Ana Reception/Ceremony with Family Post Actual Marriage Certificate Finally Recognized By the State of San Francisco is about to begin!!!"

ANA: Yay!

JOY: Yes.

JAMIE: Did you come right here? You look . . . I don't know if you want to put your things.

JOY: I don't know where I'm staying actually.

JAMIE: Oh. Well I'm sure we'll figure that out.

ANA: Before they get here. She should learn the dance. She needs to dance.

JOY: I don't—

JAMIE: Wait til you see! Who needs a wedding planner when you have the great Ana!

ANA: I'll walk you through.

JAMIE: She will blow you away. First burlesque show she took me too—our first date might I add—that she choreographed I was blown away she was so—

ANA: I can hear you and if I can hear you you're not listening! You're talking. *(Ana walks through the "ceremony")* So, walk, walk, walk. Love, love, love. Vows! *(Turning to Joy)* Will you read my vows actually—

JOY: Me?

ANA: You're a writer, right?

JOY: I'm not even half as talented as this one.

JAMIE: Oh no, I'm all about the scribbles. Drawing, not writing, please.

ANA: I want you to read it.

JOY: Ok.

ANA: Good! So after all that. *(Takes off ring and holds it up)* The rings. I play the music and it starts like this!

> *(Ana plays a song on her iphone. She starts dancing. The moves get more and more complicated. Jamie loves this and claps and she gets into it, jumps in. Joy is doing terribly.)*

ANA: I taught everybody yesterday. See?

JOY: Yeah, no. I don't.

> *(Ana and Jamie encourage her. Joy starts to dance on her own. It's awful.)*

ANA: Stop.

JOY: What?

ANA: You're kidding?

JOY: No.

JAMIE: She doesn't need to dance.

ANA: Everyone is dancing at the end. Everyone is wearing some kind of green, there are flowers, we say the vows and everyone dances at the end the way I've pictured our formal wedding for seven years.

JAMIE: Baby.

ANA: Everyone got the video. Everyone knows this dance.

JAMIE: Well we didn't know she was coming.

ANA: Who doesn't RSVP?

JAMIE: We're old friends.

ANA: She never calls you.

JAMIE: Hey. Babe.

ANA: *(Gets a text)* It's Monica. She's here with the chairs.

> *(Ana exits.)*

JOY: Wow. She's a spitfire.

JAMIE: She's a redhead. She's right. You couldn't have told us —before you got on the plane—maybe?

JOY: I really can't explain.

JAMIE: That hasn't changed.

JOY: Look I'm going, I'm fine.

JAMIE: Joy. You're not going anywhere. You look like shit. What is going on?

JOY: It's your day, I'm ruining it.

JAMIE: You leave you'll ruin my day.

JOY: Look, I don't want to fuck this up ok.

JAMIE: So you'll hop on a flight for six hours to just go back?

JOY: Don't be pushy Jamie. I don't miss you being pushy.

(Jamie pushes her. Joy tries to get around her. Jamie starts wrestling her.)

JOY: Don't make me hurt a bride.

JAMIE: I have been pushing weights for three months to look good for this. I've been boxing my ass off—you cannot get —past—me!

JOY: Fuck! Fuck! Fuck! Ahhhhh . . . ..

(They have both fallen into the sand. They lie there. Beat, then:)

JOY: This morning I woke up hung over in my own vomit. The windows were open. My cats escaped. Or I can't find them. My book has been passed on. That's 24 different publishers. That's twenty four different agents. And I don't even like it anymore. It's not me. I'm just trying to be someone else in it—to sell—sell because I don't know why—I want to write one story that someone opens and just goes—that changed me. That changed my life but I'm not changing my life. I'm drinking a lot and I tell myself it's the wine that goes with pasta but it's too much and Sherry has been falling out of love with me for a long time and I've been watching it happen like a TV show where you know it's happening and Tina— we went through such hell to get her—Do you know I got the book you illustrated with all the monkeys. We sit and we count all the monkeys. All the fucking monkeys and I think I should be good for something. I should be such a good mother. My mother was such a good mother, even though I gave her such shit. Are you going to try to have kids?

JAMIE: Ana's looking into it.

JOY: Good! Good! See you'll make a good mother. That's what I
    was thinking when I saw your invitation in the garbage after
    Sherry took Tina and left. I got off the floor. I got to the air-
    port. I got on a plane. I followed the invitation—had a driver
    drop me off to Oakland Beach and I don't know why. I don't
    know why you fucking invited me in the first place.

JAMIE: Don't you . . . ever want to share who you are with your
    first love.

JOY: I was that for you.

JAMIE: You were that for me. So making the list . . . I added you.
    I couldn't explain to Ana why, but even though she acts . . .
    she understands. I couldn't have met someone like her with-
    out being with you.

JOY: Why?

JAMIE: Oh honey. You loved me. You made me feel loved. Joy.

    (Joy is crying. Jamie holds her.)

JOY: Can you do me a favor? Can you roll me? Can you roll
    me in the water and let the waves roll over me. Let the
    water rise over me. Let me drown because I'm already
    drowning.

JAMIE: You can't drown.

JOY: Why?

JAMIE: You're a mermaid at a mermaid themed wedding and
    Ana will kill you if you don't play by the rules and the big-
    gest rule for a mermaid is she floats.

JOY: Swims.

JAMIE: You might float. I think you're a good floater. I think—
    you'll be fine.

    *(Jamie and Joy sit up. Ana returns with a chair. A little
    girl enters, holding chair too.)*

ANA: Monica's unloading the chairs. She sent Sally to help. Say
    hello Sally. She's shy. You can put that there sweety.

JAMIE: I've got it honey. You take a break, ok?

    *(Jamie helps Sally put out the chairs, clean up a bit,
    decorate some more from Ana's bag. Beat with Joy and
    Anna. Joy breaks the silence.)*

JOY: What about those vows?

ANA: I don't have them *(imitates writing)* I'm not like you . . .
I'm shit at writing. I have them *(gestures to head. Joy nods
for you to go ahead. Ana speaks from memory.)* When I met
you I didn't know what love was. I thought I did. I thought
I knew everything. The day we met here. The day you wore
your silly, pink hat and looked up at the sun, but the sun was
me. This gigantic creature of a woman with red hair over
you on your beach towel. You said I was in t he way of the
light. You were drawing the waves. But in them you drew
mermaids and creatures of the sea and fantastical things.
You said you drew for kids and I told you I made dances
for adults. I thought looking at you, drawing, looking away
from me that I was seeing beyond something. I'd look at the
world and see the beautiful stars and think what I saw was
what was. But with you. The stars are a chariot. The waves
a home. In my heart. We were always married. Now we are
wife and wife. But what a wife is with you changes . . . . and
I want it to always change. Like the water. Like us. I love
this poem:

> *You will remember that leaping stream*
> *where sweet aromas rose and trembled,*
> *and sometimes a bird, wearing water*
> *and slowness, its winter feathers.*
> *You will remember those gifts from the earth:*
> *indelible scents, gold clay,*
> *weeds in the thicket and crazy roots,*
> *magical thorns like swords.*
> *You'll remember the bouquet you picked,*
> *shadows and silent water,*
> *bouquet like a foam-covered stone.*
> *That time was like never, and like always.*
> *So we go there, where nothing is waiting;*
> *we find everything waiting there.*

JOY: You—.

ANA: It's bad! It is? GOD! Everyone uses Neruda.

JAMIE: I'm glad she has you. Will you show me? Again?

*(Ana starts to dance again. Joy tries, getting better. The
girl runs to them dancing too. Jamie jumps in. They get*

better and better! They turn to the audience. They en-
courage them to dance with them. They dance until ev-
eryone is smiling.)

END OF PLAY

SACRIFICES

Erin Moughon

ORIGINAL PRODUCTION
>   Original Binding Productions' Naked Theater 2:
>   The Ladies A festival of new one act plays
>
>   Access Theatre
>   August 8-11, 2013
>
>   Directed by R. Alex Murray
>   Produced by Tom Slot
>
>   CAST:
>   JEPHTHAH'S DAUGHTER: Jennifer Alexander
>   IPHIGENIA: Kristi Barron
>   WOMAN: Sharron Pinney
>   MIDAS' DAUGHTER: Colista K. Turner

CHARACTERS:

>JEPHTHAH'S DAUGHTER: young teenager, daughter
from the book of Judges, sacrificed by her father to
satisfy his promise to God

>IPHIGENIA: young teenager ,daughter from Greek my-
thology, sacrificed by Agamemnon in order to get
wind to sail to Troy

>WOMAN: twenties to thirties, Levite's Concubine from
the book of Judges, sacrificed by the Innkeeper instead of the Levite to the townsmen

>MIDAS' DAUGHTER: young teenager, daughter from
Greek mythology, accidentally sacrificed by Midas
when she hugged him and turned to gold

SETTING: a slumber party in the afterlife

TIME: Out of time (though after all of the sacrifices occurred)

>*A slumber party of sorts. Four chairs, or sleeping bags.
Sleeping bags are preferable. Three young women, girls
really, are talking about their lives and braiding each
others' hair. The three girls each take up a chair or bag.
A fourth older (read: 20s) woman walks in. She is unno-
ticed by the others.*

IPHIGENIA: And then he just slits my throat.

MIDAS' DAUGHTER: That's cold.

IPHIGENIA: Yeah, but you know the really messed up part?

JEPHTHAH'S DAUGHTER: What?

IPHIGENIA: The same thing happened with Isaac. God comes
down and tells a man to kill his child, and you know what
happens?

JD: He gets to live.

IPHIGENIA: He gets to live. Exactly. Because he's a boy.

MD: Boys suck.

JD: Totally. You know the same thing happened to me. My dad
swears an oath to kill the first that comes out of his house.
Guess who's the idiot to come running to daddy?

IPHIGENIA: No.

JD: Yes. And not only that, but it's the way . . . I don't even know
if I can talk about . . . It's . . . And Saul says the same thing.
I'll kill whoever broke my command. And they draw lots and
show that it's his son. And you know what happens?

IPHIGENIA: Nothing.

JD: Right. Because he's a boy.

MD: Boys suck! *(pause)* So what did happen to you?

JD: I don't want to talk about it.

MD: We told you ours.

JD: This is worse.

MD: Than suffocating as gold fills your lungs?

IPHIGENIA: Or having your throat slit?

JD: I don't want to talk about it.

IPHIGENIA: If you were a boy, you would have lived.

JD: Probably.

MD: Boys suck!

WOMAN: She was burned alive.

(All three girls turn to look at her. They jump a little.)

JD: How did you . . . ?

IPHIGENIA: You're not supposed to be here. We're waiting for
someone else.

WOMAN: There is a still a celebration of your life. All the wom-
en go out into the field for four days.

JD: Wow. That's um . . . kind of nice. Or it would be if I hadn't
been all . . . burned . . . and he didn't even put up a fight. He
just said he was sorry and gave me three months to mourn.

WOMAN: Yes.

IPHIGENIA: Who are you?

WOMAN: No one.

IPHIGENIA: You're not the girl we're waiting for. Where is she?

WOMAN: So many questions. Why are you here? I thought you
got whisked away on a wind.

IPHIGENIA: People wanted a happy ending. The story got
changed.

WOMAN: Isn't that always the case?

MD: Did your father kill you too? Though mine did it on accident. I just want it to be clear that he didn't want me to . . .
you know, die. He was very sad.

WOMAN: I'm sure he was.

MD: And why is it all of our father's killed us? What did we do? And none of the boys. Why do they get to live? Isaac, Jonathan, Telemachus. Odysseus turned the plow to not hit him. Even Orestes got to live. Why is that? I think this is a more important question. Don't you, Iphigenia?

IPHIGENIA: I still want to know who you are. You're not who we were expecting.

JD: I want to know. Why us?

IPHIGENIA: Because we're *girls*. Don't you get it? Men. The gods. All of it is against us. And we pay the price. We can't make our own decisions. We can't do anything for ourselves. The only thing we're good for is sacrificing.

WOMAN: And procreation. Don't forget procreation.

JD: Oh sex. Did you get to have sex? What's it like?

WOMAN: Why are you so dismissive of other questions?

IPHIGENIA: Because they distract from the point. We know why we're here.

WOMAN: Do you really?

IPHIGENIA: Our fathers killed us.

WOMAN: Do you know why?

IPHIGENIA: To go to war.

JD: To uphold an oath.

MD: Dumb luck.

IPHIGENIA: Really?

MD: It's not his fault! He didn't mean to kill me!

IPHIGENIA: And that makes it so much better?

MD: A little.

WOMAN: You're all wrong. *(to Midas' daughter)* Except you. You're really close.

IPHIGENIA: How do you know?

WOMAN: Before you died, who held your father's heart?

IPHIGENIA: What does that have to do with . . .

JD: I did.

MD: Me too. He said I was his world.

JD: Mine too. And I guess he did feel bad.

IPHIGENIA: What are you guys doing? We don't even know who she is. Why are you indulging her?

WOMAN: So you weren't your father's favorite?

IPHIGENIA: I was my mother's.

WOMAN: Your father didn't love you?

IPHIGENIA: He did. At one point I believed he did. But after . . .

WOMAN: So why do you think you were chosen? Why were you three the sacrifices?

IPHIGENIA: Because we're girls.

WOMAN: No. Because your fathers are idiots.

MD: My father isn't . . . well . . . that makes more sense actually.

WOMAN: Not saying that Abraham or Saul or Odysseus were much better, but yours were idiots.

JD: Why do you say that?

WOMAN: Your dad, for example, makes a pretty outrageous promise. No prompting other than he's afraid for the battle, which I guess could be good prompting. But really, who does he think is going to come out and greet him?

JD: That's true.

WOMAN: And your dad just picks you up.

MD: Well, I kind of ran into him.

WOMAN: Whatever. And you. Your dad agrees to sacrifice you.

IPHIGENIA: What's your point?

WOMAN: That it wasn't because you're girls that you died. It's because you were important to them. A punishment. A trage-dy. You can't have a tragedy without someone caring. Some-thing important being lost.

JD: That makes sense.

IPHIGENIA: So we died because they were selfish?

WOMAN: Yes and no, but yes. To be simple about it, yes.

IPHIGENIA: Why are we even listening to you? You're just in-sulting us.

JD: I didn't think she was.

IPHIGENIA: Calling us simple. Telling us we died because of someone else's mistakes. What about the boys? Their fathers made mistakes.

WOMAN: And they paid for them. In different ways. But they were able to say something . . . do something else to make penance as it were.

JD: Wow. I had never thought of it that way. That me being burned alive was punishment for my father.

IPHIGENIA: Do you hear how ridiculous that sounds?

JD: It does, and it doesn't.

IPHIGENIA: And who are you to tell us anything? You come in here and interrupt and take over and . . . and . . . who are you? YOU'RE NOT SUPPOSED TO BE HERE.

WOMAN: You're right.

IPHIGENIA: Really? I mean, of course! So what happened to you that brought you here? What gives you the right to talk to us like that?

WOMAN: You asked about sex earlier?

JD: Yes.

WOMAN: It can be wonderful. It really can be. It can also be worse than anything else you can imagine.

MD: What do you . . .

WOMAN: We were traveling. My husband had just come to my father to claim me as his concubine. He really worked for it. I thought . . . it felt like love. Or something close to it. And we were going back to his homeland. It was too dangerous to stay outside, so we found someone to take us in. At midnight a group of men surrounded the house demanding that my husband come out.

JD: Were they going to kill him?

WOMAN: Rape him. But the owner of the house refused. He offered his virgin daughter and me instead. Mostly his daughter.

MD: That's awful! So both of you were sent out.

WOMAN: Just me. She was so scared and alone. And it wasn't her fault. So I went alone.

IPHIGENIA: And they beat you and hurt you and blah blah blah. You robbed us of our fourth. We were supposed to have a fourth girl to hang out with. Not you.

WOMAN: They took turns with me. I was passed around. Sometimes two men took me at a time. Sometimes more. Again. And again. And again. If they couldn't do it themselves, they used whatever they could fit. A hand. A pole. A sword. Again. And again. And again. Until dawn when they were satisfied or too exhausted or bored. I crawled back to the doorstep and died clinging to the threshold. My husband walked out, stepped over me, and said "Woman, get up." Then, seeing I was dead, he cut me into twelve pieces and sent me to his people. As a message. As a call to action. *(to Iphigenia)* Just like you. But not like you. That's why I'm here. So someone else isn't.

(There is a silence.)

IPHIGENIA: Was it worth it?

WOMAN: I don't know.

JD: Do you regret it?

WOMAN: Of course. But it wasn't . . . it's easy to blame the men. And yes, I do blame those who did it to me or watched or didn't intervene, but it wasn't all men. It's not all boys. The boys you're talking about didn't even have a choice. It's . . . people being stupid or selfish or both. And we're left here.

MD: *(crying)* It was my fault. I jumped in his arms. He said don't. He said no. I just . . . I just wanted to hug my daddy.

JD: *(crying too)* I know what you mean. I just want to hug my daddy too.

IPHIGENIA: So why tell us this? Why bother with us at all?

WOMAN: I don't know. Maybe I thought it would help. To show that you're whole. That it was bigger than you. Maybe that doesn't help.

IPHIGENIA: Why?

WOMAN: Because we're selfish too. We want it to be about us and not a bigger cause. We want our justice and our recognition and our pain.

IPHIGENIA: That's what you want.

WOMAN: What I want is to put all of my pieces back together.

IPHIGENIA: And you're wrong. It was about me.

WOMAN: Sure. Who am I?

IPHIGENIA: Exactly. *(to Midas' daughter)* And it wasn't your fault. *(to all)* It wasn't any of our faults. It was the men. It's because we're not boys. It's because we are who we are.

MD: You think so?

JD: Really?

IPHIGENIA: I don't know. I . . . I . . . *(to Woman)* You've ruined everything. Everything! It was supposed to be the girl. She would have . . . Not you! Not you! You've made me question. I was so sure. And now I . . . I . . . I don't KNOW.

(Another silence. All three girls are near tears.)

WOMAN: At least you know they loved you.

(The girls burst into tears and hug. Woman is set apart. It continues for a moment and then blackout.)

End of play.

SOMETHING FINE

Eric Dufault

ORIGINAL PRODUCTION
Ensemble Studio Theatre. Billy Carden, Artistic Director
May 18, 2013- June 2, 2013

Directed by Larissa Lury

CAST:
BESS: Catherine Curtin
VIRGIN MARY: Diana Ruppe
HULA GIRL: Lucy DeVito

CHARACTERS

> BESS: A truck driver. Probably she's in her thirties.
> VIRGIN MARY: A dashboard figurine, but lifesize
> HULA GIRL: Also a dashboard figurine

> *In the interior of her big-rig truck, BESS drives with great determination. On her dashboard she has two plastic statuettes: a Virgin Mary and a hula girl. Loud music is playing to keep her awake. Her CB radio buzzes in. She turns down the music, and speaks with intense focus into the radio. Behind her are two figures. They are the VIRGIN MARY and HULA GIRL.*

BESS: Ten four, this is Minnie Mouse to Hamburger Helper, I'm dusting my britches on I-378, dropped off goods, following the stripes home, hell bent for leather, dropping the hammer, one foot on the floor, one hanging out the door, and she just won't do no more. Ten roger, Hamburger Helper. Down n'out.

> *(She slaps her face to stay awake. She takes a bottle of five hour energy drink and downs it. She takes another five hour energy drink and downs it. She takes out her phone and dials.)*

. . . Katy? Katy is that you . . . ? No it's . . . it's your mom! Happy Birthday, Katy!! Oh my god, your voice sounds so grown up, I . . . no I'm coming home now! No, I'll be there. Katy, I will definitely be there. . . . Well you should believe me because I'm telling the truth and it's rude to . . . Can you put your daddy on? Yes. Katy, put your daddy on. Put your daddy on. Katy, I need you to put your daddy on, put your daddy on—Hi Russ . . . Yeah, no, I got it all, I got some balloons, I got a cake and ice cream. . . . Well, it's not an ice cream cake, but it's a cake and ice cream so . . . I don't see what the . . . Russ I have been driving for like 36 hours straight and- are you trying to make me late?! Are you trying to sabotage my—. . . Okay. Okay! I'll get a goddamn ice cream cake. I'll get off at the next fucking stop. I'm not being passive aggressive. I'm saying you're a dickless shit and I'm gonna see my daughter whether you want it or not. Down n'out.

(She hangs up. Upset, she takes her small handgun from beside her and mimes firing it. To Virgin Mary:)

Fuck him, Mama. Fuck him. Fuck him.

(She nudges Hula Girl with her gun.)

Better shake those fucking hips, girlie.

(HULA GIRL's hips shake. The VIRGIN MARY looks irritated.)

HULA GIRL: I like Interstate 378. I think it's my favorite Interstate. Do you know why, Virgin Mary? I think I may have mentioned it before?

VIRGIN MARY: Because of the telephone—

HULA GIRL: It's because of the telephone poles! Because they look like palm trees! Do you know what a palm tree is, Virgin Mary?

VIRGIN MARY: A palm tree is a tree that's too much of a bitch to grow any branches.

HULA GIRL: . . . No, no that's not . . . palm trees are just one of many plants native to Hawaii, including guavas, pineapples, candlenuts, kukui nuts, java plums—and sometimes? If I sort of blur my eyes? I can pretend that the telephone poles really are palm trees. And the wind is a tropical breeze. And the car horns are schools of dolphins at play. And that's when my dancing gets really good.

Hula Girl closes her eyes, pretends, and dances. With her body language she invites Virgin Mary to do the same. We begin to hear the soothing tropical music. Bess begins to nod off.

VIRGIN MARY: Fuck the java plums.

HULA GIRL: . . . What?

VIRGIN MARY: Fuck 'em. And fuck the dolphins. What does a dolphin look like? Tell me what it looks like.

HULA GIRL: Well it has a . . . it has a head . . .

VIRGIN MARY: You've never seen a dolphin. You're not from Hawaii. You've never even been to Hawaii.

HULA GIRL: . . . Well, yeah, but . . . . Are you okay, Virgin Mary? All this language . . . and last night—

VIRGIN MARY: What? What about last night?

HULA GIRL: Nothing. Sorry.

> *(BESS has fallen asleep at the wheel. Cars begin to honk.)*

VIRGIN MARY: Whatever. I'd just like one trip where we didn't have to talk about palm trees or java plums or motherfucking Hawaii.

> *(Suddenly, the intense sound of honking traffic. BESS wakes up, terrified.)*

BESS: Fuck fuck fuck fuck fuck!

> *(She drastically rights the wheel. She's breathing very heavily.)*

BESS: *(to VIRGIN MARY)* You gotta keep your eyes on the road, Mama.

HULA GIRL: Well, even if I haven't been to Hawaii, one day I will! And when I get off the plane, they'll put a lei— a traditional garland of Hawaiian flowers— around my neck. And I'll look out at all the smiling faces and say "Aloha". In Hawaiian, aloha means both hello and goodbye.

VIRGIN MARY: You really think one day you'll go to Hawaii?

HULA GIRL: Of course, Virgin Mary. Why? You don't think I will? What? Say it. If you don't think I'll go to Hawaii then say it.

VIRGIN MARY: Hula Girl . . . I promise you. You are never ever going to Hawaii.

> *(This makes HULA GIRL very, very sad. She dances sadly.)*

HULA GIRL: I thought the Virgin Mary was supposed to be nice.

VIRGIN MARY: Well I'm not the Virgin Mary. We just bear an unfortunate resemblance.

> *(BESS pulls the truck into a gas station. She stops the car. She gets out, picks up her gun and slips it into her waist. She exits offstage to the gas station.)*

HULA GIRL: I heard you crying last night.

VIRGIN MARY: . . . That wasn't crying. That was praying. My praying just happens to sound like crying. Look it's not . . . you're not going to Hawaii! Face it! Because we are plastic reproductions! We are hollow, soulless objects and there are millions of others exactly like us. So you don't have to dance. And I don't have to be nice.

HULA GIRL: . . . You don't think we have souls?

(Suddenly, there are three gun shots heard offstage.)

VIRGIN MARY: I don't think we have souls.

(BESS re-enters, totally shell-shocked, holding in one hand her gun, and in the other a very large Slushee cup. Her shirt is covered in slushee. She enters the truck cabin and dials her phone.)

BESS: Hello police. I am Bess Rector. I operate a 1998 Mach CH612 truck. I am at a gas station after Exit 13 on Interstate 378. I went to get an ice cream cake. And at the counter there was a . . . a man with a Dora the Explorer mask. And I thought it was strange because it looked like it was made for children and the string was really digging into his head. And then he turned around, and I saw he had a gun in his hand. And I took out my firearm, and I shot him. And he shot at me. And I shot him again. And he hit the . . . the slushee machine so there's all sorts of . . . slushee on the floor. And the second shot went through the . . . the bangs of the Dora the Explorer mask. So the mask is still on but it's broken and . . . No, I'm. I'm okay. I feel weird, though. I drank about seven bottles of five-hour energy. That's thirty-five hours of energy. Maybe that's why I feel weird.

(A beat. She takes a sip of the slushee.)

No, I'm still here. I have to get home. It's my daughter's fourth birthday. . . . . Okay. I'll . . . I'll be here. I'm the one in the truck with the sticker of Minnie Mouse squatting and taking a piss.

(She hangs up. A beat. She takes her straw and lets a drop of slushee drip onto the Virgin Mary. The VIRGIN MARY feels the slushee dripping down her back.)

HULA GIRL: Virgin Mary? Are you okay?

VIRGIN MARY: Do you want to know what we are, Hula Girl? What we really are?

HULA GIRL: Um—

VIRGIN MARY: Lately I've been feeling . . . I don't know. Whatever. And last night I needed . . . I can't describe it well. And
I looked up at the sky, through the windshield, through the
bugs and the stains, over the telephone wires, and I saw it.
I saw the Star of Bethlehem. And it was beautiful, and I felt
like it was pulling me, pulling some deep part of me inside
my stomach, beneath my heart, and oh god, it felt so good,
it felt like an answer, it felt like all the answers that we're
supposed to hear but never seem to get, and then I realized . . .
it wasn't the Star of Bethlehem. It was an airplane. But it
wasn't just an airplane. It was Hooters Air.

HULA GIRL: Hooters Air . . .

VIRGIN MARY: The restaurant. Hooters. They have an airplane.
Hooters Air. And that's what we are. We're not Stars of Bethlehem, we're motherfucking Hooters Air. Cheap and empty
and burning in the night! And it's just . . . it's not fair.

HULA GIRL: It's not fair that she got to be her and I had to be
me.

HULA GIRL: . . . Virgin Mary . . . are we besties? I mean, you're
pretty much the only person I know, so we pretty much have
to be besties.

VIRGIN MARY: . . . I guess we're besties.

HULA GIRL: I think we're besties, too. There's this word, this
special Hawaiian word—

VIRGIN MARY: *(very quietly)* . . . Why can't I perform just one
miracle?

HULA GIRL: What?

VIRGIN MARY: . . . Why can't I perform just one fucking miracle?

(BESS dials and speaks into her phone.)

BESS: . . . Hi Katy. Hi baby. I just wanted to call you. I just wanted to say hi and . . . and do you watch that show? Do you
watch that show *Dora the Explorer?* Okay, I don't want you
watching that show any more. Katy . . . Katy, yes the monkey, I get that you like the monkey, but you're not watching it
any more. Katy. Stop talking about the monkey. Stop talking
about the monkey. Katy, I am your mother stop talking about
the fucking monkey! . . . I'm sorry I shouted. I shouldn't
have shouted. I love you. I love you. Say you love me. I love

you. I love you. . . . Russ? Why did she give you the phone. I didn't ask her to give you the phone. Let me talk to her . . . I didn't say that. I didn't use that word . . . No, I'm coming Russ. I'm coming! I have the fucking ice cream cake and I'm coming and I've planned this for months and-don't hang up! Don't hang up! Don't hang up!

(He's hung up.)

Fuck. Fuck. Fuck. Fuck. Fuck!

(She rears up furiously, grabs the hula girl statuette off of her dashboard, and breaks it in frustration. It falls to the ground. HULA GIRL's body suddenly contorts in an enormously violent manner and falls to the floor.)

VIRGIN MARY: Hula Girl!

HULA GIRL: It's . . . it's okay. I'm okay. Look, I'm fine, I can still dance, see? See?

(She tries pathetically to dance; it hurts.)

No, I can't. I can't dance. Oh my God. Ow. Ouch.

VIRGIN MARY: Hula Girl, just . . . just don't move! Don't try to hula!

HULA GIRL: Oh man. Oh wow, it's really bad—

VIRGIN MARY: No! No, it's fine! Hey, I have an idea! Why don't we talk about Hawaii! You like Hawaii!

HULA GIRL: I do like Hawaii . . . Virgin Mary, in Hawaii . . . they have special Hawaiian words for everything, like poi and . . . hula. And they have . . . they have this word, au-makua, have you ever heard that word before?

VIRGIN MARY: No, tell me about it—

HULA GIRL: It . . . it means "soul". Because Hawaiians . . . they think everything has aumakuas. The people. And the dolphins. And the pineapples. And the surfboards . . .

BESS: Oh fuck.

(She picks up her gun.)

VIRGIN MARY: Just keep talking.

HULA GIRL: People can care so much about their surfboards. So they have to have aumakuas. Why else would people care much? I think you have an aumakua, Virgin Mary. Do you know what aumakua translates into in English?

VIRGIN MARY: What?

HULA GIRL: "Something fine."

(Bess picks up and examines the broken Hula Girl.)

VIRGIN MARY: . . . When you take me to Hawaii, Hula Girl, we're definitely going surfing.

HULA GIRL: What? We are? We're going?

VIRGIN MARY: Oh yeah! Are you kidding?! We'll eat java plums, we'll uh go to volcanoes, right? They have volcanoes there, you've told me that.

HULA GIRL: But I don't want . . . your robe . . . to get lava on it.

VIRGIN MARY: We'll ride dolphins—

HULA GIRL: *(motioning to invisible dolphins)* Look, Virgin Mary! Dolphins! Dolphins with their . . . heads. They're beautiful. I didn't know what they looked like, but they're so beautiful.

VIRGIN MARY: And you can teach me all of your Hawaiian words ...

HULA GIRL: Like aloha. Aloha means both hello and goodbye. Did you know that? Aloha, Virgin Mary. Aloha.

(She dies. BESS places the broken hula girl on the dashboard.)

BESS: Fuck it. Fuck it. Fuck it.

(Suddenly, the phone rings. She looks at it, surprised, and picks up.)

. . . Hello? Russ? Why're you—I don't care. I don't care why you're calling. Congratulations. You're getting what you wanted. I was at a gas station getting an ice cream cake and shot a robber dead. So I guess I'm not coming. I guess you're always right. I guess I'm a terrible mother. . . . Stop talking so loudly. You're talking too loudly. . . . I was gonna give her the Hula Girl. For her birthday. Because she always liked it. Because she always liked to make it dance. I'd sit in the truck with her . . . back when you and I were still . . . you know . . . and Katy and I would both do the hula . . . . Can you be honest with me, Russ? . . . Does she hate me? I mean . . . I understand if she does, but . . . Wait, what? She said that about me? Are you . . . are you lying? Are you sure? . . . That's so nice of her. Oh God, Russ. I almost died. I almost died. I almost died. I almost died.

(She begins to break down a bit. We begin to hear police sirens in the background that get progressively louder.)

Oh God. I haven't slept in forever. Oh God. Thank you. Thank you. Thank you. Thank you.

(She addresses the statuette of the Virgin Mary and begins to thank it.)

BESS: Thank you. Thank you. Thank you. Thank you. Thank you. Thank you. Thank you. Thank you. Thank you.

VIRGIN MARY: . . . You're welcome.

(Blackout)

END OF PLAY

STONEHENGE

Patricia Milton

ORIGINAL PRODUCTION

STONEHENGE was first performed as part of *GIRL PLAY 2013*, The Fourth Lesbian Play Festival, June 21, 22 & 23, 2013 at the Women's Theatre Project, Wilton Manors, 600 NE 21st Court, Wilton Manors, FL.

Directed by Marj O'Neill Butler

CAST:
EMMA: Jessica Marion Welch
JANE: Casey Dressler
AVERY: Noah Levine

CHARACTERS:

> EMMA: female, twenties
> JANE: female, twenties to thirties
> AVERY: male, twenties

> *A crowded pub, evening, present day. JANE, nervous, and EMMA. EMMA drinking a pint.*

JANE: He doesn't like me.

EMMA: You don't know that.

JANE: He walks in, sees us, and he says "Hi!" to *you*— and then he heads for the bathroom.

EMMA: So he had to relieve himself.

JANE: He's been in there for 25 minutes!

EMMA: Um, well, you know, maybe he had to . . . You know.

JANE: Right. I probably won't like *him*.

EMMA: Maybe you won't. But I hope you'll—

JANE: That other one was a doozy.

EMMA: Okay, we / already—

JANE: In the country illegally. Checking in on his cell phone with his parole officer, me sitting right there—

EMMA: I said *okay*! Do you want a beer?

JANE: No. What I want, Emma—

EMMA: Oh my god. Shh! Here he comes. Just be yourself. Wait, don't be yourself. Be pleasant.

> *(AVERY approaches the table carrying a paper bag.)*

EMMA: Avery! Hi.

AVERY: Emma. Hi, you must be—

JANE: I'm Jane. Hi.

AVERY: Emma's told me a lot about you.

EMMA: (*sotto voce*) In the bathroom for 25 minutes?

AVERY: (*He shrugs, puts the bag on the table.*) So, Jane,—

JANE: I don't like him. (*to AVERY*) Nothing personal.

EMMA: Sit down. Please, sit down, she's just being—herself.

> *(AVERY sits.)*

AVERY: I'm really a good guy.

JANE: (*to AVERY*) I appreciate the sincere self-recommendation.

AVERY: Wow. (*to EMMA*) Cool, and can I borrow a ten from you?

JANE: And he's *broke*?

EMMA: Can you stop being hostile for one second?

AVERY: You two, uh, having, like, a spat or something?

EMMA: (*to JANE*) Don't say anything!

AVERY: Do you / want—

EMMA: Don't *YOU* say anything either! Now. I happened to think Avery, here, was kind of perfect. *Is* kind of perfect. He's cute—

AVERY: Thanks. I think of myself as ruggedly handsome—

EMMA: And although he's not all that well set up in the financial department, what you want is a good heart, and some smarts, right?

AVERY: The economy sucks right now.

EMMA: Don't get defensive. *I'm* talking. Okay?

JANE: I don't like his hair color. (*to AVERY*) I don't like your hair color.

AVERY: It's actually . . . I use Loreal™.

EMMA: I didn't know that!

AVERY: Yeah. Because I'm worth it. My hair's. . . really, white. When you do a lot of cocaine, it can drain your hair of its color.

JANE: Oh my god.

AVERY: It used to be red. I don't do a lot of cocaine any more.

JANE: This is what you bring me? (*To AVERY*) What do you do now, like, reasonable amounts of cocaine?

EMMA: *You* said the bios and the data at the sperm bank were too impersonal!

JANE: Well, when I see them in the flesh, I keep getting reminded why I'm a lesbian.

AVERY: There's no need to attack my gender.

EMMA: Avery, go get yourself a beer, would you? Here.

(*EMMA gives him money, and AVERY exits.*)

EMMA: You are determined to ruin this, aren't you?

JANE: No! No. I'm just. . . he's not right.

EMMA: Why do I get the feeling anyone I find won't be "right?"

JANE: You know what? You scare me. Do you really want "that" in our lives for 20 years?
Where did you even meet him?

EMMA: He was at this poetry slam. . .

JANE: Jesus, he's a *poet*?

EMMA: You used to like poetry. Oh, for Christ's sake. How are we even still together, let alone trying to conceive? I must be crazy.

JANE: I want a *baby*. With you. With you, Emma, not with some broke poet guy. Did that sound classist?

EMMA: Yes. And biologically impossible.

JANE: You lack the skills, is what I'm saying. We've got to get you off the daddy shopping gig.

EMMA: Not "daddy" shopping. Sperm shopping. It's not exactly the same thing. And a poet is as good as . . . (*trails off as she regards the paper bag.*) Oh, God. Jane, do you think? The bag?

JANE: What? What, "oh, Jane, do I think?" (*catching her drift*) Ooooooooooooh. 25 minutes in the bathroom. Jesus, this guy.

EMMA: Do you . . . do you suppose . . .? I hope he used a thermos, or something.

JANE: Yeah, there's a stain, on the bottom. Leaking, and that would indicate he did not use a thermos. (*beat*) Open it.

EMMA: I am not going to open it. If he's wrong for you, if he's wrong for us, then forget the bag. Let's just forget him. Forget Avery, forget I ever suggested him.

JANE: Emma, I care about *you*. I love you. Our relationship. . .

EMMA: You don't even trust me—our fucking "relationship"—

JANE: No, it's good. It's a good relationship.

EMMA: How? In that it has no logic, and we drive each other crazy?

JANE: Yes. But it works, anyway. The love. The love makes it work.

EMMA: It's like some kind of a slow mo disaster. It's this—big pile of rocks and rubble, this relationship!

JANE: You know, I was thinking that. No, really. Not "rubble," though. Wait, listen to me. It's. . . it's like Stonehenge.

EMMA: (*beat. This sinks in*) "Stonehenge." Oh, fine. Falling apart, a *ruin*, / like a—

JANE: No. Stonehenge. Mighty and mysterious, and who the hell knows how it got built, how the stones got there, how the foundation got constructed to last so damn long . . . and—

And it's actually really well—made, right? Durable, for the ages. "Inside a ruin may lie a treasure." That's Rumi.

EMMA: (*getting onboard*) Sure, okay. And the current civilization doesn't understand what it means, its internal, spiritual meaning—

JANE: Yes! And maybe a stone falls over, here and there, every. . . oh, once a century or something. But it's built to last. With 45-ton slabs, Emma! And adding a little new stone, a little baby: that will be just as mysterious, and majestic, and . . . poetic. . . as— As a poem. Like, well, like Rumi. Oh, hell. Maybe Avery's okay.

EMMA: Oh, no. He is *not* okay. If this bag—

JANE: That's points in his favor. It's a good sign. That means he's ready, and willing.

EMMA: A little *overly* willing, if you ask me.

JANE: The eagerness is good. It bodes well. As long as the coke habit—

EMMA: He doesn't do coke any more. I'm 100% almost completely sure.

AVERY returns. No beer.

AVERY: The crowd to get beers is ridiculous. I'll try again in a few.

JANE: Look, I'm sorry I was so hard on you, just now. I . . . I want you to know, I appreciate your, uh—

EMMA: Willingness. Enthusiasm! Both of us. We kind of want to start over, from here.

AVERY: That's great. I'd like that. Sorry we got off to—

JANE: No, it was me.

AVERY: I wrote a poem for you guys. For your family. Just— Like a haiku.

JANE: (*soft*) Well, that's terrific. Thank you, Avery. I'd like to hear it.

AVERY: (*takes a piece of paper from his pocket*) Morning rain retreats. / Spring sun welcomes and beams on / Our dreaming baby.

(Short pause, JANE and EMMA look at each other.)

EMMA: It's sweet!

AVERY: Cool! Hey, I know, let me open this! We can share.

AVERY opens the bag as the women gasp.

AVERY takes out a white take-out box and hands out forks. He eats from the box.

EMMA: *(to AVERY)* But. . . 25 minutes in the can?

AVERY: (*mouth full*) What? Oh . . . I *know*! Prune Danish for breakfast. Never again.

END OF PLAY.

SUPERNOVA IN RESEDA

Jerrod Bogard

ORIGINAL PRODUCTION
   Theatre Breaking Through Barriers in June 2013 at Theatre
   Row's Clurman

   Director: Christopher Burris
   Stage Manager: Emily Goforth
   Dramaturg: Julius Novick

   CAST:
   LAUREN: Samantha Debicki
   MURIEL: Tonya Pinkins
   SIMON: Lawrence Merritt

CHARACTERS:

> LAUREN: A young, fiery manager/publicist (twenty-five to thirty-five).
>
> MURIEL: A seasoned, jaded manager/publicist (fifty-five to sixty-five).
>
> SIMON: A retired B-list action star (sixty-five to eighty).

SETTING: The present. Simon's home office in Hollywood.

> *LIGHTS UP in Simon's home-office in Reseda, Hollywood, CA.*

MURIEL: What's this about, Simon? Why am I Getting onto the 405 after 3pm? Am I Evil Knievel? What has caused you to put my life in danger in this way? What terrible business could not be discussed over face-time or on the phone or via fucking carrier pigeon? What is it?

SIMON: Reseda just isn't the same without you, my dear. Any problems getting through security?

MURIEL: *(setting her purse down)* Security. You're making Gerardo wear a gun now.

SIMON: One cannot be too careful these days. Doesn't it look formidable?

MURIEL: It looks like you gave your gardener a gun.

SIMON: Muriel Mengals, Lauren Goldberg.

LAUREN: It's very nice to—

MURIEL: *(without looking at her)* Nice to meet you.

> *(to Simon)*
>
> Out with it, Simon. I told you how inconvenient this is for me. And yet I have come—out of respect for our professional relationship of 35-years and our friendship of 22.

SIMON: Now see—I thought we had a 26-year friendship.

MURIEL: I don't count the early '90's. Can we get to the chase, or cut to the point, or can you at the very least tell me you have some booze? Yes thank you, I'll have a drink. No, I don't care what. Why-oh-fucking-why have you summoned me here? *(pause)* Is your girl going to get the drink or am I?

SIMON: Lauren is not my assistant.

LAUREN: It's very nice to meet you, Miz Mengals. Lauren Goldberg.

SIMON: Lauren is with Simpson-Weller.

MURIEL: *(after a beat- to Simon)* What the fuck is this?

SIMON: Muriel—

MURIEL: What. The fuck. Is this?

(sizing up the situation—surmising she is being fired)

You haven't booked in five years, Simon. Is this my fault?

LAUREN: Well, it is not Mr. Thomas's fault. Of that we are sure.

MURIEL: I am above and beyond the call of duty here. You know it was me who returned the German Shepard you stole from the PETA fundraiser shoot. And when you caused a drunken pile up on Wilshire Boulevard, I sent my assistant to take your place. He's still on house arrest. I finally book you a respectable gig—

LAUREN: *(to Simon)* The diabetes telethon?

SIMON: *(to Lauren)* I spiked the juice at craft services.

MURIEL: And sent half the volunteers into a diabetic coma! . . . I have been sweeping up the messes—working my lipoed ass off while you barricade yourself in this faux-mahogany, 70's tribute room like a latter day Howard Hughes. But sure. No. It's all your manager's fault. So you what- you lure me up here—into the God-damn canyon—to what- to *shame* me? In some power-play hatchet job? Have you gone completely senile? Are you entirely out of your mind this time?

SIMON: Muriel, I'm dying.

MURIEL: *(without a beat)* Oh we will get to that. . . . And "Mister Thomas?" Is that supposed to be a mark of respect for your status or for your fragility? Why doesn't she just call you *Gramps*? Jesus, Simon. . . . Now-what-now? You're fucking dying?

SIMON: I have seventy-five tumors. Or some atrocious thing like that.

MURIEL: What?

SIMON: I have cancer. But,. . . it's not that bad.

MURIEL: What?

SIMON: It's actually rather good precisely because it *is* so fucking bad.

MURIEL: *(to Lauren)* Is he making any sense to you?

(to Simon)

You, now, make sense.

LAUREN: May I?

MURIEL: Somebody!

LAUREN: Mr. Thomas—Simon, . . . Simon has cancer. He was just explaining to me that it has progressed beyond the point that he wishes to pursue treatment. He's decided to. . .

SIMON: Ride it out. I've decided to ride it out.

MURIEL: *(she takes a deep breath)* I would tell you I don't have time for this, Simon, but I already know that my time doesn't matter to you.

LAUREN: Miz Mengals,—

SIMON: *(asking her to back off)* Lauren, please.

(then to Muriel)

Sweetie. It's OK. Muriel is speechless for the first time. Give her a moment.

Lauren, would you get us some drinks?

LAUREN: *(asserting her position)* No.

(Both Muriel and Simon admire Lauren's moxie. Then their gazes rest on her with the resolve of age's wisdom.)

LAUREN: *(with dignity)* Of course.

(Lauren crosses to the bar. In the time that Lauren is away, Muriel lets her exterior soften, and we begin to see her as Simon's old friend.)

MURIEL: You're a son of a bitch.

SIMON: Yes.

MURIEL: Simon the martyr. Take on the world, but God forbid you ask for any help.

(pause)

When?

SIMON: When did I find out or when do I die? *(pause)* Doctor told me last month. Another doctor told me the month before that. I first heard the word last year some time. . . . Some time around April. . . . On the sixth. . . . It was a Tuesday. . . . 3:14 in the afternoon.

MURIEL: And so you haven't been—But you've sought treatment options.

SIMON: None at all.

MURIEL: For God's sake why not? And why am I hearing about this from a God-damn stranger? *(pause)* How long?

SIMON: I'll be gone by February.

LAUREN: *(returning with drinks)* Just in time!

> *(She sets down the drinks: Coffee for Simon and herself, Vodka for Muriel.)*

SIMON: If we time it right.

MURIEL: Time what right?

SIMON: Well, my bags are packed, metaphorically speaking.

MURIEL: Just in time. In time for what?

LAUREN: For the Oscars.

> *(Lauren and Simon sip their drinks.)*

> *(Muriel moves to take a big drink and then, thinking better of it, sets the drink down untouched. She needs her wits.)*

MURIEL: Alright. Lauren Goldberg. I'll bite. Why the Oscars.

> *(Simon and Lauren share a glance.)*

> *(He nods to her. And she begins. . .)*

LAUREN: In 1994 the Academy of Arts & Sciences instituted the tradition of running an obituary reel on Oscar night. They began by honoring just a dozen or so Hollywood icons, but over the last fifteen years the "in memoriam" segment has exploded. Last year it featured 53 fallen Hollywood insiders. Among them: actors, directors, producers, technicians, even a well-liked publicist.

MURIEL: *(raising her glass)* Something to aspire to.

SIMON: People have worked much harder for far less.

MURIEL: So you're hoping to get a spot on the bucket reel if you croak at exactly the right time.

> *(takes that drink now)*

So that makes me what—the Dr. Kevorkian of managers?

LAUREN: Unfortunately it's not as simple as just dying at the right moment.

MURIEL: Can't anything be simple?

LAUREN: While the obit reel has become a stalwart of the awards show, it's reached the capacity for the time they can allow. As it is they have it playing before a commercial break.

MURIEL: Tough act to follow.

LAUREN: So while they've capped the number of people who can be mentioned in the reel, the number of candidates continues to grow. Last year they turned down over three hundred names.

SIMON: Andy Griffith.

MURIEL: Phyllis Diller.

LAUREN: Competition has never been steeper, and the obit reel is becoming one of *the* categories to watch.

MURIEL: OK, well I'm still lost. Mr. Thomas—Simon—this shit-bag never won an Academy Award. He's never even been to the Academy Awards.

LAUREN: He went in 1968, '69, '76, '89, and had an invitation in 2001 but declined to go.

SIMON: You don't have to have won an Oscar to be included.

LAUREN: The opening and the final spot being the most coveted, the opening spot is sometimes given to a person who has a terrific reputation,

SIMON: Popularity.

LAUREN: But who hasn't necessarily been honored by the Academy—in an official sense.

MURIEL: And you think.

SIMON: I want that spot.

(Muriel takes a big drink.)

SIMON: Muriel? What do you think?

LAUREN: You have concerns? You think perhaps that this is somehow . . . unethical.

MURIEL: If it was ethical it wouldn't be happening in Hollywood. No, it's that this has never even entered my—and it wouldn't have—I mean frankly, this would never have occurred to me in a million years. And I'm a sick twisted bitch.

SIMON: Exactly. So I wanted you two to meet.

MURIEL: And here we are. And you've got your little plan. But you're not firing me—you wouldn't have asked me to come all the way down here.

LAUREN: Mr. Thomas would like us to work together on this project.

MURIEL: Project. Phsh. . . . Why?

SIMON: Nobody knows my career like you do. There's no one who can best encapsulate what I've done in this town—for this town. No one better to remember everything and, the way it was, not how it's seen now. Do you—do you know what I—

MURIEL: I do know, but you're not jumping off moving trains anymore, Simon. You're not that guy! Simon, forgive me, but this is dark.

SIMON: Dark!? Dark is my life now. I wake up and it's dark. I plod my day through in this darkness, Mimi, and no light spills into these halls. There are no people, no voices. It's a darkness of sound in this damned house! You know I have left in my life's wake a trail of nothingness—for all the explosions and all the gunfights—a void. And the projector aint spinning and the light—is—out. Help me. Cause it can shine again. I know it can. Like the good ol' days and into eternity. Right? Into their hearts. A billion people saying, O', O', Oh we've lost something brilliant. Some bright star is out. And that darkness—it can be shared, and felt, . . . and, and mourned. I want to be on that list.

MURIEL: I'll draft a campaign. We'll get started. We'll need to get you some work. We'll need to get you out there. Some charity. Some cause. But will you have the strength, I don't—

SIMON: No.

MURIEL: That's what I'm saying! If you're not going to—

SIMON: No.

LAUREN: It is crucial, Miz Mengals, that we all be on the same page with this project. It won't be enough to simply run patterns from "the old playbook."

MURIEL: I'm getting that 405-feeling again.

LAUREN: Simon Thomas. He's led a mediocre career . . . of moderate-stardom. To make up for that, he has got to go out like a supernova.

MURIEL: Simon, are you listening to this?

SIMON: Are you?

(Lauren retrieves a plastic case from the desk.)

LAUREN: It's a pageant, Miz Mengals, and we have got to be the belle of the ball. Some newspaper clippings at a soup kitchen aren't going to cut it. *(Lauren opens the case and produces a pistol.)* Are you aware that 5 out of 6 handguns used by criminals in this country are obtained through the black market?

MURIEL: So you couldn't just get one for Gerardo.

SIMON: They came as a set!

LAUREN: If Simon is making his final exit, ask yourself, what could be a bigger exit than for the former poster-boy of Smith & Wesson to face off, to "show-down" if-you-will, with the American Gun Lobby. Picture: a full-on media blitz of Simon Thomas in activist roles, reality television, short documentaries, and finally, a trip to Southern Mexico where an unfortunate run-in with a gun-running cartel will lead to his kidnapping. The state department will intervene. A tribute concert in the Hollywood Bowl. An autobiography—finished with letters from his imprisonment. And ultimately, a violent,

SIMON: *(apprehensive)* Mm-mm?

LAUREN: or quasi-violent, . . . final ending. The dénouement. A dramatic demise—met on live streaming video—Internationally viewed by hundreds of millions of new and ever-adoring fans.

SIMON: All the world's a stage.

LAUREN: A fan base with muscle, a fan base we wouldn't dare disappoint come Hollywood's biggest night.

MURIEL: The Oscars.

SIMON: Immortality.

LAUREN: Are you in? Muriel?

MURIEL: No.

SIMON: Mimi.

LAUREN: This is unfortunate. And disappointing.

MURIEL: Do you know what's disappointing? When awards are given to children and to dead people. Do you know why? Because these people have not earned anything; they have merely gone where life has put them. Simon, it's officially hell on the 405. Again, you have my derision for bringing me here today to meet this adolescent twat and hear your hare-brained scheme for world domination. Thank you for the drink. Have fun with the Cancer. Goodbye.

LAUREN: We can't let you leave.

MURIEL: Excuse me?

(Lauren points the pistol at Muriel.)

LAUREN: This is an airtight plan, but only if we keep it air tight.

MURIEL: Simon. Listen to me now. Once upon a time I may have found this lunacy charming. But no longer. Now you have got to accept where things are and move on.

SIMON: But don't you see, that's exactly what I'm doing!

LAUREN: It's a shame that you broke in to Mr. Thomas's house today. That under the stress of a floundering career, and triggered by the loss of your biggest client, you decided to break into his home and threaten him with a gun you purchased illegally from a Mexican cartel. You would have achieved your tragic aim were it not for the chance visit of Mr. Thomas's new manager and publicist, Lauren Goldberg of Simpson-Weller.

SIMON: And who knew. . . that would mark the beginning of an unprecedented Hollywood comeback. That Simon Thomas, one-time soap star turned Hollywood's go-to side-kick turned voice over fad turned reclusive shut-in, would rise again, and during his final days become an icon of the anti-gun movement in this country, forever turning the tide of Hollywood——no—of American—

LAUREN: Of *world* history.

SIMON: Oh, we strut and fret our hour upon the stage. And then—

(Muriel rushes at Lauren and grabs for the pistol. They struggle. The PISTOL FIRES. The pistol falls to the floor. Both women step back. After a beat: Simon falls into a chair, gripping his stomach.)

SIMON: I've shot this scene. . . a thousand times.

(He dies.)

(Long pause.)

MURIEL: We can spin this.

LAUREN: Oh yeah.

CURTAIN.

Unveiled

J. Thalia Cunningham

ORIGINAL PRODUCTION

Unveiled was originally produced by CACC South as part of the Pittsburgh New Works Festival, Pittsburgh, Pennsylvania in September 2013. The production was directed by Lora Oxenreiter.

CAST:
ADRIENNE: Dara Stern
MASUDA: Elyse Alberts
DR. SORA ZADRAN: Louise Fox
AMANULLAH: Nitai Das Monge

Unveiled was produced as part of Short & Sweet Festival Malaysia, Kuala Lumpur, Malaysia in October 2013, where it won the award for best script. The production was directed by Matthew Koh.

CAST:
ADRIENNE: Natalie Heng
MASUDA: Mia Sabrina Mahadir
DR. SORA ZADRAN: Nik Waheeda

CHARACTERS:

> ADRIENNE: American woman, late thirties or older, tough, smart, her intelligence and ability to move mountains doesn't extend to her cultural sensitivity
>
> MASUDA: Female, late twenties to thirties, DR. ZADRAN's interpreter
>
> DR. SORA ZADRAN: Female, Afghan Minister of Women's Affairs, forties or older, but looks older than actual age, very wise, speaks and thinks using Afghan proverbs
>
> AMANULLAH: Male, twenties, works for DR. ZADRAN (could be stagehand)

PLACE: Kabul, Office of the Ministry of Women's Affairs

TIME: The Present

> *At rise: ADRIENNE sits in DR. SORA ZADRAN's office. MASUDA, is positioned between ZADRAN and the visitor. ADRIENNE's black bra is visible under a somewhat sheer top and she is bareheaded. Both ZADRAN and MASUDA wear shalwaar kameez with large chadri draped over head and shoulders. There should be a clear behavioral distinction between the interaction of MASUDA with ADRIENNE and MASUDA with ZADRAN. After MASUDA speaks with ZADRAN, both women frequently beam, smiling graciously and politely at ADRIENNE, despite the content of their actual conversation. Several of these have been written in as stage directions. The remainder are at the discretion of the director.*

ADRIENNE: Translate into Pushtu for the minister that we're the women of RAW.

MASUDA: Raw? You want place to cook food?

ADRIENNE: R. A. W. Rampant American Women.

MASUDA: *(to ZADRAN)* The acronym for their NGO.

ZADRAN: I thought RAW had something to do with wrestling.

MASUDA: *(turns back to American as both Afghan women smile graciously.)* The Minister says you are most welcome to Afghanistan.

ADRIENNE: *(slapping papers on desk)* Tell her here are our goals and objectives for you. An Afghanistan expert sits on our board of directors.

MASUDA: *(to ZADRAN)* They think we're incapable of creating our own goals and objectives?

ZADRAN: How often does their expert come to Afghanistan? Birds only fly high as their wings take them.

(both Afghan women beam fixed smiles at American woman)

MASUDA: The Minister appreciates your interest and asks when your Afghanistan expert last visited our country. Perhaps they have met.

ADRIENNE: Well . . . she's never *been* to Afghanistan. But she gives wonderful lectures about your suffering.

MASUDA: How very kind of her.

ADRIENNE: *(handing over brochure)* And she printed these brochures for us to pass out.

MASUDA: *(examining brochure and handing it to ZADRAN)* "Getting to know your Afghan." Published by the Westminster . . . Kennel Club?

ZADRAN: The last NGO thought an Afghan was something you crochet and drape over the sofa. Ask her if there are any Afghans on their board.

(Afghan women beam staged smiles at American)

MASUDA: The Minister is grateful for your efforts and asks whether your board of directors includes any Afghans. Afghan *people.*

ADRIENNE: No, but we want to fast track Afghan women into the 21st century.

MASUDA: *(to ZADRAN)* Have we ever fast tracked anything, let alone social change?

ZADRAN: A disastrous recipe for fundamentalism to flourish. Worst recipe in existence—other than the naranj pilau I made last night.

MASUDA: I've tasted your pilau. It's soggy because you use too much water.

(to ADRIENNE)

The Minister thanks you and asks your plans.

ADRIENNE: *(reciting parrot-like)* Tell her we want to create jobs for women so they can sustain their families. Life-changing skills and economic opportunities will put your troubled country on the path to prosperity and peace. Empower you and free you from the burqa religion so . . .

MASUDA: *(to ZADRAN)* Here comes a burqa religion diatribe. The last NGO said "empowerment" 67 times. Shall I keep count again?

ZADRAN: They don't understand our tribal culture influences us more than religion.

MASUDA: Because America has no tribal culture. Or any other kind—of culture, I mean.

ZADRAN: What happened to their native American Indian tribes?

MASUDA: Drank into an alcoholic stupor. The sober ones opened casinos.

(to ADRIENNE)

The Minister appreciates your kindness. But we prefer wearing chadri, or burqa, as you call it.

ADRIENNE: That's ridiculous.

(She reaches into her tote bag and removes chadri.)

Someone gave me this to wear. But I refuse to cover my head for a bunch of male chauvinists.

(She stuffs chadri back into bag.)

MASUDA: To us, covering ourselves is a symbol of resistance. A useful disguise. Throughout our wars, Afghan women transported messages, weapons and forbidden publications underneath their chadris.

ADRIENNE: *(Reaching into a tote bag and unrolls large poster of woman in burqa.)* Here's our PR campaign. The Afghan woman victimized by the triumvirate of poverty, ignorance and fear. Powerful image. Encourages donors to give money for aid intervention. We held a fundraiser with the theme, "Tragedy Behind the Veil." Fabulous event in a private winery.

MASUDA: How very generous.

ADRIENNE: Dr. Alogia, the pet psychiatrist, and her dog, Thymus, attended as our celebrity guests. We used the money for a conference on Afghan Women's Human Rights.

MASUDA: *(to ZADRAN)* How do I respond to a celebrity dog with psychiatric issues raising funds in a winery?

ZADRAN: Ask whether any of the funds ever reached Afghanistan.

MASUDA: The Minister compliments your efforts to educate the public and wondered how money you raised was spent in Afghanistan.

ADRIENNE: We used the money to raise awareness of your oppression. Wanted donors to realize that setting Afghan women up in business sustains thousands of families, and accelerates an entire community, creating an explosive effect.

MASUDA: The Russians left us sufficient explosives. What about raising awareness of our abilities?

ADRIENNE: Once you're free from those burqas, we'll develop some abilities for you.

MASUDA: We prefer not to accelerate explosively, but to progress at a more moderate pace.

ADRIENNE: You must change your life situation. See our logo? Doves in flight. Metaphor for your captivity.

MASUDA: *(to ZADRAN)* What do you think of this "metaphor for our captivity?"

ZADRAN: Her aspirations are in heaven, but her brains are in her feet.

MASUDA: The Minister wishes you to know Afghan women seek improvement in their lives, not change.

ADRIENNE: Don't worry, we're trained in cultural competency. Our needlework program enables Afghan women to sew from home. Practical work for you homemakers and mothers. Safer, too. You can achieve financial independence without risking your security or threatening traditional roles.

MASUDA: *(to ZADRAN)* Yet another handicrafts-and tailoring-at-home program.

ZADRAN: More unemployed women tailors? If our women do any more sewing and weaving, we'll have enough textiles to blanket Kabul.

MASUDA: The Minister thanks you for your program, but expresses concern that already, too many women tailors can't find work.

ADRIENNE: We also developed a home-bound chicken-raising project. We'll support any women-run business for six months. That's the amount of funding we got. Here's our questionnaire. What is your business license number, date and place of issue? What were your sales the past two years? Please report in dollars. How many employees do you have? Answer yes or no: I can use a computer. I can email. I know how to do an Internet search. I know Excel. I know Skype.

MASUDA: How do chicken-raising and needlework projects expand abilities of Afghan women?

ADRIENNE: We'll offer meaningful employment, traditional work at our NGO, too. Women helping women.

MASUDA: *(to ZADRAN)* Our women may also work at their NGO.

ZADRAN: Who is this Skype? Someone who works with them?

MASUDA: Don't know. It's not a Pushtun name.

ZADRAN: Find out what sort of work they envision at their NGO.

MASUDA: The Minister asks the sort employment you offer Afghan women at your NGO.

ADRIENNE: We'll need women to do housekeeping, laundry, food preparation. Plenty of opportunities.

MASUDA: *(to ZADRAN)* Traditional work, all right.

ZADRAN: Even if a knife is made of gold, a person won't stab her own heart with it.

MASUDA: The Minister applauds your generous offer, but asks if cleaning your offices, washing your clothes and preparing your food fits your definition of elevating our status.

ADRIENNE: Augments our numbers for the annual report. But that's not all.

MASUDA: There's more?

ADRIENNE: To motivate you and raise your awareness, we're bringing a famous American play and plan to give performances to women throughout Afghanistan.

MASUDA: A theatre play will motivate us? For what? A theatrical career?

ADRIENNE: If women don't see this, they'll always suffer from repression.

MASUDA: What is this play?

ADRIENNE: It's called *"The Vagina Monologues."*

MASUDA: Excuse me?

ZADRAN: What did she say?

ADRIENNE: *"The Vagina Monologues."*

MASUDA: *(to ZADRAN)* The Vagina Monologues?

(to ADRIENNE)

What is this theatre piece about?

ADRIENNE: It celebrates women's sexuality and strength, exposing violations women endure worldwide.

MASUDA: *(to ZADRAN)* To celebrate our sexuality.

ADRIENNE: We'll give performances on V-Day.

MASUDA: V-Day? What this is?

ADRIENNE: V stands for Victory, Valentine, and Vagina.

MASUDA: *(to ZADRAN)* She likes that word.

ADRIENNE: It's a global movement to stop violence against women and girls. Wait until you hear the monologue, "The Little Coochie Snorcher that Could."

MASUDA: *(to ZADRAN)* What is a coochie snorcher?

ZADRAN: I don't know, but it sounds as though it should see a doctor.

ADRIENNE: That's just the beginning. We're also going to build you a women's health clinic.

MASUDA: *(to ZADRAN)* What do you think about a new women's health clinic?

ZADRAN: A tree doesn't move unless there is wind. Tell her the truth.

MASUDA: The Minister wishes to inform you that such a clinic already exists. Our women feel comfortable going there. Could you assist us by repairing the roof? Money saved could be used elsewhere.

ADRIENNE: Nope, we're going to build you a brand-new facility.

MASUDA: *(to ZADRAN)* A brand-new clinic.

ZADRAN: *(tapping MASUDA on the arm)* I bet you those lapis earrings we saw in the bazaar a donor wants a clinic named for him. Or her.

MASUDA: The Minister appreciates your kindness, but wishes to understand why you prefer to fund a new clinic rather than repairing our present one.

ADRIENNE: A donor earmarked a hefty contribution for a clinic named for her.

MASUDA: With ear-marks, the *donor* is the one who needs those lapis earrings.

ZADRAN: *(to MASUDA)* Perhaps they use those coochie snorch-
ers to earn money.

ADRIENNE: We want gender equality.

MASUDA: *(to ZADRAN)* I knew the "G" word was coming.

ZADRAN: The "G" word? See if they intend to address *real* gender equality.

MASUDA: The Minister supports gender equality and asks your
plans for aiding Afghan men.

ADRIENNE: Afghan men?

MASUDA: You mentioned equal opportunity.

ADRIENNE: Afghan men shackle your development. Afghan
men are exploiters, tyrants or terrorists. We'll fix gender im-
balance by focusing on Afghan women.

MASUDA: How will you do this?

ADRIENNE: Employment. Opportunities for the woman to become the breadwinner. Wear the pants in the family. Bring
home the bacon.

MASUDA: *(to ZADRAN)* She wants women to bring home the
bacon.

> *(to ADRIENNE)*

We do not eat bacon here. It is not halal.

ZADRAN: Sometimes it's easier to wage war with wise enemies
than be at peace with foolish friends.

MASUDA: The Minister concurs with your desire for employment and equal opportunity.

> *(AMANULLAH enters, placing teapot and glasses on
> table, then exits.)*

Tashakor, Amanullah.

> *(As MASUDA rises to serve the tea, she limps badly,
> then stumbles and falls. The others assist her to a chair.
> MASUDA winces in pain).*

ADRIENNE: Are you all right?

MASUDA: Thank you. It's nothing.

ADRIENNE: Nothing? You can barely walk.

> *(MASUDA and ZADRAN exchange glances)*

MASUDA: I'm fine. I tripped in the road yesterday.

ZADRAN: *(in perfect English)* Tell her. Perhaps she'll understand.

ADRIENNE: You speak English?

ZADRAN: Of course.

ADRIENNE: Why pretend you don't?

ZADRAN: An interpreter shields me. My verbal veil.

ADRIENNE: What happened to her?

ZADRAN: Tell her, Masuda.

MASUDA: Please, Sora, no.

ADRIENNE: Her husband beat her, didn't he?

MASUDA: My mother-in-law. My sisters-in-law.

> (*MASUDA removes her chadri and rolls up her sleeve. One arm is in a sling; the other arm and one leg in blood-stained bandages*).

ADRIENNE: Women . . .beat you? Why?

MASUDA: For shaming the family.

ADRIENNE: How did you do that?

MASUDA: Working here. With the Minister.

ADRIENNE: Earning money to support your family? They should be proud.

MASUDA: It's dishonorable.

ADRIENNE: Why?

ZADRAN: You come here with your programs offering assistance only to Afghan women. Our men have suffered from decades of war, too. In our tradition, we prefer that our men provide for us. Where are the training programs for men? You don't give equal opportunities.

ADRIENNE: That's why we're here. For equal opportunity.

ZADRAN: Five fingers are brothers but are not equals. Afghan men must live with the indignity of not providing for their families. They burn with shame of either starving or eating food the woman earned. Every anguish passes except the anguish of hunger. Employment for one Afghan woman creates shame and dishonor for an entire family. The cost is greater than her earning potential.

ADRIENNE: Why hasn't anyone said something?

ZADRAN: Our culture teaches us to say what we think people want to hear. Besides, women fear if they speak up, they'll lose their chance for training.

ADRIENNE: Women should take care of each other.

ZADRAN: Women also take care of the family honor.

ADRIENNE: How does honor enter into it?

ZADRAN: Responsibility for safeguarding family honor belongs to women. If a woman brings about shame, other women in the family must remedy the situation.

ADRIENNE: I thought just men beat women here.

ZADRAN: You come to our country telling us what to do. None of you asks us what we want.

ADRIENNE: No woman ever told us what she wanted.

ZADRAN: Did you ask? Afghans view women working outside their traditional roles as reminding us of our poverty, insulting man's dignity and doubting men's ability to provide. The rich can afford honor; the poor must eat shame.

ADRIENNE: Don't you want more freedom?

ZADRAN: Not like yours. Helping our men will bring us more freedom.

MASUDA: Don't you see? Our men become angry because NGOs don't pay attention to their needs. Your women's programs make our lives worse, not better.

ADRIENNE: What do you propose we do?

ZADRAN: You NGOs conduct surveys, but nothing happens. You don't get to know us, talk to us, ask us, before deciding what to do. We want progress at an Afghan pace, not at Western speed.

ADRIENNE: Our funding is directed towards helping women. Not men.

ZADRAN: Then, you'll continue to cripple us and foster corruption.

ADRIENNE: We never thought Afghan women would . . .

MASUDA: But it happens in America, too.

ZADRAN: I have heard of it. Mr. Tiger Woods' wife attacked him with a golf club. Mrs. Lorena Bobbitt, she cut off her husband's . . . his . . .

ADRIENNE: Penis.

ZADRAN: We do not say these words in public.

MASUDA: These events in America. Afghans cannot fathom such things.

ADRIENNE: Lorena Bobbit did it only after her husband raped her.

ZADRAN: I read Mr. Bobbitt was acquitted.

ADRIENNE: He had a good lawyer.

ZADRAN: What about the mother, Mrs. Susan Smith, who killed her two children?

MASUDA: We cannot bear to hear these stories. We would die for our husbands and children.

ZADRAN: How do you think we feel, knowing the world views us as downtrodden?

ADRIENNE: *(rising)* I can't make any promises . . .

ZADRAN: Then you're better than the NGOs that make promises they don't keep.

(ZADRAN escorts ADRIENNE to the door, embracing and kissing her, first on the right cheek, then the left. ZADRAN returns to MASUDA, draping her chadri back in place so that she is well covered, avoiding her injuries, gently tucking in stray wisps of hair so they are not visible. Outside the office, ADRIENNE pauses, reaches into her tote bag, pulls out mobile phone and dials.)

ADRIENNE: Hello? Libby? That you? *(pause)* . . .Uh-huh. I just did . . . *(pause)* No, it won't work . . .I'll explain later . . . *(pause)* We're going to have to rethink this . . .

(ADRIENNE reaches again into her tote bag, removes large chadri, wrapping it clumsily over her head, chest and shoulders. She sighs, yanks chadri forward to cover her hair completely, and exits.)

(Blackout)

End of Play

WHOSE BAG IS IT, ANYWAY?

Michele Markarian

ORIGINAL PRODUCTION

WHOSE BAG IS IT, ANYWAY? was a semi-finalist in the 19th Annual 15 Minute Play festival presented by American Globe Theatre and Turnip Theatre Company, New York New York.

Directed by Jason Taylor

CAST:
MOM: Michele Markarian
DAUGHTER: Heather Bildman
DAD: Jim Loutzenhiser

CHARACTERS:

MOM: A forty-five to fifty year old woman. She wears a jogging suit.

DAUGHTER: A seventeen-year old senior in high school. She is dressed for a casual night with friends.

DAD: A forty-five to fifty year old man. He is dressed for an evening in front of the television at home.

SCENE: A living room in America.

TIME: The present.

SETTING: A living room in America. There is a table, with two or three chairs around it, perhaps a couch or a bookcase in the background.

AT RISE: It is early evening. MOM and DAD are seated at the table, reading. A bong and a bag of marijuana are in the center of the table.

(DAUGHTER enters from offstage)

MOM: Hey, honey. Going out tonight?

DAUGHTER: Yeah.

DAD: Where are you off to?

DAUGHTER: A bunch of us are hanging out at Jen's house.

DAD: Oh. Sounds like fun.

MOM: How are you getting there?

DAUGHTER: Linda's picking me up.

(notices bong and bag of marijuana)

What's this?

MOM: You know what this is.

DAD: You can't fool us.

DAUGHTER: Where did you find this?

MOM: We have our ways.

DAD: We're not as "uncool" as you might think.

DAUGHTER: Seriously. Where did you get this?

(MOM and DAD look at DAUGHTER sternly)

MOM: Where do you think we'd get it?

DAD: Who do you think we'd get it from?

DAUGHTER: I have no idea!

MOM: Really.

> *(MOM and DAD look at each other, then at DAUGH-TER. Silence)*

DAUGHTER: I'm going to wait outside.

DAD: Not so fast, young lady.

DAUGHTER: What? What did I do?

> *(MOM nods towards bong and bag)*

DAUGHTER: That's not mine!

MOM: Oh.

DAD: Okay.

MOM: So . . .

DAUGHTER: It's not mine! What do you want me to say? It's not mine!

> *(MOM and DAD break into grins)*

DAD: We know that, honey!

MOM: And I hope you know that we would never go through your things. You know that, right, honey?

DAUGHTER: Yeah.

MOM: I mean, you do know that . . .

DAUGHTER: Yeah, I know.

DAD: Good.

DAUGHTER: So . . . what are you doing with that stuff?

DAD: It has a name, you know.

DAUGHTER: You named it?

DAD: No, but it has a proper name.

MOM: It's not just that stuff.

DAD: No. It has a name.

MOM: Right?

DAUGHTER: Uh huh.

MOM: You know what this is, right?

DAUGHTER: Mom, duh. Of course I know what it is.

DAD: How would you know what it is?

DAUGHTER: Because. Everyone know what it is. My God, I'm not a kid.

MOM: Have you tried it?
DAUGHTER: That?
MOM: Yeah.
DAUGHTER: No!
DAD: Really?
DAUGHTER: Really. No.
MOM: Oh, good.

(She grabs DAD'S hand).

DAD: We're not too late.
DAUGHTER: Too late for what?

(MOM and DAD beam at DAUGHTER)

DAD: Look. We weren't born yesterday. It's a tough world out
   there. A world where kids are doing all kinds of unsavory
   things. Dope. PCP. XTHC. You name it.
MOM: I'm sure you're under a lot of pressure as a teenager to
   participate in some pretty unhealthy and illegal activities.
DAUGHTER: Not really.
MOM: Honey.

(She reaches out for DAUGHTER'S hand).

DAUGHTER: What are you getting at?
MOM: Well—
DAD: We want to get you stoned.
DAUGHTER: *(in disbelief)* What?
MOM: We would like you to get high. With us.
DAUGHTER: What?
DAD: Just hear us out.
MOM: Look. At some point in the near future, you're gonna be
   at a party and someone's going to approach you with a jay,
   or a bong, and you're going to feel compelled by your peers
   to take a hit.
DAUGHTER: I—
DAD: We'd rather you tried it in the safety of your own home,
   with people who care about you, and with pot procured from
   a reliable source.
DAUGHTER: I—I don't believe this.
MOM: What?
DAUGHTER: I don't believe my parents are asking me to get
   high!

DAD: Better us than some high school burnout who'll try to take advantage of your altered state!

DAUGHTER: I don't want to get high!

MOM: At least this way, you'll see what it feels like to be high so that you can be prepared for the future.

DAUGHTER: What future?

DAD: The future when you'll be partaking socially!

DAUGHTER: But I don't want to get high!

MOM: Oh, you say that now, but . . . ..

DAUGHTER: Seriously! I don't want to get high!

DAD: Really?

DAUGHTER: Really!

MOM: But—this is something you're going to have to face at some point, sweetheart. Okay, maybe not in high school, but in college.

DAUGHTER: I don't want to get high!

DAD: Not even a taste?

DAUGHTER: No!

MOM: Oh.

DAD: Huh.

(MOM and DAD brood)

DAUGHTER: I'm sorry.

MOM: *(Shrugs)* It's okay.

DAD: You know, it's—it's not for—you don't even want to try it?

DAUGHTER: No.

(Silence)

MOM: I just don't want you to be hurt.

DAUGHTER: How can I be hurt if I'm not going to try it?

MOM: I guess.

DAD: Are you sure?

DAUGHTER: I told you, I don't want to get high.

MOM: Okay.

DAD: It's okay. We heard you the first time.

DAUGHTER: You seem disappointed.

MOM: No. We're not—are we?

(Looks at DAD)

DAD: No. Who needs to get stoned, anyway?

DAUGHTER: That's not why you did this?

MOM: Did what?

DAUGHTER: This whole bag thing. That's not why you did it, is it? So that you two could get stoned?

DAD: *(Indignant)* No!

MOM: How could you even think that? We could get stoned anytime we want. We just don't want to. Right?

> *(Looks at DAD)*

DAD: Right.

DAUGHTER: So where did you get it?

MOM: Get what?

DAD: What are you talking about?

DAUGHTER: You know. The dope. Where did you get it?

MOM: Dope? Did you just refer to this as dope?

DAD: Where did you learn that phrase, young lady?

DAUGHTER: Don't turn this on me. Where did you get it?

> *(MOM and DAD are silent)*

Alright. Fine. Do I have to call your friends?

> *(MOM and DAD look at each other)*

MOM: What friends?

DAUGHTER: Oh, I don't know. Maybe the Chauncys? Should I call them?

> *(Picks up cordless phone)*

Maybe they can tell me where you picked this up?

MOM: No!

DAD: Dick Chauncy sits on the Town Planning Board, for chrissakes!

DAUGHTER: I'm just saying, maybe he knows—

DAD: He knows nothing.

> *(Takes phone away from DAUGHTER).*

DAUGHTER: You're acting awfully upset.

DAD: Just get the Chauncys out of your head, will you?

DAUGHTER: So where did you get the stuff?

> *(MOM and DAD sit silently. They look around, uncomfortable)*

DAUGHTER: Okay. Be that way. But no one's moving from this table until you tell me where you got it.

MOM: Fine.

DAD: I don't need to be anywhere .

MOM: Nope. I'm not the one going anywhere.

(Silence)

MOM:	DAD:
It was—	Someone—

MOM: You go 'head.

DAD: No, you.

MOM: Okay. It was for the Little League team. You know, one of those boys outside of the 7 Eleven with a can and some little bags trying to make money for the Little League team.

DAD: Yeah. Twelve bucks a bag.

MOM: It was very reasonable.

DAD: I'll say.

DAUGHTER: You expect me to believe that a boy was standing outside the 7-Eleven selling weed to raise money for Little League?

MOM: You don't have to believe it—

DAD: But it's true.

DAUGHTER: Okay. Fine. Whatever. Why don't we just flush this bag down the toilet and forget we had this conversation, okay?

MOM: Okay.

DAD: Sure.

(He gets up to take bag of weed to the bathroom)

Are you sure you don't want to—

DAUGHTER: Positive.

MOM: I just feel badly that you don't trust your Dad and I enough to confide in us.

DAUGHTER: There's nothing to confide!

MOM: Okay. I just want you to know, though, that if there's anything—

DAUGHTER: Anything?

MOM: Absolutely.

DAUGHTER: Well, there is something—

MOM: *(leans in, nods encouragingly)*

DAUGHTER: Have you ever been on the Pill?

MOM: I'm sorry, honey, I didn't hear you. Are kids pushing pills on you these days?

DAUGHTER: No, not pills. The Pill. Birth control.

MOM: Excuse me? What did you say?

DAUGHTER: Birth control pills.

MOM: Harold, get in here.

DAD: *(Runs in from bathroom)* What? What is it?

MOM: Tell him.

DAUGHTER: Nothing. Just forget it!

MOM: Your daughter—our little girl—was asking me about birth control pills!

DAD: She—what?

MOM: You heard me. Don't make me say it again.

DAD: Birth control pills?

DAUGHTER: Forget it! Forget I said anything!

DAD: What do you think this is, some kind of free love clinic?

MOM: Now look what you've done. You've upset your father.

DAUGHTER: You asked me—

DAD: No! We were trying to prepare you for college party life, not an orgy!

MOM: I—I can't even talk about this. Which one of your friends put this idea in your head?

DAUGHTER: Nobody! I'm going to go wait downstairs for Linda.

(The doorbell rings)

I have to go. That's Linda.

DAD: Be home by 12:00—no, make that 11:00, you hear me?

MOM: And no more talk of this—this filth! Don't forget, you are a lady!

DAD: And if anyone at this gathering decides to do up some birth control pills, you come home immediately, young lady.

DAUGHTER: Goodbye.

(She kisses them each on the cheek and leaves)

DAD: Kids.

(Shakes head)

I don't get it.

MOM: I'm so—disturbed. What is this generation coming to?

(Silence)

DAD: I saved a little bit of the pot.

  (DAD pulls out the water pipe)

MOM: Fire it up.

  (DAD packs the pipe as LIGHTS FADE.)

  END OF PLAY

WITH HER OLD BOYFRIEND THERE WERE PATTERNS

Eric Pfeffinger

ORIGINAL PRODUCTION

With Her Old Boyfriend There Were Patterns was first produced by the Source Festival in Washington DC, June 16-30, 2013.

Directed by Kate Bryer

CAST:
JENNA NOW: Hyla Matthews
JENNA THEN: Emma Jackson
CRAIG/OMAR: Josh Adams
JENNA'S FRIEND: Gwen Grastorf
JENNA'S OTHER FRIEND: Hannah Blechman

CHARACTERS:
      JENNA NOW: a woman, late twenties
      JENNA THEN: the same woman, early twenties
      CRAIG: a man, late twenties   can/should be
      OMAR: a man, late twenties   played by same actor
      JENNA'S FRIEND a woman, twenties
      JENNA'S OTHER FRIEND a woman, twenties

THE TIME: The present, and also the past

THE PLACE: A bedroom and elsewhere

Two spaces: then (mostly, but not exclusively, a bedroom in a small apartment) and now. JENNA THEN sits on the bed reading an art book. JENNA NOW stands apart, addresses the audience:

JENNA NOW: There *were*. Habits, I mean. Repetitive—behaviors. Not like—what's the word?—normal people.

    (CRAIG enters, flossing. To JENNA THEN:)

CRAIG: A highway worker was killed in Frankfurt, Germany, when his machine struck a World War II bomb buried under a busy autobahn. Threw the construction vehicle like five hundred feet. I mean, you know: whoa.

    (CRAIG finishes flossing, exits.)

JENNA NOW: Like the way he flossed twice a night.

    (CRAIG reenters, flossing.)

CRAIG: I'm just saying, that's more than sixty years later . . . it's just—you know, that's craftsmanship.

JENNA NOW: Not obsessive, just predictable. Some might find that appealing.

    (JENNA THEN shrugs. CRAIG reenters the bedroom with a history book.)

Know what he was like? Wallpaper. That sounds like an insult. But almost everyone has wallpaper. Patterned wallpaper. Regular, predictable. What else was there? He liked history.

Bought books about battles at sale tables. Called himself a buff.

CRAIG: This is a great book.

(beat)

Know what I think I—?

JENNA THEN: —you're a buff, I know.

JENNA NOW: No one under fifty should want to be a buff. Always he was talking about land mines.

CRAIG: The earliest "land torpedoes" were deployed against the Seminole Indians in 1840.

JENNA THEN: Mm.

CRAIG: . . . Bet that got their attention.

JENNA THEN: . . . mm-hm.

CRAIG: —Boom.

JENNA THEN: Yes good.

(JENNA THEN and CRAIG go to the museum.)

JENNA NOW: We met at a photography exhibit I helped curate. Battlefields. I thought he was there for the photography, turned out he was there for the battlefields.

JENNA THEN: You like the photographs?

CRAIG: I like the battlefields.

JENNA NOW: No reason I shouldn't have seen it.

JENNA THEN: I curated.

CRAIG: *(has no idea what that means)* Aaaaahh!

JENNA NOW: There are times looking back when you think it would have been so easy to step right—

JENNA THEN: Wanna get a drink?

JENNA NOW: —instead of left.

CRAIG: Boom.

(JENNA THEN joins her FRIENDS in a coffee shop.)

JENNA NOW: His title at the university was Assistant Director in Charge of Development . . .

JENNA THEN: . . . but he never changes!

JENNA NOW: That was a joke I'd use with my friends.

(The FRIENDS laugh appreciatively with JENNA THEN.)

JENNA FRIEND: Good one.

JENNA OTHER'S FRIEND: That's hilarious.

JENNA FRIEND: He never changes, that's great, he's totally arrested!

JENNA OTHER'S FRIEND: But, I mean, a total catch.

JENNA FRIEND: Yes, a keeper.

JENNA NOW: "He never changes." Good joke, I thought. We laughed, anyway.

(More appreciative laughter.)

(Culminating in a group "Ooooohhh," deflating, decelerating.)

JENNA THEN: Oh, my.

JENNA NOW: His patterns would emerge gradually, familiar and remembered elements like—this is actually what I thought—like a colored blot that resurfaces recurrently from underneath other blots in a de Koonig.

JENNA THEN: "Woman and Old Boyfriend, oil on canvas."

(The FRIENDS stare blankly at JENNA THEN.)

JENNA NOW: I never used that with my friends.

JENNA FRIEND: Later.

JENNA OTHER'S FRIEND: Later.

JENNA THEN: Later.

(The FRIENDS disperse and JENNA THEN returns to the bedroom, strips efficiently to her bedclothes, and gets into bed alongside CRAIG, reading her book. He's still reading, too.)

CRAIG: Modern anti-personnel mines, you know, the kind that are detonated remotely by trip-wires? They can weigh less than a pound. Less than a pound!

JENNA NOW: Let me give you an example of something.

CRAIG: That's not very much, see. . . . For to kill somebody with.

(Through the following, CRAIG and JENNA THEN enact what JENNA NOW describes.)

JENNA NOW: We'd be reading in bed. Side-by-side. He'd be lying to my right—always to my right—and he would reach over and take my right hand, gently, and kiss my thumb-knuckle, a movement so casual, and I so involved in my book, I wouldn't even notice it at all. Then, invariably—it was ridiculous that I never came to anticipate this—he would hold my right hand tight, really really tight, against his shaggy chest, and with his other hand he would reach over silently, like he was just reaching for a handful of popcorn, and he would start tickling me.

> *(CRAIG does so. JENNA THEN convulses and begins to laugh and shriek and flail. This goes on for a while. JENNA NOW continues:)*

My back would arch. My book go flying. My fingers, wrists, toes, knees bend. Sharply. Like—this is what I actually thought—Uri Geller's spoons. My head thrown back into the pillow. He never even looked over. Not a single "kitchy koo." Just tickled. And tickled. I fling my body all over the bed, kicking the sheets untucked, breathing hair into my mouth, clapping my free hand to my forehead, sliding my legs off the bed.

JENNA THEN: No please no no no no please!

JENNA NOW: I start to think, irrationally: My God, he's never going to stop. He's going to tickle me like this, in this bed, until I die, which could take days. This is no way to go. What will my friends think? I'll do anything. If he would just. Stop. Stop. STOP. I'm—pretty ticklish.

JENNA THEN: I'm very ticklish STOP!

JENNA NOW: Eventually, of course, he does.

JENNA THEN: STOP!

JENNA NOW: Stop.

> *(CRAIG stops.)*

He let go and went back to reading, smiling a little while I sprawled, ungainly, across my half of the bed. Like a Philip Pearlstein. Like a chalk outline. Giggling aftershocks.

CRAIG: It's late. Want me to set the alarm?

JENNA NOW: Didn't happen all the time.

JENNA THEN: —Didn't have to . . .

JENNA NOW: But I don't say how often, in case it was too much.

> *(CRAIG and JENNA THEN get out of bed, throw on clothes, meet over some cardboard boxes.)*

Time went by.

CRAIG: *(taking a book from JENNA THEN's box:)* Mine.

JENNA NOW: It ended, eventually. Big surprise. We separated the books, the military from the art history. The Jeff Shaara from the Robert Hughes. He'd just stare at me. Like a Modigliani.

CRAIG: (taking a book from JENNA THEN's box:) Mine.

(CRAIG takes a box and exits.)

JENNA NOW: Years passed. I never thought about him. Or his behaviors. If I did, ever think about them at all, ever, which I didn't, I might have likened them to an Andy Warhol print. "Old Boyfriend Diptych. Acrylic and silkscreen enamel on canvas." But I never did.

(JENNA THEN exits. JENNA NOW gradually comes to inhabit the bedroom space.)

He moved, actually. Got a really good job at another university. Director of Development for its brand new School of Terrorism Studies. I moved, too. I packed and unpacked, crossed a bunch of states, took a new job, and then another.

JENNA FRIEND: Bye!

JENNA OTHER'S FRIEND: We have to visit, or something! We totally have to!

(to JENNA'S FRIEND:)

Whatever happened to her?

JENNA FRIEND: She was kinda weird.

JENNA NOW: Cut my hair and grew it out again. Went shopping for suits thinking about how I'd never pictured myself ever shopping for suits. Moved in with Omar.

(OMAR enters. If he's played by the same actor who plays CRAIG, then he wears an obvious and theatrical device—a fake mustache, say, or a wig—to distinguish him. Dressed for bedtime, he takes CRAIG's side of the bed. He reads. JENNA NOW undresses for bed.)

When a book about Verdun or Laos with a sale price penciled on its inside cover turns up in my collection like a splinter working its way to the surface, Omar looks at it funny and I donate it to the public library. So, well, yeah.

(JENNA NOW gets into bed alongside OMAR. They ex-

change a brief, familiar kiss. She begins to read. JEN-NA THEN occupies JENNA NOW's former space and watches.)

Things are good.

(JENNA NOW and OMAR read in silence.)

JENNA THEN: They'll be good. A new boyfriend. Long-term. Co-worker. First one since who's easy and organic. Like a Rothko.

(OMAR gives JENNA NOW an affectionate look. Reaches over and takes her right hand.)

The first one who'll make me think: "Hm." Think: "Well . . ." Like: "Maybe so."

(OMAR lifts JENNA NOW's hand to his lips.)

Until, that is, I snag his nostril violently with my thumbnail.

(Suddenly, instinctively, afraid of being tickled, JENNA NOW panics and jerks her hand away.)

JENNA NOW: No no don't!!

(OMAR clasps his nose and writhes, cursing and wailing in pain.)

JENNA THEN: And I tear a bit of his nose away from him like a tuft of bloody tissue paper.

JENNA NOW: OhmygodI'msosorry!

JENNA THEN: That won't be so great.

(Lights down on OMAR's agony. Curtain.)

End of play.

PLAYS FOR THREE OR MORE ACTORS

Actors Theatre of Louisville
www.actorstheatre.org
Amy Wegener
awegener@actorstheatre.org

Acts on the Edge, Santa Monica
mariannesawchuk@hotmail.com

American Globe Theatre
Turnip Festival, Gloria Falzer
gfalzer@verizon.net

Appetite Theatre Company
Bruschetta: An Evening of Short
Plays, www.appetitetheatre.com

Artists' Exchange, Cranston RI
Rich Morra
rich.morra@artists-exchange.org

Artistic New Directions
Janice Goldberg - Co Artistic Director
ANDJanice@aol.com
Kristine Niven - Co Artistic Director
KNiven@aol.com
www.ArtisticNewDirections.org

The Arts Center, Carrboro NC
10x10 in the Triangle
Jeri Lynn Schulke, director
theatre@artscenterlive.org
www.artscenterlive.org/performance/
opportunities

A-Squared Theatre Workshop
My Asian Mom Festival Joe Yau
jyauza@hotmail.com

Association for Theatre in Higher
Education New Play Development
Workshop, Charlene A. Donaghy
charlene@charleneadonaghy.com
http://www.athe.org/displaycommon.
cfm?an=1&subarticlenbr=70

Auburn Players Community Theatre
Short Play Festival
Bourke Kemmedy
email: bourkekennedy@gmail.com

The Barn Theatre
www.thebarnplayers.org/tenminute/

Barrington Stage Company
10X10 New Play Festival
Julianne Boyd is the Artistic Director
jboyd@barringtonstageco.org
www.barringtonstageco.org

Belhaven University, Jackson,
Mississippi
One Act Festival
Joseph Frost, Department Chair
theatre@belhaven.edu

Blue Slipper Theatre, Livingston,
Montana
Marc Beaudin, Festival Director
blueslipper10fest@gmail.com
www.blueslipper.com

Boston Theatre Marathon
Boston Playwrights Theatre
www.bostonplaywrights.org
Kate Snodgrass
ksnodgra@bu.edu
(Plays by New England Playwrights
only)

Boulder Life Festival, Boulder,
Colorado
Dawn Bower, Director of Theatrical
Program
dawn@boulderlifefestival.com
www.boulderlifefestival.com

The Box Factory
Judith Sokolowski, President
boxfactory@sbcglobal.net
www.boxfactoryforthearts.org

The Brick Theater's
"Tiny Theater Festival"
Michael Gardner, Artistic Director
mgardner@bricktheater.com
www.bricktheater.com

The Brooklyn Generator
Erin Mallon
brooklyngenerator@outlook.com
https://www.facebook.com/TheBrook-
lynGenerator/info

Camino Real Playhouse
www.caminorealplayhouse.org

Chalk Repertory Theatre Flash Festival
produced by Chalk Repertory Theatre
Ruth McKee: ruthamckee@aol.com
www.chalkrep.com

Chameleon Theater Circle,
Burnsville, MN 55306
www.chameleontheatre.org
jim@chameleontheatre.org
Cherry Picking
cherrypickingnyc@gmail.com

Chicago Indie Boots Festival
www.indieboots.org

City Theatre
www.citytheatre.com
Susan Westfall: susan@citytheatre.com

City Theatre of Independence
Powerhouse Theatre
Annual Playwrights Festival
Powerhouse Theatre
www.citytheatreofindependence.org

Colonial House Theatre
Colonial quickies
colonialplayhousetheater@40yahoo.com

Company of Angels at the Alexandria
501 S. Spring Street, 3rd Floor
Los Angeles, CA 90013
(213) 489-3703 (main office)
armevan@sbcglobal.net

Darkhorse Dramatists
www.darkhorsedramatists.com
darkhorsedramatists@gmail.com
Distilled Theatre Co.
submissions.dtc@gmail.com

Driftwood Players
www.driftwoodplayers.com
shortssubmissions@driftwoodplay-
ers.com,tipsproductions@drift-
woodplayers.com

Drilling Company
Hamilton Clancy
drillingcompany@aol.com

Driftwood Players
www.driftwoodplayers.com

Durango Arts Center 10-Minute Play
Festival
www.durangoarts.org

Theresa Carson
TenMinutePlayDirector@gmail.com

Eden Prairie Players
www.edenprairieplayers.com

Eastbound Theatre 10 minute Festival
(in the summer: themed)
Tom Rushen: ZenRipple@yahoo.com

East Haddam Stage Company
Kandie Carl
Kandie@ehsco.org

Eden Prairie Players
www.concordspacecom/2012/11/18/
submit-concords-1010-play-festival/
ReedSchulkereedschulke@yahoo.
com

Edward Hopper House (Two on the
Aisle Playwriting Competition)
Nyack, NY
Rachael Solomon
edwardhopper.house@verizon.net
www.edwardhopperhouse.org

Emerging Artists Theatre
Fall EATFest
www.emergingartiststheatre.org

En Avant Playwrights
Ten Lucky Festival
www.enavantplaywrights.yuku.com/
topic/4212/Ten-Tucky-Festival-KY-
deadline-10-1-no-fee#.UE5-nY5ZGQI

Ensemble Theatre of Chattanooga
Short Attention Span Theatre Festival
Contact Person: Garry Posey (Artistic
Director)
garryposey@gmail.com
www.ensembletheatreofchattanooga.
com

Fell's Point Corner Theatre 10 x 10
Festival
Contact Person: Richard Dean Stover
rick@fpct.org
www.fpct.org

Fine Arts Association
Hot from the Oven: Fresh on Delivery
ahedger@fineartsassociation.org

Firehouse Center for the Arts, New-
buryport MA
New Works Festival
Kimm Wilkinson, Director
www.firehouse.org
Limited to New England playwrights
Fire Rose Productions
www.fireroseproductions.com
kazmatura@gmail.com

The Fringe of Marin Festival
Contact Person: Annette Lust
jeanlust@aol.com\
Fury Theatre
katie@furytheare.org
Fusion Theatre Co.
http://www.fusionabq.org
info@fusionabq.org

Future Ten
info@futuretenant.org

Gallery Players
Annual Black Box Festival
info@galleryplayers.com

Gaslight Theatre
www.gaslight-theatre.org
gaslighttheatre@gmail.com
GI60
Steve Ansell
screammedia@yahoo.com

Generic Theatre Co.
www.generictheatre.org
contact@generictheatre.org

The Gift Theater
TEN Festival
Contact: Michael Patrick Thornton
www.thegifttheatre.org

Good Works Theatre Festival
Good Acting Studio
www.goodactingstudio.com

Half Moon Theatre
www.halfmoontheatre.org

Heartland Theatre Company
Themed 10-Minute Play Festival
Every Year
Contact Person:
Mike Dobbins (Artistic Director)
boxoffice@heartlandtheatre.org
www.heartlandtheatre.org

Hella Fresh Fish
freshfish2submit@gmail.com

Hobo Junction Productions
Hobo Robo Festival
Literary Manager:
Spenser Davis
hobojunctionsubmissions@gmail.
com
www.hobojunctionproductions.com

The Hovey Players, Waltham MA
Hovey Summer Shorts
www.hoveyplayers.com

Illustrious Theatre Co.
www.illustrioustheatre.org
illustrioustheatre@gmail.com

Image Theatre
Naughty Shorts
jbisantz@comcast.net

Independent Actors Theatre
Columbia, MO
Short Women's Play Festival
Emily Rollie, Artistic Director
e.rollie@iatheatre.org
www.iatheatre.org

Island Theatre 10-minute Play Festival
www.islandtheatre.org

Kings Theatre
www.kingstheatre.ca

Lake Shore Players
www.lakeshoreplayers.com
Joan Elwell
office@lakeshoreplayers.com

La Petite Morgue (Fresh Blood)
Kellie Powell
Lapetitemorgue@gmail.com
www.lapetitemorgue.blogspot.com

Lebanon Community Theatre
Playwriting Contest
Plays must be at least 10 minutes and
no longer than 20 minutes.
www.lct.cc/PlayWriteContest.htm

Lee Street Theatre, Salisbury, NC
Original 10-Minute Play Festival
Justin Dionne, managing artistic director
info@leestreet.org
www.leestreet.org

Little Fish Theatre
Pick of the Vine Festival
holly@littlefishtheatre.org
www.littlefishtheatre.org/wp/partici-
pate/submit-a-script/

Live Girls Theatre
submissions@lgtheater.org

LiveWire Chicago VisionFest
livewirechicago@gmail.com
Artistic Director:
Joel Ewing
joel.b.ewing@gmail.com
I think they do an annual festival
of 10 minute plays with a specific
theme

Lourdes University Drama Society
One Act Play Festival, Sylvania,
Ohio
Keith Ramsdell,
Drama Society Advisor
dramasociety@lourdes.edu
www.lourdes.edu/dramasociety.
aspx

Luna Theater
Contact: GregCampbell
lunatheater@gmail.com
www.lunatheater.org

Madlab Theatre
Theatre Roulette
Andy Batt
andy@madlab.net
www.madlab.net/MadLab/Home.
html

Magnolia Arts Center, Greenville, NC
Ten Minute Play Contest
info@magnoliaartscenter.com
www.magnoliaartscenter.com
Fee charged

ManhattanRepertoryTheatre, New
York, NY
Ken Wolf
manhattanrep@yahoo.com
www.manhattanrep.com

McLean Drama Co.
www.mcleandramacompany.org
Rachel Bail: rachbail@yahoo.com

Miami 1-Acts Festival (two sessions)
Winter (December) and Summer (July)
Steven A. Chambers, Literary Manager: schambers@new-theatre.or
Ricky J. Martinez, Artistic Director
rjmartinez@new-theatre.org
www.new-theatre.org

Milburn Stone One Act Festival
www.milburnstone.org

Mildred's Umbrella
Museum of Dysfunction Festival
www.mildredsumbrella.com
info@mildredsumbrella.com

Monkeyman Productions
The Simian Showcase
submissions@monkeymanproductions.com.
www.monkeymanproductions.com

Nantucket Short Play Competition
Jim Patrick
www.nantucketshortplayfestival.com
nantucketshortplay@comcast.net

Napa Valley Players
8 x 10: A Festival of 10 Minute Plays
www.napavalleyplayhouse.org

Newburgh Free Academy
tsandler@necsd.net

New American Theatre
www.newamericantheatre.com
Play Submissions: JoeBays44@earthlink.net

New Urban Theatre Laboratory
5 & Dime
Jackie Davis, Artistic Director:
jackie.newurbantheatrelab@gmail.com

New Voices Original Short
Play Festival
Kurtis Donnelly
kurtis@gvtheatre.org
NFA New Play Festival

Newburgh Free Academy
201 Fullerton Ave, Newburgh, NY
12550
Terry Sandler
terrysandle@hotmail.com
(may not accept electronic submissions)

North Park Playwright Festival
New short plays (no more than 15
pages, less is fine)
Submissions via mail to:
North Park Vaudeville and Candy
Shoppe
2031 El Cajon Blvd.
San Diego, CA 92104
Summer Golden, Artistic Director.
www.northparkvaudeville.com

Northport One-Act Play Festival
Jo Ann Katz
joannkatz@gmail.com
www.northportarts.org

NYC Playwrights
Play of the Month Project
http://nycp.blogspot.com/p/play-of-month.html

Northwest 10 Festival of 10-Minute
Plays
Sponsored by Oregon Contemporary
Theatre
www.octheatre.org/nw10-festival
NW10Festival@gmail.com

Nylon Fusion
nylonsubmissions@gmail.com
www.nylonfusioncollective.org

Over Our Head Players, Racine WI
www.overourheadplayers.org/oohp15
Pan Theater, Oakland, CA
Anything Can Happen Festival
David Alger, pantheater@comcast.net
http://www.facebook.com/sanfranciscoimprov

Pandora Theatre, Houston, Texas
Vox Feminina
Melissa Mumper, Artistic Director
pandoratheatre@sbcglobal.net

Paw Paw Players One Act Festival
www.ppvp.org/oneacts.htm

Pegasus Theater Company (in Sonoma
County, north of San Francisco)
Tapas Short Plays Festival
www.pegasustheater.com/html/sub-
missions.html
Lois Pearlman lois5@sonic.net

Philadelphia Theatre Company
PTC@Play New Work Festival
Jill Harrison:
jillian.harrison@gmail.com
www.philadelphiathatrecompany.org

PianoFight Productions, L.A.
ShortLivedLA@gmail.com

Piney Fork Press Theater
Play Festival
Johnny Culver,
submissionspineyforkpress.com
www.pineyforkpress.com

Playhouse Creatures
Page to Stage
newplays@playhousecreatures.org

Play on Words Productions
playonwordsproductions@gmail.com
Artist Director: Megan Kosmoski

Playmakers Spokane
Hit& Run
Sandra Hosking
playmakersspokane@gmail.com
www.sandrahosking.webs.com

Playwrights' Arena
Flash Theater LA
Jon Lawrence Rivera
jonlawrencerivera@gmail.com
www.playwrightsarena.org

Playwrights' Round Table
Orlando, FL
Summer Shorts
Chuck Dent charlesrdent@hotmail.
com www.theprt.com

Playwrights Studio Theater
5210 W. Wisconsin Ave.
Milwaukee, WI 53208
Attn: Michael Neville, Artistic Dir.

Renaissance Guild
www.therenaissanceguild.org
actoneseries@therenaissanceguild.org

Ruckus Theatre
Allison Shoemaker
theruckus@theruckustheater.org
www.ruckustheater.org

Salem Theatre Co.
Moments of Play
New England playwrights only
mop@salemtheatre.com

Salve Regina
www.salvetheatreplayfestival.sub-
mishmash.com/submit

Santa Cruz Actor's Theatre
Eight Tens at Eight
Wilma Chandler, Artistic Director
ronziob@email.com
http://www.sccat.org

Secret Room Theatre
Contact: Alex Dremann
alexdremann@me.com
www.secretroomtheatre.com

Secret Rose Theatre
www.secretrose.com
info@secretrose.com

Secret Theatre (Midsummer Night
Festival), Queens, NY.
Odalis Hernandez
odalis.hernandez@gmail.com
www.secrettheatre.com/

She Speaks, Kitchener, Ontario.
Paddy Gillard-Bentley
paddy@skyedragon.com
Women playwrights

Shelterbelt Theatre, Omaha, NB
From Shelterbelt with Love
McClain Smouse
associate-artistic@shelterbelt.org
submissions@shelterbelt.org
www.shelterbelt.org

Shepparton Theatre Arts Group
"Ten in 10" is a performance of 10
plays each running for 10 minutes
every year.
info@stagtheatre.com
www.stagtheatre.com

Short+Sweet
Literary Manager, Pete Malicki
Pete@shortandsweet.org
http://www.shortandsweet.org/short-
sweet-theatre/submit-script

Silver Spring Stage,
Silver Spring, MD
Jacy D'Aiutolo
oneacts2012.ssstage@gmail.com
www.ssstage.orgSixth Street Theatre

Snowdance 10-Minute Comedy
Festival
Rich Smith
Snowdance318@gmail.com
Six Women Play Festival
www.sixwomenplayfestival.com

Source Festival
jenny@culturaldc.org

Southern Repertory Theatre 6 x6
Aimee Hayes
literary@southernrep.com
www.southernrep.com/

Stage Door Productions
Original One-Act Play Festival
www.stagedoorproductions.org

Stage Door Repertory Theatre
www.stagedoorrep.org

Stage Q
www.stageq.com

Stageworks/Hudson
Play by Play Festival
Laura Margolis is the Artistic Director
literary@stageworkshudson.org
www.stageworkshudson.org

Stonington Players
HVPanciera@aol.com

Stratton Summer Shorts
Stratton Players
President: Rachel D'onfro
www.strattonplayers.com
info@strattonplayers.com

Subversive Theatre Collective
Kurt Schneiderman, Artistic Director
www.subversivetheatre.org
info@subversivetheatre.org

Ten Minute Playhouse (Nashville)
Nate Eppler, Curator
newworksnashville@gmail.com
www.tenminuteplayhouse.com

Ten Minute Play Workshop
www.tenminuteplayworkshop.com

Ten Tuckey Festival
doug@thebardstown.com

The Theatre Lab
733 8th St., NW
Washington, DC 20001
https://www.theatrelab.org/
Buzz Mauro
buzz@theatrelab.org, 202-824-0449

Theatre Odyssey, Sarasota, Florida
Tom Aposporos Vice President
www.theatreodyssey.org
Theatre One Productions
theatreoneproductions@yahoo.com

Theatre Out, Santa Ana CA
David Carnevale
david@theatreout.com
LGBT plays

Theatre Oxford 10 Minute Play Contest
http://www.theatreoxford.com
Alice Walker
10minuteplays@gmail.com

Theatre Three
www.theatrethree.com
Jeffrey Sanzel: jeffrey@theatrethree.com

Theatre Westminster
Ten Minute New (And Nearly New)
Play Festival
Terry Dana Jachimiak II
jachimtd@westminster.edu

TouchMe Philly Productions
www.touchmephilly.wordpress.com
touchmephilly@gmail.com

Towne Street Theatre
Ten-Minute Play Festival
info@townestreet.org

Unrenovated Play Festival
unrenovatedplayfest@gmail.com

Walking Fish Theatre
freshfish2submit@gmail.com

Wide Eyed Productions
www.wideeyedproductions.com
playsubmissions@wideeyedproductions.com

Wild Claw Theatre:
Death Scribe 10 Minute Radio Horror
Festival
www.wildclawtheatre.com/index.html
literary@wildclawtheatre.com

Winston-Salem Writers
Annual 10 Minute Play Contest
www.wswriters.org
info@wswriters.org

Write Act
www.writeactrep.org
John Lant: j316tlc@pacbell.net